"*Tozer on Christian Leadership* delivers the kind of timeless spiritual insights that distinguished A.W. Tozer in the last century . . . and that the twenty-first century church would do well to heed. Though these devotional readings are primarily meant to challenge and inspire Christian leaders, they will stir the heart of any Christian dedicated to thinking more biblically, serving the Lord more effectively and knowing God more intimately. The sensitive craftsmanship of compiler Ron Eggert in adding Scripture and prayer to each day's selection perfectly compliments the spirit of Tozer's writing and directs the reader to God—as Dr. Tozer would have wanted."

Doug Salser, Executive Director
Literature Ministries International

"Ron Eggert has done it again. For those of us who depend on the timeliness of Tozer to feed our messages, *Tozer on Christian Leadership* is a 'must' resource. For those to whom Tozer is unknown, the well-planned daily devotional approach is a good introduction. . . . For those who are afraid of using material from sources older than this morning's newspaper, read Tozer. If you're worried about relevance . . . read Tozer. Tozer is addictive because he takes you to the very throne of God."

Charles Morris, President and Speaker
"Haven" international radio program

TOZER ON
CHRISTIAN LEADERSHIP

TOZER FOR TODAY

DEVOTIONAL SERIES

TOZER
ON
CHRISTIAN
LEADERSHIP

A 366-DAY DEVOTIONAL

COMPILED BY RONALD EGGERT

WingSpread Publishers
Camp Hill, Pennsylvania

WingSpread Publishers
3825 Hartzdale Drive · Camp Hill, PA 17011
www.wingspreadpublishers.com

A division of Zur Ltd.

Tozer on Christian Leadership
ISBN: 978-1-60066-120-4
LOC Control Number: 2007923982
© 2001 by Zur Ltd.

Previously published by Christian Publications, Inc.
First Christian Publications Edition 2001
First WingSpread Publishers Edition 2007

Scripture taken from
The Holy Bible: King James Version.

Dedication

To my four children,
Jodi, Jon, Jeremy and Jessica (who is with the Lord)

I have no greater joy than to hear that my
children walk in truth. (3 John 4)

Love, Dad

PREFACE

$\mathcal{A}$iden Wilson Tozer was born April 21, 1897, on a small farm among the spiny ridges of Western Pennsylvania. Within a few short years, Tozer, as he preferred to be called, would earn the reputation and title "twentieth-century prophet."

When he was fifteen years old, Tozer's family moved to Akron, Ohio. One afternoon as he walked home from his job at Goodyear, he overheard a street preacher say, "If you don't know how to be saved . . . just call on God." When he got home, he climbed the narrow stairway to the attic where, heeding the preacher's advice, Tozer was launched into a lifelong pursuit of God.

In 1919, without formal education, he was called to pastor a small storefront church in Nutter Fort, West Virginia. That humble beginning thrust him and his wife, Ada, into a forty-four-year ministry with The Christian and Missionary Alliance.

Thirty-one of those years were spent at Chicago's Southside Alliance Church. The congregation, captivated by Tozer's preaching, grew from eighty to 800.

His humor, written and spoken, has been compared to that of Will Rogers—honest and homespun. Congregations could one moment be swept by gales of laughter and the next sit in a holy hush.

But Tozer's forte was his prayer life, which often found him walking the aisles of a sanctuary or lying face down on the floor. Tozer biographer James L. Snyder notes that "his preaching as well as his writings were but extensions of his prayer life." An earlier biographer and confidante, David J. Fant, wrote, "He spent more time on his knees than at his desk."

Tozer's final years of pastoral ministry were at Avenue Road Church in Toronto, Canada. On May 12, 1963, his pursuit of God was realized when he died of a heart attack at age sixty-six. In a small cemetery in Akron, Ohio, his tombstone bears this simple epitaph: "A Man of God."

Tozer once said, "The rewards of godly leadership are so great and the responsibilities of the leader so heavy that no one can afford to take the matter lightly."

Our prayer for these pages is that they may be used by God to help you shoulder your responsibility and reap the rewards.

Please note:

Each passage cited is followed by a code and number which represent the name of the book and the page from which the quote was taken. A list of the reference codes and a Scripture index are provided in the back of the book.

Ron Eggert holds a Th.M. from Dallas Theological Seminary and served in pastoral and youth ministries for thirty years. He is currently a regional representative for Mastermedia International, a ministry of evangelism and discipleship with executives in the film and television industry. Ron lives with his wife Dianna in Garland, Texas. They have three grown children.

January

Personal Life

Some things may be neglected with but little loss to the spiritual life, but to neglect communion with God is to hurt ourselves where we cannot afford it. ROR009

THUS SAITH THE LORD

Thy word is a lamp unto my feet, and a light unto my path.

—Psalm 119:105

*E*very new year is an uncharted and unknown sea. No ship has ever sailed this way before. The wisest of earth's sons and daughters cannot tell us what we may encounter on this journey. Familiarity with the past may afford us a general idea of what we may expect, but just where the rocks lie hidden beneath the surface or when that "tempestuous wind called Euroclydon" may sweep down upon us suddenly, no one can say with certainty. . . .

Now more than at any other time in generations, the believer is in a position to go on the offensive. The world is lost on a wide sea, and Christians alone know the way to the desired haven. While things were going well, the world scorned them with their Bible and hymns, but now the world needs them desperately, and it needs that despised Bible, too. For in the Bible, and there only, is found the chart to tell us where we are going on this rough and unknown ocean. The day when Christians should meekly apologize is over—they can get the world's attention not by trying to please, but by boldly declaring the truth of divine revelation. They can make themselves heard not by compromise, but by taking the affirmative and sturdily declaring, "Thus saith the Lord." TWP009-010

Lord, guide me carefully as I seek You in Your Word. Then use me mightily as Your servant as I boldly proclaim Your word in leading others. Amen.

THE SET
OF
OUR SAILS

But Daniel purposed in his heart that he would not defile himself with the portion of the king's meat, nor with the wine which he drank.

—Daniel 1:8

*T*hough we do not hear much of it in this age of spineless religion, there is nevertheless much in the Bible about the place of moral determination in the service of the Lord. "Jacob vowed a vow," and it was the beginning of a very wonderful life with God. . . .

Daniel "purposed in his heart," and God honored his purpose. Jesus set His face like a flint and walked straight toward the cross. Paul "determined not to know any thing among you, save Jesus Christ, and him crucified" (1 Corinthians 2:2). . . .

These are only a few of the many men . . . of the Bible who have left us a record of spiritual greatness born out of a will firmly set to do the will of God. . . .

Let us, then, set our sails in the will of God. If we do this we will certainly find ourselves moving in the right direction, no matter which way the wind blows. SOS011-013

Lord, help us to serve You unreservedly. We are often pulled in other directions, but keep us focused and faithful, undeterred and undefiled. In Jesus' name, Amen.

FACE DOWN, LISTENING

And Abram fell on his face: and God talked with him, saying, As for me, behold, my covenant is with thee, and thou shalt be a father of many nations.

—Genesis 17:3-4

The Scriptures declare, "Abram fell on his face" as the Lord talked with him (Genesis 17:3). Abraham was reverent and submissive. Probably there is no better picture anywhere in the Bible of the right place for mankind and the right place for God. God was on His throne speaking, and Abraham was on his face listening!

Where God and man are in relationship, this must be the ideal. God must be the communicator, and man must be in the listening, obeying attitude. If men and women are not willing to assume this listening attitude, there will be no meeting with God in living, personal experience. . . .

Yes, Abraham was lying facedown in humility and reverence, overcome with awe in this encounter with God. He knew that he was surrounded by the world's greatest mystery. The presence of this One who fills all things was pressing in upon him, rising above him, defeating him, taking away his natural self-confidence. God was overwhelming him and yet inviting and calling him, pleading with him and promising him a great future as a friend of God! MMG021-022

> *Lord, we don't spend nearly enough time facedown before You. Draw me to a position of humility and reverence, I pray. Amen.*

A
FRIEND
OF GOD

And the scripture was fulfilled which saith, Abraham believed God, and it was imputed unto him for righteousness: and he was called the Friend of God.

—James 2:23

*W*hat higher privilege and experience is granted to mankind on earth than to be admitted into the circle of the friends of God? . . .

It is well for us to remember that Divine-human friendship originated with God. Had God not first said "You are My friends," it would be inexcusably brash for any man to say, "I am a friend of God." But since God claims us for His friends, it is an act of unbelief to deny the offer of such a relationship. . . .

The spiritual giants of old were those who at some time became acutely conscious of the presence of God. They maintained that consciousness for the rest of their lives. . . .

The essential point is this: These were men who met and experienced God! How otherwise can the saints and prophets be explained? How otherwise can we account for the amazing power for good they have exercised over countless generations?

Is it not that indeed they had become friends of God? Is it not that they walked in conscious communion with the real Presence and addressed their prayers to God with the artless conviction that they were truly addressing Someone actually there? MMG013-014

I pray that I might catch a glimpse of what it means to walk in conscious communion with You, and might increasingly move into the intimate joy of experiencing You as a personal Friend. Amen.

LET GOD ALONE

But let patience have her perfect work, that ye may be perfect and entire, wanting nothing.

—James 1:4

$\mathcal{G}$od is saying, "I stand ready to pour a little liquid fire into your heart, into your spiritual being!"

We respond: "No, Lord, please excuse me. That sounds like fanaticism—and I would have to give up some things!" So we refuse His desire, even though we want all the benefits of His cross.

There is this thoughtful phrase in *The Cloud of Unknowing*: "He wills thou do but look on Him and let Him alone." Let God alone. In other words, let Him work! Don't stop Him. Don't prevent Him from kindling your heart, from blessing you and leading you out of a common state into that of special longing after Him. . . .

"Look on Him—and let Him work, let Him alone." Get your hands down to your side and stop trying to tell God where to cut. Stop trying to make the diagnosis for God. Stop trying to tell God what to give you. He is the Physician! You are the patient. . . .

Let Him work and your spiritual life will begin to blaze like the rising sun. ITB063-064

Lord, I'll try to stay out of Your way, take my hands off and let You work! Amen.

THE COMPELLING CALL

For though I preach the gospel, I have nothing to glory of: for necessity is laid upon me; yea, woe is unto me, if I preach not the gospel!

—1 Corinthians 9:16

*T*he true minister is one not by his own choice but by the sovereign commission of God. From a study of the Scriptures one might conclude that the man God calls seldom or never surrenders to the call without considerable reluctance. The young man who rushes too eagerly into the pulpit at first glance seems to be unusually spiritual, but he may in fact only be revealing his lack of understanding of the sacred nature of the ministry.

The old rule, "Don't preach if you can get out of it," if correctly understood, is still a good one. The call of God comes with an insistence that will not be denied and can scarcely by resisted. Moses fought his call strenuously and lost to the compulsion of the Spirit within him; and the same may be said of many others in the Bible and since Bible times. Christian biography shows that many who later became great Christian leaders at first tried earnestly to avoid the burden of the ministry; but I cannot offhand recall one single instance of a prophet's having applied for the job. The true minister simply surrenders to the inward pressure and cries, "Woe is unto me, if I preach not the gospel!" GTM087-088

Lord, I'm here in this ministry not because I chose to be, but because I've sensed Your call on my life. Help me always to be faithful to that call, in the power of Your Holy Spirit. Amen.

THE CALL OF GOD

And I thank Christ Jesus our Lord, who hath enabled me, for that he counted me faithful, putting me into the ministry.

—1 Timothy 1:12

"*Y*our calling," said Meister Eckhart to the clergy of his day, "cannot make you holy; but you can make it holy." No matter how humble that calling may be, a holy man can make it a holy calling. A call to the ministry is not a call to be holy, as if the fact of his being a minister would sanctify a man; rather, the ministry is a calling for a holy man who has been made holy some other way than by the work he does. The true order is: God makes a man holy by blood and fire and sharp discipline. Then he calls the man to some special work, and the man being holy makes that work holy in turn. . . .

Every person should see to it that he is fully cleansed from all sin, entirely surrendered to the whole will of God and filled with the Holy Spirit. Then he will not be known as what he *does*, but as what he *is*. He will be a man of God first and anything else second. WTA059-060

Keep me focused today on being the person You want me to be, no matter how significant or insignificant the work You ask me to do. Amen.

PEOPLE FOLLOW LEADERS

Be ye followers of me, even as I also am of Christ.

—1 Corinthians 11:1

The history of Israel and Judah points up a truth taught clearly enough by *all* history, viz., that the masses are or soon will be what their leaders are. The kings set the moral pace for the people. . . .

Whatever sort of man the king turned out to be, the people were soon following his leadership. They followed David in the worship of Jehovah, Solomon in the building of the Temple, Jeroboam in the making of a calf and Hezekiah in the restoration of the temple worship.

It is not complimentary to the masses that they are so easily led, but we are not interested in praising or blaming; we are concerned for truth, and the truth is that for better or for worse religious people follow leaders. A good man may change the moral complexion of a whole nation; or a corrupt and worldly clergy may lead a nation into bondage. . . .

Today Christianity in the Western world is what its leaders were in the recent past and is becoming what its present leaders are. The local church soon becomes like its pastor. GTM059-060

Strengthen us in the power of Your Holy Spirit, that we might be leaders worth following. Amen.

MEDITATE LONG AND OFTEN

I remember the days of old; I meditate on all thy works; I muse on the work of thy hands. I stretch forth my hands unto thee: my soul thirsteth after thee, as a thirsty land.

—Psalm 143:5-6

*A*mong Christians of all ages and of varying shades of doctrinal emphasis there has been fairly full agreement on one thing: They all believed that it was important that the Christian with serious spiritual aspirations should learn to meditate long and often on God.

Let a Christian insist upon rising above the poor average of current religious experience and he will soon come up against the need to know God Himself as the ultimate goal of all Christian doctrine. Let him seek to explore the sacred wonders of the Triune Godhead and he will discover that sustained and intelligently directed meditation on the Person of God is imperative. To know God well he must think on Him unceasingly. Nothing that man has discovered about himself or God has revealed any shortcut to pure spirituality. It is still free, but tremendously costly. TIC135

Slow me down, Lord, and quiet my heart. Favor me with an acute awareness of Your presence as I meditate quietly. I want to know You, God, so I can indeed move well beyond that "poor average of current religious experience." Amen.

LONGING AFTER GOD

Now therefore, I pray thee, if I have found grace in thy sight, shew me now thy way, that I may know thee, that I may find grace in thy sight.

—Exodus 33:13

Come near to the holy men and women of the past and you will soon feel the heat of their desire after God. They mourned for Him, they prayed and wrestled and sought for Him day and night, in season and out, and when they had found Him the finding was all the sweeter for the long seeking. Moses used the fact that he knew God as an argument for knowing Him better. "Now therefore, I pray thee, if I have found grace in thy sight, shew me now thy way, that I may know thee, that I may find grace in thy sight" (Exodus 33:13); and from there he rose to make the daring request, "I beseech thee, shew me thy glory" (33:18). God was frankly pleased by this display of ardor, and the next day called Moses into the mount, and there in solemn procession made all His glory pass before him. POG015

Restore to us today this deep longing, I pray in Jesus' name. Amen.

LONGING FOR GOD

As the hart panteth after the water brooks, so panteth my soul after thee, O God. My soul thirsteth for God, for the living God: when shall I come and appear before God?

—Psalm 42:1-2

O God, I have tasted Thy goodness, and it has both satisfied me and made me thirsty for more. I am painfully conscious of my need of further grace. I am ashamed of my lack of desire. O God, the Triune God, I want to want Thee; I long to be filled with longing; I thirst to be made more thirsty still. Show me Thy glory, I pray Thee, that so I may know Thee indeed. Begin in mercy a new work of love within me. Say to my soul, "Rise up, my love, my fair one, and come away." Then give me grace to rise and follow Thee up from this misty lowland where I have wandered so long. In Jesus' name. Amen. POG020

> *"I want to want Thee; I long to be filled with longing; I thirst to be made more thirsty still." Amen.*

To Think God's Thoughts

> *This book of the law shall not depart out of thy mouth; but thou shalt meditate therein day and night, that thou mayest observe to do according to all that is written therein: for then thou shalt make thy way prosperous, and then thou shalt have good success.*
>
> —Joshua 1:8

To think God's thoughts requires much prayer. If you do not pray much, you are not thinking God's thoughts. If you do not read your Bible much and often and reverently, you are not thinking God's thoughts. . . .

There also has to be a lot of meditation. We ought to learn to live in our Bibles. Get one with print big enough to read so it does not punish your eyes. Look around until you find a good one, and then learn to love it. Begin with the Gospel of John, then read the Psalms. Isaiah is another great book to help you and lift you. When you feel you want to do it, go on to Romans and Hebrews and some of the deeper theological books. But get into the Bible. Do not just read the little passages you like, but in the course of a year or two see that you read it through. Your thoughts will one day come up before God's judgment. We are responsible for our premeditative thoughts. They make our mind a temple where God can dwell with pleasure, or they make our mind a stable where Christ is angry, ties a rope and drives out the cattle. It is all up to us. RRR042

Lord, help us to lead Your people wisely, despite the barrage of outside influences we face every day. Amen.

THE KNOWLEDGE OF GOD

For when for the time ye ought to be teachers, ye have need that one teach you again which be the first principles of the oracles of God; and are become such as have need of milk, and not of strong meat.

—Hebrews 5:12

*P*robably the most widespread and persistent problem to be found among Christians is the problem of retarded spiritual progress. Why, after years of Christian profession, do so many persons find themselves no farther along than when they first believed? . . .

The causes of retarded growth are many. It would not be accurate to ascribe the trouble to one single fault. One there is, however, which is so universal that it may easily be the main cause: *failure to give time to the cultivation of the knowledge of God.* . . .

The Christian is strong or weak depending upon how closely he has cultivated the knowledge of God. . . .

Progress in the Christian life is exactly equal to the growing knowledge we gain of the Triune God in personal experience. And such experience requires a whole life devoted to it and plenty of time spent at the holy task of cultivating God. God can be known satisfactorily only as we devote time to Him. ROR010-012

> *Lord, I'd like to devote the remaining years of my life and ministry to the "holy task of cultivating God." Help me to know You first, and then out of the overflow of that growing knowledge can come whatever ministry You choose to bless me with. Amen.*

PERSONAL FEEDING ON GOD'S WORD

O how love I thy law! it is my meditation all the day.

—Psalm 119:97

I remember James M. Gray, the noted Bible teacher, telling of a Christian brother, a Michigan farmer, whose spiritual life had suddenly blossomed until there was an overflowing of God's presence. Many in the man's community recognized the change in his life and personality and sought spiritual counsel from him. Dr. Gray had opportunity to ask the man about the transformation of his spiritual life and witness.

"Dr. Gray, I began to devote myself to the Scriptures for my own need," the man humbly explained. "Something happened when God opened my spiritual understanding as I studied the book of Ephesians. I cannot really explain what the Lord is doing for me and through me, but it has come through prayerful meditation in the Word of God."

None of us can expect to get the rich, transforming blessings from God apart from the Scriptures. . . .

Too many of us ministers and Sunday school teachers are content to reach for a commentary on the Scriptures. What we need most is to search the Scriptures for ourselves. MMG047

Deliver me today from the shortcuts, and help me to discipline myself to long, concentrated study of the Scriptures themselves. Amen.

HEARING FROM GOD

Then went out to him Jerusalem, and all Judaea, and all the region round about Jordan, and were baptized of [John] in Jordan, confessing their sins.

—Matthew 3:5-6

*L*et me give you some reasons why I believe God could honor John the Baptist in that day in which he lived.

First, John had the ability to live and meditate in solitude. He knew the meaning of quietness. He was in the desert until the time of his showing forth unto Israel as a prophet. He came out of his lonely solitude to break the silence like a drumbeat or as the trumpet sounds. The crowds came—all gathered to hear this man who had been with God and who had come from God.

In our day we just cannot get quiet enough and serene enough to wait on God. Somebody has to be talking. Somebody has to be making noise. But John had gone into the silence and had matured in a kind of special school with God and the stars and the wind and the sand. . . .

I do not believe it is stretching a point at all to say that we will most often hear from God in those times when we are silent. CES130-131

> *Oh, Lord, help me to carve out of my busy schedule some time with "God and the stars and the wind and the sand." Amen.*

ALONE WITH GOD

> *And Jesus went up into a moun-
> tain, and there he sat with his
> disciples.*
>
> —John 6:3

*J*ust prior to [His] miraculous multiplying of the bread and fish, Jesus "went up into a mountain, and there he sat with his disciples"(John 6:3). That fact is noteworthy. It seems plain that Jesus withdrew purposely from the great press of people who had been pursuing Him.

There are some things that you and I will never learn when others are present. I believe in church and I love the fellowship of the assembly. There is much we can learn when we come together on Sundays and sit among the saints. But there are certain things that you and I will never learn in the presence of other people.

Unquestionably, part of our failure today is religious activity that is not preceded by aloneness, by inactivity. I mean getting alone with God and waiting in silence and quietness until we are charged with God's Spirit. Then, when we act, our activity really amounts to something because we have been prepared by God for it. . . .

Now, in the case of our Lord, the people came to Him, John reports, and He was ready for them. He had been quiet and silent. . . . Looking upward, He waited until the whole hiatus of divine life moved down from the throne of God into His own soul. FBR130,133

> *Lord, I come in quietness and silence to wait for You to
> fill me. Amen.*

THE NEED FOR SOLITUDE

And when he had sent the multitudes away, he went up into a mountain apart to pray: and when the evening was come, he was there alone.

—Matthew 14:23

$\mathscr{M}$odern civilization is so complex as to make the devotional life all but impossible. It wears us out by multiplying distractions and beats us down by destroying our solitude, where otherwise we might drink and renew our strength before going out to face the world again.

"The thoughtful soul to solitude retires," said the poet of other and quieter times; but where is the solitude to which we can retire today? Science, which has provided men with certain material comforts, has robbed them of their souls by surrounding them with a world hostile to their existence. "Commune with your own heart upon your bed and be still" is a wise and healing counsel, but how can it be followed in this day of the newspaper, the telephone, the radio and the television? These modern playthings, like pet tiger cubs, have grown so large and dangerous that they threaten to devour us all. What was intended to be a blessing has become a positive curse. No spot is now safe from the world's intrusion.

OGM125-126

Lord, help us somehow to escape today and retire to solitude, even if only for a brief time. Amen.

HEALING SILENCE

And when he had sent them away, he departed into a mountain to pray.

—Mark 6:46

*V*ery few of us know the secret of bathing our souls in silence. It was a secret our Lord Jesus Christ knew very well. There were times when He had to send the multitudes away so He could retire alone into the silence of the mountainside. There He would turn the God-ward side of His soul toward heaven and for a long time expose Himself to the face of His Father in heaven. . . .

My eyes and ears and spirit are aware of the immaturities in the so-called evangelicalism of our time. The more noise we make, the more we advertise, the more bells we jingle, the happier we seem to be. All of the signs of immaturity are among us.

We are seeing a general abhorrence of being alone, of being silent before the Lord. We shrink from allowing our souls to be bathed in the healing silences. MMG103-104

> *Father, grant that we might not forsake the quest for solitude and silence until we have really mastered this discipline, no matter how busy our lives continue to be. Amen.*

STAY
IN THE
SECRET PLACE

My voice shalt thou hear in the morning, O Lord; in the morning will I direct my prayer unto thee, and will look up.

—Psalm 5:3

$\mathcal{R}$etire from the world each day to some private spot, even if it be only the bedroom (for a while I retreated to the furnace room for want of a better place). Stay in the secret place till the surrounding noises begin to fade out of your heart and a sense of God's presence envelops you. Deliberately tune out the unpleasant sounds and come out of your closet determined not to hear them. Listen for the inward Voice till you learn to recognize it. Stop trying to compete with others. Give yourself to God, and then be what and who you are without regard to what others think. Reduce your interests to a few. Don't try to know what will be of no service to you. Avoid the digest type of mind—short bits of unrelated facts, cute stories and bright sayings. Learn to pray inwardly every moment. After a while you can do this even while you work. Practice candor, childlike honesty, humility. Pray for a single eye. Read less, but read more of what is important to your inner life. Call home your roving thoughts. Gaze on Christ with the eyes of your soul. Practice spiritual concentration. OGM128-129

Lord, direct me today to those things that would most enhance my walk with You, and enable me to serve You better. Amen.

PERSONAL DISCIPLINE

And every man that striveth for the mastery is temperate in all things. Now they do it to obtain a corruptible crown; but we an incorruptible.

—1 Corinthians 9:25

*A*nother trap into which the preacher is in danger of falling is that he may do what comes naturally and just take it easy. I know how ticklish this matter is and, while my writing this will not win me friends, I hope it may influence people in the right direction. It is easy for the minister to be turned into a privileged idler, a social parasite with an open palm and an expectant look. He has no boss within sight; he is not often required to keep regular hours, so he can work out a comfortable pattern of life that permits him to loaf, putter, play, doze and run about at his pleasure. And many do just that.

To avoid this danger the minister should voluntarily impose upon himself a life of labor as arduous as that of a farmer, a serious student or a scientist. No man has any right to a way of life less rugged than that of the workers who support him. No preacher has any right to die of old age if hard work will kill him. GTM094-095

Help us to work hard and faithfully, driven by a sense of passion. Amen.

DEPENDENCE ON GOD

And it shall be, that thou shalt drink of the brook; and I have commanded the ravens to feed thee there.

—1 Kings 17:4

We can learn important lessons by considering God's disciplines in dealing with Elijah. As Elijah fled to the wilderness following his first confrontation with King Ahab, God said to him, "Elijah, go to the brook Cherith, and I will feed you there." God sent big, black buzzards—ravens, scavenger birds—each morning and evening with Elijah's meals. What humiliation! All his life Elijah had been self-sufficient. Now he waited on scavenger birds to deliver him his daily bread. . . .

Elijah was like so many faithful preachers of the Word who are too true and too uncompromising for their congregations.

"We don't have to take that," the people protest. And they stop contributing to the church. More than one pastor knows the meaning of economic strangulation. Preach the truth, and the brook dries up! But the Lord knows how to deal with each of us in our humiliations. He takes us from truth to truth. MMG096

Lord, I commit myself anew today to never compromise the truth, even if it costs me my job. Amen.

BE
THOU
EXALTED

The LORD liveth; and blessed be my rock; and exalted be the God of the rock of my salvation.

—2 Samuel 22:47

O God, be Thou exalted over my possessions. Nothing of earth's treasures shall seem dear unto me if only Thou art glorified in my life. Be Thou exalted over my friendships. I am determined that Thou shalt be above all, though I must stand deserted and alone in the midst of the earth. Be Thou exalted above my comforts. Though it mean the loss of bodily comforts and the carrying of heavy crosses, I shall keep my vow made this day before Thee. Be Thou exalted over my reputation. Make me ambitious to please Thee even if as a result I must sink into obscurity and my name be forgotten as a dream. Rise, O Lord, into Thy proper place of honor, above my ambitions, above my likes and dislikes, above my family, my health and even my life itself. Let me sink that Thou mayest rise above. Ride forth upon me as Thou didst ride into Jerusalem mounted upon the humble little beast, a colt, the foal of an ass, and let me hear the children cry to Thee, "Hosanna in the highest."

POG101-102

Be Thou exalted in my life. Amen.

IT MAY NOT BE CONVENIENT

> *But I keep under my body, and bring it into subjection: lest that by any means, when I have preached to others, I myself should be a castaway.*
>
> —1 Corinthians 9:27

What must our Lord think of us if His work and His witness depend upon the convenience of His people? The truth is that every advance that we make for God and for His cause must be made at our inconvenience. If it does not inconvenience us at all, there is no cross in it! If we have been able to reduce spirituality to a smooth pattern and it costs us nothing—no disturbance, no bother and no element of sacrifice in it—we are not getting anywhere with God. We have stopped and pitched our unworthy tent halfway between the swamp and the peak.

We are mediocre Christians!

Was there ever a cross that was convenient? Was there ever a convenient way to die? I have never heard of any, and judgment is not going to be a matter of convenience, either! Yet we look around for convenience, thinking we can reach the mountain peak conveniently and without trouble or danger to ourselves.

Actually, mountain climbers are always in peril and they are always advancing at their inconvenience. ITB048

> *Lord, help me to serve You faithfully, with full discipline, whether it's convenient or not. Amen.*

GOD IS IN THAT!

And now, Lord, behold their threatenings: and grant unto thy servants, that with all boldness they may speak thy word, by stretching forth thine hand to heal; and that signs and wonders may be done by the name of thy holy child Jesus.

—Acts 4:29-30

Some are concerned because there are not more miracles and wonders wrought in our midst through faith. In our day, everything is commercialized. And I must say that I do not believe in commercialized miracles.

"Miracles, Incorporated"—you can have it!

"Healing, Incorporated"—you can have that, too! . . . I have my doubts about signs and wonders that have to be organized, that demand a letterhead and a president and a big trailer with lights and cameras. God is not in that!

But the person of faith who can go alone into the wilderness and get on his or her knees and command heaven—God is in that. The preacher who will dare to stand and let his preaching cost him something—God is in that. The Christian who is willing to put himself in a place where he must get the answer from God and God alone—the Lord is in that! FBR033-034

Lord, forgive me for so often trying to box up my plans and organize Your work so it can all be controlled and explained. Take over, Lord, and do Your thing, not mine, today. Amen.

PEOPLE ARE WHAT THEY THINK ABOUT

Keep thy heart with all diligence; for out of it are the issues of life.

—Proverbs 4:23

$\mathcal{E}$very person is really what he or she secretly admires. If I can learn what you admire, I will know what you are, for people are what they think about when they are free to think about what they will.

Now, there are times when we are forced to think about things that we do not care to think about at all. All of us have to think about income taxes, but income taxes are not what we want to think about. The law makes us think about them every April. You may find me humped over Form 1040, just like everyone else, but that is not the real me. It is really the man with the tall hat and the spangled stars in Washington who says, "You can't let it go any longer!" I assure you it is not consentingly done! But if you can find what I think about when I am free to think about whatever I will, you will find the real me. That is true of every one of us.

Your baptism and your confirmation and your name on the church roll and the big Bible you carry—these are not the things that are important to God. You can train a chimpanzee to carry a Bible. Every one of us is the sum of what we secretly admire, what we think about and what we would like to do most if we became free to do what we wanted to do. FBR096

Lord, may the secret thoughts of my heart be pure thoughts, pleasing to You, completely under the control of Your Holy Spirit. Amen.

YOUR THOUGHTS A SANCTUARY

I dwell in the high and holy place, with him also that is of a contrite and humble spirit, to revive the spirit of the humble, and to revive the heart of the contrite ones.

—Isaiah 57:15

I have been thinking recently about how important my thoughts are. I don't have to *do* wrong to get under blistering conviction and repent. I can lose the fellowship of God and sense of His presence and a sense of spirituality by just *thinking* wrong. God has been saying to me, "I dwell in your thoughts. Make your thoughts a sanctuary in which I can dwell. See to it." You can't do anything with your heart—that is too deep—but you can control your thoughts. . . .

Your theology is your foundation. The superstructure is your spiritual experience built on that foundation. But the high bell towers where the carillons are—those are your thoughts. And if you keep those thoughts pure the chimes can be heard ringing out "Holy, Holy, Holy" on the morning air.

Make your thoughts a sanctuary God can inhabit, and don't let any of the rest of your life dishonor God. See to it that not a foot of ground is unholy. See to it that every hour and every place is given over to God, and you will worship Him and He will accept it. TWE010-011

May my thoughts be a sanctuary, Father, where You can dwell comfortably. Amen.

THE HABIT OF HOLY THOUGHT

Casting down imaginations, and every high thing that exalteth itself against the knowledge of God, and bringing into captivity every thought to the obedience of Christ.

—2 Corinthians 10:5

*W*hat we think about when we are free to think about what we will—that is what we are or will soon become. . . .

Anyone who wishes to check on his true spiritual condition may do so by noting what his voluntary thoughts have been over the last hours or days. What has he thought about when free to think of what he pleased? Toward what has his inner heart turned when it was free to turn where it would? When the bird of thought was let go did it fly out like the raven to settle upon floating carcasses or did it like the dove circle and return again to the ark of God? Such a test is easy to run, and if we are honest with ourselves we can discover not only what we are but what we are going to become. We'll soon be the sum of our voluntary thoughts. . . .

The best way to control our thoughts is to offer the mind to God in complete surrender. The Holy Spirit will accept it and take control of it immediately. Then it will be relatively easy to think on spiritual things, especially if we train our thoughts by long periods of daily prayer. Long practice in the art of mental prayer (that is, talking to God inwardly as we work or travel) will help to form the habit of holy thought. BAM044,046-047

Take control of my thoughts and move me along in the development of the habit of holy thought. Amen.

CHOICES

*I have chosen the way of truth:
thy judgments have I laid before me. I have stuck unto thy
testimonies: O LORD, put me
not to shame.*

—Psalm 119:30-31

*T*he important thing about a man is not where he goes when he is compelled to go, but where he goes when he is free to go where he will. . . .

A man is absent from church Sunday morning. Where is he? If he is in a hospital having his appendix removed his absence tells us nothing about him except that he is ill; but if he is out on the golf course, that tells us a lot. To go to the hospital is compulsory; to go to the golf course, voluntary. The man is free to choose and he chooses to play instead of to pray. His choice reveals what kind of man he is. Choices always do. . . .

I think it might be well for us to check our spiritual condition occasionally by the simple test of compatibility. When we are free to go, where do we go? In what company do we feel most at home? Where do our thoughts turn when they are free to turn where they will? When the pressure of work or business or school has temporarily lifted and we are able to think of what we will instead of what we must, what do we think of then?

The answer to these questions may tell us more about ourselves than we can comfortably accept. But we had better face up to things. We haven't too much time at the most. MDP158-161

Lord, help me to make choices today that are pleasing to You. Amen.

SEEKING APPROVAL

Them that sin rebuke before all, that others also may fear.

—1 Timothy 5:20

$\mathcal{I}$ cannot believe in the spirituality of any Christian man who keeps an eye open for the approval of others, whoever they may be. The man after God's own heart must be dead to the opinion of his friends as well as his enemies. He must be as willing to cross important persons as obscure ones. He must be ready to rebuke his superior as quickly as those who may be beneath him on the ecclesiastical ladder. To reprove one man in order to gain the favor of another is no evidence of moral courage. It is done in the world all the time.

We'll never be where we should be in our spiritual lives until we are so devoted to Christ that we ask no other approbation than His smile. When we are wholly lost in Him the frantic effort to please men will come to an end. The circle of persons we struggle to please will be narrowed to One. Then we will know true freedom, but not a moment before. PON141

Lord, does anyone ever really get over the desire to seek the approval of others? That is a battle for which we are totally dependent on You for victory. Help me today to be content with only the smile of Your approval. Amen.

ACCOUNTABILITY TO GOD

And as it is appointed unto men once to die, but after this the judgment.

—Hebrews 9:27

*I*t was the belief in the accountability of man to his maker that made America a great nation. Among those earlier leaders was Daniel Webster whose blazing eyes and fiery oratory often held the Senate spellbound. In those days the Congress was composed of strong, noble statesmen who carried the weight of the nation in their hearts and minds.

Someone asked: "Mr. Webster, what do you consider the most serious thought that has ever entered your mind?"

"The most solemn thought that has ever entered my mind is my accountability to my Maker," he replied.

Men like that cannot be corrupted and bought. They do not have to worry if someone listens to their telephone calls. What they are in character and in deportment results from their belief that they will finally be accountable to God. EFE130

Lord, help me to live my life today in such a way that, should You call me tonight to stand before You and give account, I would have nothing of which I would need to be ashamed. Amen.

PERSONAL HOLINESS

> *But as he which hath called you is holy, so be ye holy in all manner of conversation; because it is written, Be ye holy; for I am holy.*
>
> —1 Peter 1:15-16

*Y*ou cannot study the Bible diligently and earnestly without being struck by an obvious fact—the whole matter of personal holiness is highly important to God!

Neither do you have to give long study to the attitudes of modern Christian believers to discern that by and large we consider the expression of true Christian holiness to be just a matter of personal option: "I have looked it over and considered it, but I don't buy it!". . .

Personally, I am of the opinion that we who claim to be apostolic Christians do not have the privilege of ignoring such apostolic injunctions. I do not mean that a pastor can forbid or that a church can compel. I only mean that morally we dare not ignore this commandment, "Be holy." . . .

But, brethren, we are still under the holy authority of the apostolic command. Men of God have reminded us in the Word that God does ask us and expect us to be holy men and women of God, because we are the children of God, who is holy. The doctrine of holiness may have been badly and often wounded—but the provision of God by His pure and gentle and loving Spirit is still the positive answer for those who hunger and thirst for a life and spirit well-pleasing to God. ICH061-062, 068

> *Oh, Lord, strengthen me today, walk with me, keep me cognizant of Your presence, guard me from any thought or action that would be displeasing to You. Amen.*

The Holy Spirit

In my sober judgment the relation of the Spirit to the believer is the most vital question the church faces today.
KDL057

THE ETERNAL SPIRIT

> *But ye shall receive power, after that the Holy Ghost is come upon you: and ye shall be witnesses unto me both in Jerusalem, and in all Judaea, and in Samaria, and unto the uttermost part of the earth.*
>
> —Acts 1:8

$\mathcal{Y}$ou know, the Church started out with a Bible, then it got a hymnbook, and for years that was it—a Bible and a hymnbook. The average church now certainly wouldn't be able to operate on just a hymnbook and the Bible. Now we have to have all kinds of truck. A lot of people couldn't serve God at all without at least a vanload of equipment to keep them happy.

Some of these attractions that we have to win people and keep them coming may be fine or they may be cheap. They may be elevated or they may be degrading. They may be artistic or they may be coarse—it all depends upon who is running the show! But the Holy Spirit is not the center of attraction, and the Lord is not the one who is in charge. We bring in all sorts of antiscriptural and unscriptural claptrap to keep the people happy and keep them coming.

As I see it, the great woe is not the presence of these religious toys and trifles—but the fact that they have become a necessity, and the presence of the Eternal Spirit is not in our midst! COU041

> *As we commit ourselves to excellence in reaching people for Christ, help us to remember that the power is not in the methods or the means, but in the Person of the Holy Spirit. Amen.*

MORATORIUM ON ACTIVITY

The fining pot is for silver, and the furnace for gold: but the LORD trieth the hearts.

—Proverbs 17:3

I suppose my suggestion will not receive much serious attention, but I should like to suggest that we Bible-believing Christians announce a moratorium on religious activity and set our house in order preparatory to the coming of an afflatus from above. So carnal is the body of Christians which composes the conservative wing of the Church, so shockingly irreverent are our public services in some quarters, so degraded are our religious tastes in still others, that the need for power could scarcely have been greater at any time in history. I believe we should profit immensely were we to declare a period of silence and self-examination during which each one of us searched his own heart and sought to meet every condition for a real baptism of power from on high. POM094

Lord, I do pray that You would move in the hearts of leaders in churches everywhere to prompt this time of silence and self-examination. Stimulate our hearts and quiet us to hear from You. Amen.

SENDING SOMETHING BETTER

Howbeit when he, the Spirit of truth, is come, he will guide you into all truth: for he shall not speak of himself; but whatsoever he shall hear, that shall he speak: and he will shew you things to come.

—John 16:13

O ur trouble is that we are trying to confirm the truth of Christianity by an appeal to external evidence. We are saying . . . "Here is a great statesman who believes the Bible. Therefore, the Bible must be true." We quote Daniel Webster, or Roger Bacon. We write books to show that some scientist believed in Christianity: therefore, Christianity must be true. We are all the way out on the wrong track, brother! That is not New Testament Christianity at all. That is a pitiful, whimpering, drooling appeal to the flesh. That never was the testimony of the New Testament, never the way God did things—never! You might satisfy the intellects of men by external evidences, and Christ did, I say, point to external evidence when He was here on the earth. But He said, "I am sending you something better. I am taking Christian apologetics out of the realm of logic and putting it into the realm of life. I am proving My deity, and My proof will not be an appeal to a general or a prime minister. The proof lies in an invisible, unseen but powerful energy that visits the human soul when the gospel is preached—the Holy Ghost!" HTB029-030

Lord, open our ears that we might hear when the Holy Spirit speaks. Amen.

THE NEED FOR ILLUMINATION

> *But the natural man receiveth not the things of the Spirit of God: for they are foolishness unto him: neither can he know them, because they are spiritually discerned.*
>
> —1 Corinthians 2:14

The doctrine of the inability of the human mind and the need for divine illumination is so fully developed in the New Testament that it is nothing short of astonishing that we should have gone so far astray about the whole thing. . . . Everywhere among conservatives we find persons who are Bible-taught but not Spirit-taught. They conceive truth to be something which they can grasp with the mind. If a man holds to the fundamentals of the Christian faith he is thought to possess divine truth. But it does not follow. There is no truth apart from the Spirit. The most brilliant intellect may be imbecilic when confronted with the mysteries of God. For a man to understand revealed truth requires an act of God equal to the original act which inspired the text. . . .

Conservative Christians in this day are stumbling over this truth. We need to reexamine the whole thing. We need to learn that truth consists not in correct doctrine, but in correct doctrine *plus the inward enlightenment of the Holy Spirit*. We must declare again the mystery of wisdom from above. A re-preachment of this vital truth could result in a fresh breath from God upon a stale and suffocating orthodoxy. POM076-077, 084

> *Lord, help me to heed this reminder that even Your inspired text is not alive until the Holy Spirit takes it and enlightens the recipients. May the Holy Spirit indeed take what I teach and imbed it in the hearts and minds of my hearers. Amen.*

PREACHERS WITHOUT POWER

*Now the end of the command-
ment is charity out of a pure
heart, and of a good conscience,
and of faith unfeigned: from
which some having swerved have
turned aside unto vain jangling;
desiring to be teachers of the law;
understanding neither what they
say, nor whereof they affirm.*

—1 Timothy 1:5-7

*A*nother thing that greatly hinders God's people is *a hardness of
heart caused by hearing men without the Spirit constantly preaching
about the Spirit.* There is no doctrine so chilling as the doctrine of
the Spirit when held in cold passivity and personal unbelief. The
hearers will turn away in dull apathy from an exhortation to be
filled with the Spirit unless the Spirit Himself is giving the exhortation through the speaker. It is possible to learn this truth and
preach it faithfully, and still be totally devoid of power. The hearers sense the lack and go away with numbed hearts. Theirs is not
opposition to the truth, but an unconscious reaction from unreal-
ity. Yet scarcely one of the hearers can tell another what the trouble
is; it is as if they had been hearing an echo and not the voice, or seeing a reflection and not the light itself. PTP055

> *Lord, that's a challenging thought. Deliver us from the
> error of preaching and teaching in our own strength,
> without the filling and the power of the Holy Spirit.
> Amen.*

JUST TURNING THE CRANK

Then he answered and spake unto me, saying, This is the word of the LORD unto Zerubbabel, saying, Not by might, nor by power, but by my Spirit, saith the LORD of hosts.

—Zechariah 4:6

It is possible to run a church and all of its activity without the Holy Spirit. You can organize it, get a board together, call a pastor, form a choir, launch a Sunday school and a ladies' aid society. You get it all organized—and the organization part is not bad. I'm for it. But I'm warning about getting organized, getting a pastor and turning the crank—some people think that's all there is to it, you know.

The Holy Spirit can be absent and the pastor goes on turning the crank, and nobody finds it out for years and years. What a tragedy, my brethren, what a tragedy that this can happen in a Christian church! But it doesn't have to be that way! "He that hath an ear, let him hear what the Spirit saith unto the churches" (Revelation 3:22). . . .

If you could increase the attendance of your church until there is no more room, if you could provide everything they have in churches that men want and love and value, and yet you didn't have the Holy Spirit, you might as well have nothing at all. For it is " 'Not by might, nor by power, but by my Spirit,' saith the LORD of hosts" (Zechariah 4:6). . . . [I]t is by the Spirit that God works His mighty works. COU038-039

Oh, Lord, in whatever ministry I am involved, I pray that Your Holy Spirit would be present with His controlling power. Amen.

WE NEED TO REPENT

> *What? know ye not that your body is the temple of the Holy Ghost which is in you, which ye have of God, and ye are not your own?*
>
> —1 Corinthians 6:19

*I*t is time for us to repent, for our transgressions against the blessed Third Person have been many and much aggravated. We have bitterly mistreated Him in the house of His friends. We have crucified Him in His own temple as they crucified the Eternal Son on the hill above Jerusalem. And the nails we used were not of iron, but of the finer and more precious stuff of which human life is made. Out of our hearts we took the refined metals of will and feeling and thought, and from them we fashioned the nails of suspicion and rebellion and neglect. By unworthy thoughts about Him and unfriendly attitudes toward Him we grieved and quenched Him days without end.

The truest and most acceptable repentance is to reverse the acts and attitudes of which we repent. . . .

We can best repent our neglect by neglecting Him no more. Let us begin to think of Him as One to be worshipped and obeyed. Let us throw open every door and invite Him in. Let us surrender to Him every room in the temple of our hearts and insist that He enter and occupy as Lord and Master within His own dwelling. POM071-072

Forgive me. Change me. Indwell me. Control me. Amen.

HE CAN BE GRIEVED

And grieve not the holy Spirit of God, whereby ye are sealed unto the day of redemption.

—Ephesians 4:30

*B*ecause He is loving and kind and friendly, the Holy Spirit may be grieved. . . . He can be grieved because He is loving, and there must be love present before there can be grief.

Suppose you had a seventeen-year-old son who began to go bad. He rejected your counsel and wanted to take things into his own hands. Suppose that he joined up with a young stranger from another part of the city and they got into trouble.

You were called down to the police station. Your boy—and another boy whom you had never seen—sat there in handcuffs.

You know how you would feel about it. You would be sorry for the other boy—but you don't love him because you don't know him. With your own son, your grief would penetrate to your heart like a sword. Only love can grieve. If those two boys were sent off to prison, you might pity the boy you didn't know, but you would grieve over the boy you knew and loved. A mother can grieve because she loves. If you don't love, you can't grieve. COU051-052

> *Lord, I think I take Your love for granted and consequently forget how grieved You are when I sin. Overwhelm me today with Your love, so that I might be more careful to not grieve You. Amen.*

SOME OTHER TIME

Verily, verily, I say unto you, He that believeth on me, the works that I do shall he do also; and greater works than these shall he do; because I go unto my Father.

—John 14:12

"*Ye* shall receive power" (Acts 1:8). "But covet earnestly the best gifts" (1 Corinthians 12:31). Anything that God has ever done for a soul He will do for anyone else, if the conditions are met. . . .

Unbelief says: Some other time, but not now; some other place, but not here; some other people, but not us. Faith says: Anything He did anywhere else He will do here; anything He did any other time He is willing to do now; anything He ever did for other people He is willing to do for us! With our feet on the ground, and our head cool, but with our heart ablaze with the love of God, we walk out in this fullness of the Spirit, if we will yield and obey. God wants to work through you!

The Counselor has come, and He doesn't care about the limits of locality, geography, time or nationality. The Body of Christ is bigger than all of these. The question is: Will you open your heart?

COU121

This thought is very convicting, Lord. I know I've been guilty of praising You for Your power and goodness, while secretly doubting that You were really going to work in my present situation. Forgive me that duplicity, Lord, and give me faith to believe You for now, for here, for me. Amen.

THE TEXT PLUS THE HOLY SPIRIT

And they come unto thee as the people cometh, and they sit before thee as my people, and they hear thy words, but they will not do them: for with their mouth they shew much love, but their heart goeth after their covetousness.

—Ezekiel 33:31

*W*hen you are trying to find out the condition of a church, do not just inquire whether it is evangelical. Ask whether it is an evangelical rationalistic church that says, "The text is enough," or whether it is a church that believes that the text plus the Holy Spirit is enough. . . .

I would rather be part of a small group with inner knowledge than part of a vast group with only intellectual knowledge. In that great day of Christ's coming, all that will matter is whether or not I have been inwardly illuminated, inwardly regenerated, inwardly purified. FBR030, 032

> *I too, Lord, "would rather be part of a small group with inner knowledge than part of a vast group with only intellectual knowledge." Fill us with Your Spirit and Your presence today. Amen.*

BURIED UNDER THE SNOW

And he did not many mighty works there because of their unbelief.

—Matthew 13:58

*H*ow many blessed truths have gotten snowed under. People believe them, but they are just not being taught, that is all. I think of our experience this morning. Here was a man and his wife, a very fine intelligent couple from another city. They named the church to which they belonged, and I instantly said, "That is a fine church!" "Oh, yes," they said, "but they don't teach what we came over here for." They came over because they were ill and wanted to be scripturally anointed for healing. So I got together two missionaries, two preachers, and an elder, and we anointed them and prayed for them. If you were to go to that church where they attend and say to the preacher, "Do you believe that the Lord answers prayer and heals the sick?" he would reply, "Sure, I do!" He believes it, but he doesn't teach it, and what you don't believe strongly enough to teach doesn't do you any good.

It is the same with the fullness of the Holy Ghost. Evangelical Christianity believes it, but nobody experiences it. It lies under the snow, forgotten. I am praying that God may be able to melt away the ice from this blessed truth, and let it spring up again alive, that the Church and the people who hear may get some good out of it and not merely say "I believe" while it is buried under the snow of inactivity and nonattention. HTB018-019

Lord, don't let me be guilty of keeping the truth of the Holy Spirit's ministry "buried under the snow." Help me to both teach and live the active presence and controlling power of the Holy Spirit today. Amen.

OUR FEAR OF EMOTIONS

> *And he leaping up stood, and walked, and entered with them into the temple, walking, and leaping, and praising God.*
>
> —Acts 3:8

*O*ne cause of the decline in the quality of religious experience among Christians these days is the neglect of the doctrine of the inward witness.

Stamping our feet to start the circulation and blowing on our hands to limber them up, we have emerged shivering from the long period of the theological deep-freeze, but the influence of the frosty years is still felt among us to such an extent that the words *witness*, *experience* and *feeling* are cautiously avoided by the rank and file of evangelical teachers. In spite of the undeniable lukewarmness of most of us we still fear that unless we keep a careful check on ourselves we shall surely lose our dignity and become howling fanatics by this time next week. We set a watch upon our emotions day and night lest we become over-spiritual and bring reproach upon the cause of Christ. Which all, if I may say so, is for most of us about as sensible as throwing a cordon of police around a cemetery to prevent a wild political demonstration by the inhabitants. BAM011

> *Lord, open up my heart to receive, and then open up my mouth to declare, the glory of Your mighty work! Amen.*

WILD-EYED FANATICS

Quench not the Spirit. Despise not prophesyings. Prove all things; hold fast that which is good.

—1 Thessalonians 5:19-21

*T*his is a crude illustration, but let me tell you what we did after planting a field of corn when I was a young fellow in Pennsylvania. To save the field of corn from the crows, we would shoot an old crow and hang him by his heels in the middle of the field. This was supposed to scare off all of the crows for miles around. The crows would hold a conference and say, "Look, there is a field of corn but don't go near it. I saw a dead crow over there!"

That's the kind of conference that Satan calls, and that is exactly what he has done. He has taken some fanatical, weird, wild-eyed Christians who do things that they shouldn't, and he has stationed them in the middle of God's cornfield, and warns, "Now, don't you go near that doctrine about the Holy Spirit because if you do, you will act just like these wild-eyed fanatics." COU063

> *Keep us, Lord, from shying away from such valuable truth and experience as the ministry of the Holy Spirit because of the excesses of a few fanatics. We lose too much, and we can't afford the loss. Amen.*

CONFIRMING SIGNS

And they went forth, and preached every where, the Lord working with them, and confirming the word with signs following.

—Mark 16:20

$\mathcal{S}$uch words as these in the second chapter of Hebrews stand as a rebuke to the unbelieving Christians of our day: "God also bearing them witness, both with signs and wonders, and with divers miracles, and gifts of the Holy Ghost, according to his own will" (Hebrews 2:4). A cold Church is forced to "interpret" such language. She cannot enter into it, so she explains it away. Not a little juggling is required, and not a few statements for which there is no scriptural authority, but anything will do to save face and justify our half-dead condition. Such defensive exegesis is but a refuge for unbelieving orthodoxy, a hiding place for a Church too weak to stand.

No one with a knowledge of the facts can deny the need for supernatural aid in the work of world evangelization. We are so hopelessly outclassed by the world's superior strength that for us it means either God's help or sure defeat. The Christian who goes out without faith in "wonders" will return without fruit. No one dare be so rash as to seek to do impossible things unless he has first been empowered by the God of the impossible. "The power of the Lord was there" is our guarantee of victory. PTP012-013

May the power of the Lord be with me in my ministry, so that I might not be "outclassed by the world's superior strength." Amen.

LESS
THAN
TRINITARIAN

The grace of the Lord Jesus Christ, and the love of God, and the communion of the Holy Ghost, be with you all. Amen.

—2 Corinthians 13:14

*O*ur blunder (or shall we frankly say our sin?) has been to neglect the doctrine of the Spirit to a point where we virtually deny Him His place in the Godhead. This denial has not been by open doctrinal statement, for we have clung closely enough to the biblical position wherever our creedal pronouncements are concerned. Our formal creed is sound; *the breakdown is in our working creed.*

This is not a trifling distinction. A doctrine has practical value only as far as it is prominent in our thoughts and makes a difference in our lives. By this test the doctrine of the Holy Spirit as held by evangelical Christians today has almost no practical value at all. In most Christian churches the Spirit is quite entirely overlooked. Whether He is present or absent makes no real difference to anyone. Brief reference is made to Him in the Doxology and the benediction. Further than that He might as well not exist. So completely do we ignore Him that it is only by courtesy that we can be called Trinitarian. The Christian doctrine of the Trinity boldly declares the equality of the Three Persons and the right of the Holy Spirit to be worshiped and glorified. Anything less than this is something less than Trinitarianism. POM060-061

Make me so aware of the power of the Holy Spirit in my life that I might give Him the recognition and worship that He so rightly deserves. Amen.

THE DAUNTING TASK

For I am not ashamed of the gospel of Christ: for it is the power of God unto salvation to every one that believeth; to the Jew first, and also to the Greek.

—Romans 1:16

*T*he greatest event in history was the coming of Jesus Christ into the world to live and to die for mankind. The next greatest event was the going forth of the Church to embody the life of Christ and to spread the knowledge of His salvation throughout the earth.

It was not an easy task which the Church faced when she came down from that upper room. . . . Left to herself the Church must have perished as a thousand abortive sects had done before her, and have left nothing for a future generation to remember.

That the Church did not so perish was due entirely to the miraculous element within her. That element was supplied by the Holy Spirit who came at Pentecost to empower her for her task. For the Church was not an organization merely, not a movement, but a walking incarnation of spiritual energy. And she accomplished within a few brief years such prodigies of moral conquest as to leave us wholly without an explanation—apart from God.
PTP007-008

> *Empower us for our work, Holy Spirit, even as You empowered the early Church. Amen.*

DEAD CHURCHES

These things saith he that hath the seven Spirits of God, and the seven stars; I know thy works, that thou hast a name that thou livest and art dead.

—Revelation 3:1

I think we are going to have to restudy this whole teaching of the place of the Holy Spirit in the Church, so the Body can operate again. If the life goes out of a man's body, he is said to be a corpse. He is what they call "the remains." It is sad, but humorously sad, that a strong, fine man with shining eyes and vibrant voice, a living man, dies, and we say, "the remains" can be seen at a funeral home. . . . The living man is gone. You have only the body. The body is "the remains."

So it is in the Church of Christ. It is literally true that some churches are dead. The Holy Spirit has gone out of them and all you have left are "the remains." You have the potential of the church but you do not have the church, just as you have in a dead man the potential of a living man but you do not have a living man. He can't talk, he can't taste, he can't touch, he can't feel, he can't smell, he can't see, he can't hear—because he is dead! The soul has gone out of the man, and when the Holy Spirit is not present in the Church, you have to get along after the methods of business or politics or psychology or human effort. COU112-113

Lord, send Your Holy Spirit in power, that we might not be a dead Church, striving to look alive, pretending to function as though alive, while the life is actually gone. Amen.

THE POWER GOD RECOGNIZES

*Woe to the rebellious children,
saith the LORD, that take counsel,
but not of me; and that cover with
a covering, but not of my spirit,
that they may add sin to sin.*

—Isaiah 30:1

The continued neglect of the Holy Spirit by evangelical Christians is too evident to deny and impossible to justify. . . .

It is not, however, the frequency of the Spirit's mention in the Bible or in other writings that matters most, but the importance attached to Him when He is mentioned. And there can be no doubt that there is a huge disparity between the place given to the Spirit in the Holy Scriptures and the place He occupies in popular evangelical Christianity. In the Scriptures the Holy Spirit is necessary. There He works powerfully, creatively; here He is little more than a poetic yearning or at most a benign influence. There He moves in majesty, with all the attributes of the Godhead; here He is a mood, a tender feeling of good will. . . .

The only power God recognizes in His church is the power of His Spirit whereas the only power actually recognized today by the majority of evangelicals is the power of man. God does His work by the operation of the Spirit, while Christian leaders attempt to do theirs by the power of trained and devoted intellect. Bright personality has taken the place of the divine afflatus. GTM108, 110-111

*O Lord, work powerfully, creatively; move in majesty.
Send the divine afflatus to overshadow our intellect and
personalities. Come in power, for Jesus' sake. Amen.*

FEBRUARY 18

THE SOUL IN THE BODY

But now hath God set the members every one of them in the body, as it hath pleased him.

—1 Corinthians 12:18

*L*et us review something here that we probably know: the doctrine of the life and operation of Christian believers on earth—starting with the fact that the Christian church is the body of Christ, Jesus Himself being the Headship of that body. Every true Christian, no matter where he or she lives, is a part of that body, and the Holy Spirit is to the church what our own souls are to our physical bodies. Through the operation of the Holy Spirit, Christ becomes the life, the unity and the consciousness of the body, which is the church. Let the soul leave the physical body and all the parts of the body cease to function. Let the Spirit be denied His place in the spiritual body, and the church ceases to function as God intended. . . .

According to the Bible, the whole body exists for its members and the members exist for the whole body. And that, of course, is the reason God gives gifts, so that the body may profit spiritually and maintain spiritual health and prosperity in its service for Jesus Christ in an unfriendly world. TRA014-016

Lord, I pray today that we in our church might be aware of Your presence, that we might be faithfully exercising the gifts You have given and that we might be a healthy Body that pleases You. Amen.

WE NEED HIM MORE AND MORE

But the Comforter, which is the Holy Ghost, whom the Father will send in my name, he shall teach you all things, and bring all things to your remembrance, whatsoever I have said unto you.

—John 14:26

I have reason to suspect that many people are trying to give leadership in Christian churches today without ever having yielded to the wise and effective leading of the Holy Spirit. He truly is the Spirit of wisdom, understanding and counsel. He alone can bring the gracious presence of the living God into our lives and ministries.

You may think it out of place for me to say so, but in our churches today we are leaning too heavily upon human talents and educated abilities. We forget that the illumination of the Holy Spirit of God is a necessity, not only in our ministerial preparation, but in the administrative and leadership functions of our churches.

We need an enduement of the Spirit of God! We sorely need more of His wisdom, His counsel, His power, His knowledge. . . . If we knew the full provision and the spiritual anointing that Jesus promised through the Holy Spirit, we would be far less dependent on so many other things. . . . I have said it before, and I say it now: We need the Holy Spirit more and more, and we need human helps less and less! JIV048

> *Lord, I fear that we are indeed lacking the enduement of the Spirit of God. Send us to our knees, Lord, that we might be reminded that we need Him more and more. Amen.*

SPIRITUAL GIFTS

Now there are diversities of gifts, but the same Spirit. And there are differences of administrations, but the same Lord. And there are diversities of operations, but it is the same God which worketh all in all.

—1 Corinthians 12:4-6

$\mathcal{T}$he time is more than ripe for a rethinking of the whole matter of spiritual gifts within the church of Christ. The subject has fallen into the hands of people for the most part extreme and irresponsible and has become associated with fanaticism in its various forms. This is a huge misfortune and is causing tremendous loss to the work of spiritual Christianity in our times.

Prejudices pro and con make the consideration of this subject extremely difficult, but its neglect is costing us more than we should be willing to pay. A revival of true New Testament Christianity must surely bring with it a manifestation of spiritual gifts. Anything short of it will create a just suspicion that the revival is something short of scriptural. NCA080-081

Thank You, Lord, that since Tozer's time there has in fact been this rethinking about spiritual gifts. May we continue to see their proper functioning and renewed manifestation. Amen.

THE ABILITY TO DO

I am the vine, ye are the branches: He that abideth in me, and I in him, the same bringeth forth much fruit: for without me ye can do nothing.

—John 15:5

A definition of the word "power" means the ability to do. You know, because it is the Greek word from which our English word "dynamite" comes, some of the brethren try to make out that the Holy Spirit is dynamite, forgetting that they have the thing upside down. Dynamite was named after that Greek word, and the Holy Spirit and the power of God were not named after dynamite. Dynamite was discovered less than 200 years ago, but this Greek word from which we get our word "power" goes back to the time of Christ. It means "ability to do"—that is all, just "ability to do." . . .

One man steps into the prize ring and can't even lift his hands. The other fellow walks in and he has power to do, and soon the fellow who did not have the ability to do is sleeping peacefully on the floor.

It is the man with the ability to do who wins. It means the dynamic ability to be able to do what you are given to do. You will receive ability to do. It will come on you. COU061-062

> *Lord, help us to not be afraid of this vital manifestation of the Holy Spirit. Come on our churches in power as we rely upon the Spirit for "the ability to do" whatever You have called us to do. Amen.*

UNGIFTED HANDS

For it is God which worketh in you both to will and to do of his good pleasure.

—Philippians 2:13

$\mathcal{T}$he important thing is that the Holy Spirit desires to take us and control us and use us as instruments and organs through whom He can express Himself in the body of Christ. Perhaps I can use my hands as a further illustration of this truth.

My hands are about average, I suppose—perhaps a little large for the size of my body, probably because I had to do a lot of farm work when I was a boy. But there is something I must tell you about these hands. They cannot play a violin. They cannot play the organ or the piano. They cannot paint a picture. They can barely hold a screwdriver to do a small repair job to keep things from falling apart at home. *I have ungifted hands....*

You will agree that it would be foolish for me to try to bring forth any delightful organ music using such ungifted hands. Is it not appalling, then, to think that we allow this very thing to happen in the body of Christ? We enlist people and tell them to get busy doing God's work, failing to realize the necessity of the Spirit's control and functioning if there is to be a spiritual result.

TRA030-031

> *Move in our midst, Holy Spirit, that everyone in the Body might actively serve, each one using the gift they have been given for Your service. Amen.*

AN INSTRUMENT FOR GOD TO USE

If any man speak, let him speak as the oracles of God; if any man minister, let him do it as of the ability which God giveth: that God in all things may be glorified through Jesus Christ, to whom be praise and dominion for ever and ever. Amen.

—1 Peter 4:11

To please God, a person must be just an instrument for God to use. For a few seconds, picture in your mind the variety of wonderful and useful appliances we have in our homes. They have been engineered and built to perform tasks of all kinds. But without the inflow of electrical power they are just lumps of metal and plastic, unable to function and serve. They cannot do their work until power is applied from a dynamic outside source.

So it is in the work of God in the church. Many people preach and teach. Many take part in the music. Certain ones try to administer God's work. But if the power of God's Spirit does not have freedom to energize all they do, these workers might just as well stay home.

Natural gifts are not enough in God's work. The mighty Spirit of God must have freedom to animate and quicken with His overtones of creativity and blessing. TRA005-006

Lord, deliver us from our dependency on natural gifts. We hunger for effectiveness in Your work, but too seldom turn loose to let Your power flow through us. Amen.

HOLINESS AND WORSHIP FIRST

Not by works of righteousness which we have done, but according to his mercy he saved us, by the washing of regeneration, and renewing of the Holy Ghost; . . . That being justified by his grace, we should be made heirs according to the hope of eternal life.

—Titus 3:5, 7

To teach that the filling with the Holy Spirit is given to the Christian to provide "power for service" is to teach truth, but not the whole truth. Power for service is but one effect of the experience, and I do not hesitate to say that it is the least of several effects. It is least for the very reason that it touches service, presumably service to mankind; and contrary to the popular belief, "to serve this present age" is not the Christian's first duty. . . .

The primary work of the Holy Spirit is to restore the lost soul to intimate fellowship with God through the washing of regeneration. . . .

God wants worshipers before workers; indeed the only acceptable workers are those who have learned the lost art of worship. It is inconceivable that a sovereign and holy God should be so hard up for workers that He would press into service anyone who had been empowered regardless of his moral qualifications. . . .

Gifts and power for service the Spirit surely desires to impart; but holiness and spiritual worship come first. TIC036-037

Oh, Lord, where has the hunger for holiness gone? Remind us of the priority of holiness and spiritual worship. Amen.

As Holy
as You
Want to Be

Having therefore these promises, dearly beloved, let us cleanse ourselves from all filthiness of the flesh and spirit, perfecting holiness in the fear of God.

—2 Corinthians 7:1

$\mathcal{I}$t may be said without qualification that every man is as holy and as full of the Spirit as he wants to be. He may not be as full as he wishes he were, but he is most certainly as full as he wants to be.

Our Lord placed this beyond dispute when He said, "Blessed are they which do hunger and thirst after righteousness: for they shall be filled" (Matthew 5:6). Hunger and thirst are physical sensations which, in their acute stages, may become real pain. It has been the experience of countless seekers after God that when their desires became a pain they were suddenly and wonderfully filled. The problem is not to persuade God to fill us, but to want God sufficiently to permit Him to do so. The average Christian is so cold and so contented with His wretched condition that there is no vacuum of desire into which the blessed Spirit can rush in satisfying fullness. BAM008

Lord, quiet my heart today and fill me with this holy longing. I don't want to be contented with my present condition; I long for that vacuum of desire into which the Holy Spirit can rush. Amen.

DESIRE TO BE FILLED

And be not drunk with wine, wherein is excess; but be filled with the Spirit.

—Ephesians 5:18

*A*gain, before you can be filled with the Spirit you must desire to be filled. Here I meet with a certain amount of puzzlement. Somebody will say, "How is it that you say to us that we must desire to be filled, because you know we desire to be? Haven't we talked to you in person? Haven't we called you on the phone? Aren't we out here tonight to hear the sermon on the Holy Spirit? Isn't this all a comforting indication to you that we are desirous of being filled with the Holy Spirit?"

Not necessarily, and I will explain why. For instance, are you sure that you want to be possessed by a spirit other than your own? even though that spirit be the pure Spirit of God? even though He be the very gentle essence of the gentle Jesus? even though He be sane and pure and free? even though He be wisdom personified, wisdom Himself, even though He have a healing, precious ointment to distill? even though He be loving as the heart of God? That Spirit, if He ever possesses you, will be the Lord of your Life! HTB042-043

Even so come, Holy Spirit! Amen.

A BOTTLE IN THE OCEAN

> *. . . to know the love of Christ, which passeth knowledge, that ye might be filled with all the fulness of God.*
>
> —Ephesians 3:19

*P*entecost means that the Deity came to mankind to give Himself to man, that man might breathe Him in as he breathes in the air, that He might fill men. Dr. A.B. Simpson used an illustration which was about as good as any I ever heard. He said, "Being filled with the fullness of God is like a bottle in the ocean. You take the cork out of the bottle and sink it in the ocean, and you have the bottle completely full of ocean. The bottle is in the ocean, and the ocean is in the bottle. The ocean contains the bottle, but the bottle contains only a little bit of the ocean. So it is with a Christian."

We are filled unto the fullness of God, but, of course, we cannot contain all of God because God contains us; but we can have all of God that we can contain. If we only knew it, we could enlarge our vessel. The vessel gets bigger as we go on with God. COU068

> *Enlarge my vessel, Lord, and fill me with more and more of the fullness of Yourself. Amen.*

WAKE UP
THE LION
IN YOU!

*Not that we are sufficient of
ourselves to think any thing as
of ourselves; but our sufficiency
is of God.*

—2 Corinthians 3:5

$\mathcal{T}$hat is the difference between Christianity and all the Oriental cults and religions. All cult religions try to wake up what you already have, and Christianity says, "What you have is not enough—you will need the enduement which is sent from above!" That is the difference. The others say, "Stir up the thing that is in you," and they expect this to be enough.

By way of illustration, if there were four or five lions coming at you, you would never think of saying to a little French poodle, "Wake up the lion in you." That would not work—it would not be enough. They would chew the little fellow up and swallow him, haircut and all, because a French poodle just isn't sufficient for a pack of lions. Some power outside of himself would have to make him bigger and stronger than the lions if he were to conquer.

That is exactly what the Holy Spirit says He does for the Christian believer, but the cult religions still say, "Concentrate and free your mind and release the creative powers that lie within you." COU142-143

*Lord, in our self-reliance we're all too often guilty of
digging deep for that inner self-sufficiency. Our New
Age culture fosters that error. Teach us how futile this
pursuit is; show us Your power. Amen.*

Pastoral Ministry

The work of a minister is altogether too difficult for any man. We are driven to God for wisdom. TWP086

A DIFFERENT MAN IN THE PULPIT

Ye are witnesses, and God also, how holily and justly and unblameably we behaved our-selves among you that believe.

—1 Thessalonians 2:10

$\mathcal{I}$ am afraid of the pastor that is another man when he enters the pulpit from what he was before. Reverend, you should never think a thought or do a deed or be caught in any situation that you couldn't carry into the pulpit with you without embarrassment. You should never have to be a different man or get a new voice and a new sense of solemnity when you enter the pulpit. You should be able to enter the pulpit with the same spirit and the same sense of reverence that you had just before when you were talking to someone about the common affairs of life.

WMJ025

> *Lord, help me to be a man of impeccable integrity. Give me the grace to be the same man, whether in the pulpit, in a board meeting, caught in rush hour traffic or at dinner with my wife. Amen.*

In Need of a Physician

The LORD is my shepherd; I shall not want. He maketh me to lie down in green pastures: he leadeth me beside the still waters. He restoreth my soul.

—Psalm 23:1-3

*H*uman nature being what it is, the man of God may soon adopt an air of constant piety and try to appear what the public thinks he is. The fixed smile and hollow tones of the professional cleric are too well known to require further mention.

All this show of godliness, by the squeeze of circumstances and through no fault of the man himself, may become a front behind which the man hides, a plaintive, secretly discouraged and lonely soul. Here is no hypocrisy, no intentional double living, no actual desire to deceive. The man has been mastered by the circumstances. He has been made the keeper of other people's vineyards but his own vineyard has not been kept. So many demands have been made upon him that they have long ago exhausted his supply. He has been compelled to minister to others while he himself is in desperate need of a physician. GTM115

> *Lord, I pray for pastors everywhere today who are indeed exhausted and depleted. The task is so overwhelming and the demands so extreme. Come today with a fresh breath of Your Spirit to refresh, renew and restore. Amen.*

ACQUAINTANCE, NOT HEARSAY

And they said one to another, Did not our heart burn within us while he talked with us by the way, and while he opened to us the scriptures?

—Luke 24:32

"*I*t is one thing," said Henry Suso, "to hear for oneself a sweet lute, sweetly played, and quite another thing merely to hear about it."

And it is one thing, we may add, to hear truth inwardly for one's very self, and quite another thing merely to hear *about* it. . . .

We are turning out from the Bible schools of this country year after year young men and women who know the theory of the Spirit-filled life but do not enjoy the experience. These go out into the churches to create in turn a generation of Christians who have never felt the power of the Spirit and who know nothing personally about the inner fire. The next generation will drop even the theory. That is actually the course some groups have taken over the past years.

One word from the lips of the man who has actually heard the lute play will have more effect than a score of sermons by the man who has only heard that it was played. Acquaintance is always better than hearsay. ROR087-088

Lord, as I wait upon You I want to hear afresh the real sound of the lute. Fill me with a firsthand knowledge of You, so that my message might always be that of an alert eyewitness. Amen.

WORTHY TO LEAD

Paul, an apostle, (not of men, neither by man, but by Jesus Christ, and God the Father, who raised him from the dead.)

—Galatians 1:1

*C*onformity to the Word of God is always right, but obedience to religious leaders is good only if those leaders prove themselves worthy to lead. Leadership in the church of Christ is a spiritual thing and should be so understood by everyone. It takes more than a ballot to make a leader. . . .

If the church is to prosper spiritually she must have spiritual leadership, not leadership by majority vote. It is highly significant that when the apostle Paul found it necessary to ask for obedience among the young churches he never appealed to them on the grounds that he had been duly elected to office. He asserted his authority as an apostle appointed by the Head of the church. He held his position by right of sheer spiritual ascendancy, the only earthly right that should be honored among the children of the new creation. WOS162-164

Renew within me, even today, a sense of my divine call. Then help me to live a holy life, exemplary in faithfulness, so that I might indeed be a leader worthy to lead. Amen.

FAITH MUST BE DEMONSTRATED

For by [faith] the elders obtained a good report.

—Hebrews 11:2

*T*he lesson that comes to us through the many dramatic illustrations of faith in Hebrews 11 brings us back to my earlier statement: Faith in God is to be demonstrated, not defined. Just as God's church demonstrates Christian love, this demonstration of godly, humble faith is God's ideal for His church.

It is not enough for preachers in their pulpits to try to define love. The love that God has promised must be demonstrated in the lives of the believers in the pews. It must be practiced as well by the man who occupies the pulpit.

We should put the matter of faith in that same category. God wants His people, including the ministers, to demonstrate all of the outworking of faith in their daily lives and practices. JAF008

Lord, the pattern set forth in Hebrews 11 seems so unattainable! Strengthen me by Your Spirit to be able to demonstrate this type of unshakable faith. Amen.

A GOOD HUSBANDMAN

Father, I will that they also, whom thou hast given me, be with me where I am; that they may behold my glory, which thou hast given me: for thou lovedst me before the foundation of the world.

—John 17:24

I believe that a pastor who is content with a vineyard that is not at its best is not a good husbandman. It is my prayer that we may be a healthy and fruitful vineyard and that we may be an honor to the Well Beloved, Jesus Christ the Lord, that He might go before the Father and say, "These are mine for whom I pray, and they have heard the Word and have believed on Me." I pray that we might fit into the high priestly prayer of John 17, that we would be a church after Christ's own heart so that in us He might see the travail of His soul and be satisfied. . . .

The church should be a healthy, fruitful vineyard that will bring honor to Christ, a church after Christ's own heart where He can look at the travail of His soul and be satisfied. RRR112, 119

Lord, I long that Jesus Christ might indeed be satisfied with my own life and the lives of those whom He has called me to lead. Help me to be a faithful husbandman in whatever vineyard You place me. Amen.

PERSONAL IDENTITY

Let no man despise thy youth; but be thou an example of the believers, in word, in conversation, in charity, in spirit, in faith, in purity.

—1 Timothy 4:12

This problem of personal identity not infrequently troubles the faithful minister. The congregation has called him as their pastor and teacher, but the members have a hard time forgetting the saintly predecessor who died or who was called to another ministry. They find it hard to make room for the new minister—mainly because he is not enough like the former one. His voice is different. So are his gestures. His hair is not gray. His wife is not as friendly.

Be careful! God blesses people for their faith and obedience, not because they are old or young, bald or gray, pleasant voiced or raspy. God expects each one of us to let Him use us in helping people to a walk of spiritual blessing and victory. Not necessarily must we have had a long record as heroes in the faith to qualify. JAF070

Lord, I pray for any of my brothers who may be facing this struggle today. Challenge the congregation to move on and love their new pastor. Give grace to the pastor; help him to faithfully demonstrate faith and obedience. Weld pastor and people together in a deep love relationship. Amen.

A SHAKY FOUNDATION

Thus saith the LORD, Let not the wise man glory in his wisdom, neither let the mighty man glory in his might, let not the rich man glory in his riches: but let him that glorieth glory in this, that he understandeth and knoweth me.

—Jeremiah 9:23-24

*I*t is true that much church activity is thrown back upon a shaky foundation of psychology and natural talents. . . .

We live in a day when charm is supposed to cover almost the entire multitude of sins. Charm has taken a great place in religious expression. I am convinced that our Lord expects us to be tough enough and cynical enough to recognize all of this that pleases the unthinking in our churches: the charm stuff, the stage presence in the pulpit, the golden qualities of voice. . . .

I feel sorry for the church that decides to call a pastor because "his personality simply sparkles!" I have watched quite a few of those sparklers through the years. In reality, as every kid knows at Fourth of July time, sparklers can be an excitement in the neighborhood—but only for about one minute! Then you are left holding a hot stick that quickly cools off in your hand. TRA032-033

> *Lord, confirm for each of us as pastors our divine call, that we might indeed build on a strong foundation. Then bring conviction and repentance to any in our congregations who are judging us with the wrong criteria. Amen.*

I KNOW I'LL BE IN TROUBLE

But even after that we had suffered before, and were shamefully entreated, as ye know, at Philippi, we were bold in our God to speak unto you the gospel of God with much contention.

—1 Thessalonians 2:2

*I*t is good for us to remember how strong [God] is—and how weak we are. I settled this issue a long time ago. I tell you I have talked to God more than I have talked to anyone else. I have reasoned more with God and had longer conferences with God than with anybody else.

And what did I tell Him? Among other things, I told Him, "Now, Lord, if I do the things I know I should do, and if I say what I know in my heart I should say, I will be in trouble with people and with groups—there is no other way!

"Not only will I be in trouble for taking my stand in faith and honesty, but I will certainly be in a situation where I will be seriously tempted of the devil!"

Then, after praying more and talking to the Lord, I have said, "Almighty Lord, I accept this with my eyes open! I know the facts and I know what may happen, but I accept it. I will not run. I will not hide. I will not crawl under a rug. I will dare to stand up and fight because I am on your side—and I know that when I am weak, then I am strong!" ITB146

Lord, I'm convicted by Tozer's statement that he has "talked to God more than [he has] talked to anyone else." Help me to talk with You more. Amen.

FENCING WITH MASTERS

For the time will come when they will not endure sound doctrine; but after their own lusts shall they heap to themselves teachers, having itching ears; and they shall turn away their ears from the truth, and shall be turned unto fables.

—2 Timothy 4:3-4

*E*veryone who has come to the years of responsibility seems to have gone on the defensive. Even some of you who have known me for years are surely on the defensive—you have your guard up all the time!

I know that you are not afraid of me, but you are afraid, nevertheless, of what I am going to say. Probably every faithful preacher today is fencing with masters as he faces his congregation. The guard is always up. The quick parry is always ready.

It is very hard for me to accept the fact that it is now very rare for anyone to come into the house of God with guard completely down, head bowed and with the silent confession: "Dear Lord, I am ready and willing to hear what You will speak to my heart today!"

We have become so learned and so worldly and so sophisticated and so blasé and so bored and so religiously tired that the clouds of glory seem to have gone from us. CES108-109

Lord, quiet my own heart before You and give me that humble spirit of listening. Whenever I come before You may I be "ready and willing to hear what You will speak to my heart today." Amen.

THE ECONOMIC SQUEEZE

But watch thou in all things, endure afflictions, do the work of an evangelist, make full proof of thy ministry.

—2 Timothy 4:5

A number of factors contribute to bad spiritual leadership....

The economic squeeze. The Protestant ministry is notoriously underpaid and the pastor's family is often large. Put these two facts together and you have a situation ready-made to bring trouble and temptation to the man of God. The ability of the congregation to turn off the flow of money to the church when the man in the pulpit gets on their toes is well known. The average pastor lives from year to year barely making ends meet. To give vigorous moral leadership to the church is often to invite economic strangulation, so such leadership is withheld. But the evil thing is that *leadership withheld is in fact a kind of inverted leadership.* The man who will not lead his flock up the mountainside leads it down without knowing it. GTM061-062

Lord, again I pray for any pastor who may be facing this "economic squeeze" today. Help him to be faithful and give strong leadership no matter the cost. Then, Lord, I pray that even today You would grant one of Your special, generous provisions as a powerful reminder of Your great faithfulness. Amen.

BOWING TO THE GIVERS

But my God shall supply all your need according to his riches in glory by Christ Jesus.

—Philippians 4:19

*R*emember, *my giving will be rewarded not by how much I gave but by how much I had left.* Ministers are sometimes tempted to shy away from such doctrine as this lest they offend the important givers in their congregation. But it is better to offend men than to grieve the blessed Spirit of God which dwells in the church. No man ever yet killed a true church by withdrawing his gifts from it because of a personal pique. The Church of the First-born is not dependent upon the patronage of men. No man has ever been able really to harm a church by boycotting it financially. The moment we admit that we fear the displeasure of the carnal givers in our congregations we admit also that our congregations are not of heaven but of the earth. A heavenly church will enjoy a heavenly and supernatural prosperity. She cannot be starved out. The Lord will supply her needs. GTM183

Thank You, heavenly Father, for Your incredibly generous provision and faithfulness—both to us as individuals and to the churches we lead. Amen.

SUPERNATURAL ENERGIES

But they that wait upon the Lord shall renew their strength; they shall mount up with wings as eagles; they shall run, and not be weary; and they shall walk, and not faint.

—Isaiah 40:31

*I*t is possible to work far beyond the normal strength of the human constitution and yet experience little or no fatigue because the energy for the work has been provided, not by the burning up of human tissue, but by the indwelling Spirit of power. This has been realized by a few unusual souls, and the pity is that they *are* unusual.

Attention has recently been focused upon the fact that ministers suffer a disproportionately high number of nervous breakdowns compared with other men. The reasons are many, and for the most part they reflect credit on the men of God. Still I wonder if it is all necessary. I wonder whether we who claim to be sons of the new creation are not allowing ourselves to be cheated out of our heritage. Surely it should not be necessary to do spiritual work in the strength of our natural talents. God has provided supernatural energies for supernatural tasks. The attempt to do the work of the Spirit without the Spirit's enabling may explain the propensity to nervous collapse on the part of Christian ministers. SIZ184-185

Lord, today I pray for that pastor who is about to give up and quit from sheer exhaustion. Give him that supernatural enabling. Amen.

SHEEP ARE LED

O come, let us worship and bow down: let us kneel before the LORD our maker. For he is our God; and we are the people of his pasture, and the sheep of his hand.

—Psalm 95:6-7

*C*attle are driven; sheep are led; and our Lord compares His people to sheep, not to cattle.

It is especially important that Christian ministers know the law of the leader—that he can lead others only as far as he himself has gone. . . .

The minister must experience what he would teach or he will find himself in the impossible position of trying to drive sheep. For this reason he should seek to cultivate his own heart before he attempts to preach to the hearts of others. . . .

If he tries to bring them into a heart knowledge of truth which he has not actually experienced he will surely fail. In his frustration he may attempt to drive them; and scarcely anything is so disheartening as the sight of a vexed and confused shepherd using the lash on his bewildered flock in a vain attempt to persuade them to go on beyond the point to which he himself has attained. . . .

The law of the leader tells us who are preachers that it is better to cultivate our souls than our voices. . . . We cannot take our people beyond where we ourselves have been, and it thus becomes vitally important that we be men of God in the last and highest sense of that term. PON151-153

Lord help me to listen to You and be spiritually nurtured,
to have my soul cultivated by You in silence and solitude.
Amen.

GOD IS NOT A RAILWAY PORTER

Who hath measured the waters in the hollow of his hand, and meted out heaven with the span, and comprehended the dust of the earth in a measure, and weighed the mountains in scales, and the hills in a balance?

—Isaiah 40:12

We must be concerned with the person and character of God, not the promises. Through promises we learn what God has willed to us, we learn what we may claim as our heritage, we learn how we should pray. But faith itself must rest on the character of God.

Is this difficult to see? Why are we not stressing this in our evangelical circles? Why are we afraid to declare that people in our churches must come to know God Himself? Why do we not tell them that they must get beyond the point of making God a lifeboat for their rescue or a ladder to get them out of a burning building? How can we help our people get over the idea that God exists just to help run their businesses or fly their airplanes?

God is not a railway porter who carries your suitcase and serves you. God is God. He made heaven and earth. He holds the world in His hand. He measures the dust of the earth in the balance. He spreads the sky out like a mantle. He is the great God Almighty. He is not your servant. He is your Father, and you are His child. He sits in heaven, and you are on the earth. FBR044-045

God, I fall on my face before You in worship today. Forgive me for those times I have treated You as though You were my servant. I am Your servant, Lord, and I humbly bow before You today. Amen.

SPIRITUAL DISCERNMENT

> *Give therefore thy servant an understanding heart to judge thy people, that I may discern between good and bad: for who is able to judge this thy so great a people?*
>
> —1 Kings 3:9

*T*hat so-called Bible religion in our times is suffering rapid decline is so evident as to need no proof, but just what has brought about this decline is not so easy to discover. I can only say that I have observed one significant lack among evangelical Christians which might turn out to be the real cause of most of our spiritual troubles. Of course, if that were true, then the supplying of that lack would be our most critical need.

The great deficiency to which I refer is the lack of spiritual discernment, especially among our leaders. How there can be so much Bible knowledge and so little insight, so little moral penetration, is one of the enigmas of the religious world today. . . .

If not the greatest need, then surely one of the greatest is for the appearance of Christian leaders with prophetic vision. We desperately need seers who can see through the mist. Unless they come soon, it will be too late for this generation. And if they do come, we will no doubt crucify a few of them in the name of our worldly orthodoxy. But the cross is always the harbinger of the resurrection.

WTA111-112

*Therefore give to Your servant an understanding heart
to judge Your people, that I may discern between good
and evil. Amen.*

DISCERNING
LEADERSHIP

For I know this, that after my departing shall grievous wolves enter in among you, not sparing the flock. Also of your own selves shall men arise, speaking perverse things, to draw away disciples after them.

—Acts 20:29-30

*W*ithin the circles of evangelical Christianity itself there has arisen in the last few years dangerous and dismaying trends away from true Bible Christianity. A spirit has been introduced which is surely not the Spirit of Christ, methods employed which are wholly carnal, objectives adopted which have not one line of Scripture to support them, a level of conduct accepted which is practically identical with that of the world—and yet scarcely one voice has been raised in opposition. And this in spite of the fact that the Bible-honoring followers of Christ lament among themselves the dangerous, wobbly course things are taking. . . .

The times call for a Spirit-baptized and articulate orthodoxy. They whose souls have been illuminated by the Holy Ghost must arise and under God assume leadership. There are those among us whose hearts can discern between the true and the false, whose spiritual sense of smell enables them to detect the spurious afar off, who have the blessed gift of *knowing*. Let such as these arise and be heard. Who knows but the Lord may yet return and leave a blessing behind Him? PON006-007

Lord, grant to me "the blessed gift of knowing." And then be pleased to use me for Your glory today. Amen.

SPIRITUAL LEADERSHIP OF ANOINTED MEN

For David, after he had served his own generation by the will of God, fell on sleep, and was laid unto his fathers, and saw corruption.

—Acts 13:36

*T*he life ideal was described by the apostle in the Book of Acts: "For David, after he had served his own generation by the will of God, fell on sleep" (Acts 13:36).

We submit that it would be difficult, if not impossible, to improve upon this. It embraces the whole sphere of religion, appearing as it does in its three directions: God, the individual, society. Within that simple triangle all possible human activities are carried on. To each of us there can be but these three dimensions: God, myself, others. Beyond this we cannot go, nor should we even attempt to go. If we serve God according to His own will, and in doing so serve our generation, we shall have accomplished all that is possible for any human being.

David was smart enough to serve God and his generation before he fell asleep. To fall asleep before we have served our generation is nothing short of tragic. It is good to sleep at last, as all our honored fathers have done, but it is a moral calamity to sleep without having first labored to bless the world. No man has any right to die until he has put mankind in debt to him.

NCA067

Lord, keep me faithful. Let me serve my present generation well, for Your glory, before You take me home. Amen.

WHERE ARE THE PROPHETS?

O GOD, thou art my God; early will I seek thee: my soul thirsteth for thee, my flesh longeth for thee in a dry and thirsty land, where no water is; to see thy power and thy glory, so as I have seen thee in the sanctuary.

—Psalm 63:1-2

*B*ut it is within our hearts and our beings that God searches and looks. It is our spiritual heart life that is to be simple. It is in our hearts that we are to meditate and be silent. It is deep within our beings that we must be courageous and open to God's leadings.

If there ever was an hour in which the church needed courageous men of prophetic vision, it is now. Preachers and pastors? They can be turned out in our schools like automobiles off the assembly line.

But prophets? Where are they?

The simple, humble and courageous men who are willing to serve and wait on God in the long silences, who wait to hear what God says before they go to tell the world—these do not come along too often. When they do, they seek only to glorify their God and His Christ! CES134-135

Oh Lord, I long to be one of those "courageous men of prophetic vision." I quiet my heart today; I will "wait on God in the long silences;" and then I'll go with only the word that I receive from You—only for Your glory. Amen.

PROPHETIC PREACHERS

And of the children of Issachar, which were men that had understanding of the times, to know what Israel ought to do; the heads of them were two hundred.

—1 Chronicles 12:32

A prophet is one who knows his times and what God is trying to say to the people of his times. . . .

Today we need prophetic preachers—not preachers of prophecy merely, but preachers with a gift of prophecy. The word of wisdom is missing. We need the gift of discernment again in our pulpits. It is not ability to predict that we need, but the anointed eye, the power of spiritual penetration and interpretation, the ability to appraise the religious scene as viewed from God's position, and to tell us what is actually going on. . . .

What is needed desperately today is prophetic insight. Scholars can interpret the past; it takes prophets to interpret the present. Learning will enable a man to pass judgment on our yesterdays, but it requires a gift of clear seeing to pass sentence on our own day. . . .

Another kind of religious leader must arise among us. He must be of the old prophet type, a man who has seen visions of God and has heard a voice from the Throne. OGM019-022

> *Lord, I pray for that gift of prophetic insight. Move me beyond the knowledge You've enabled me to gain through education, reading and study. I pray that I might lead as one "who has seen visions of God and has heard a voice from the throne." Amen.*

A NEW TYPE OF PREACHER

But none of these things move me, neither count I my life dear unto myself, so that I might finish my course with joy, and the ministry, which I have received of the Lord Jesus, to testify the gospel of the grace of God.

—Acts 20:24

*I*f Christianity is to receive a rejuvenation, it must be by other means than any now being used. If the Church in the second half of this century is to recover from the injuries she suffered in the first half, there must appear a new type of preacher. . . .

Another kind of religious leader must arise among us. He must be of the old prophet type, a man who has seen visions of God and has heard a voice from the Throne. When he comes (and I pray God there will be not one but many), he will stand in flat contradiction to everything our smirking, smooth civilization holds dear. He will contradict, denounce and protest in the name of God and will earn the hatred and opposition of a large segment of Christendom. Such a man is likely to be lean, rugged, blunt-spoken and a little bit angry with the world. He will love Christ and the souls of men to the point of willingness to die for the glory of the One and the salvation of the other. But he will fear nothing that breathes with mortal breath. SIZ128-129

> *Send to Your church today many who have "seen visions of God and . . . heard a voice from the Throne." Amen.*

WE LANGUISH FOR MEN

Then Paul answered, What mean ye to weep and to break mine heart? for I am ready not to be bound only, but also to die at Jerusalem for the name of the Lord Jesus.

—Acts 21:13

*T*he Church at this moment needs men, the right kind of men—bold men. . . .

We languish for men who feel themselves expendable in the warfare of the soul, who cannot be frightened by threats of death because they have already died to the allurements of this world. Such men will be free from the compulsions that control weaker men. They will not be forced to do things by the squeeze of circumstances; their only compulsion will come from within—or from above.

This kind of freedom is necessary if we are to have prophets in our pulpits again instead of mascots. These free men will serve God and mankind from motives too high to be understood by the rank and file of religious retainers who today shuttle in and out of the sanctuary. They will make no decisions out of fear, take no course out of a desire to please, accept no service for financial considerations, perform no religious act out of mere custom; nor will they allow themselves to be influenced by the love of publicity or the desire for reputation. OGM011-012

Lord, what would it take for me to be that kind of man? Do in me whatever work You need to do today, that I might die to the allurements of the world and serve You with high motives. Amen.

HOW MUCH I COULD HAVE DONE

And this they did, not as we hoped, but first gave their own selves to the Lord, and unto us by the will of God.

—2 Corinthians 8:5

*B*efore the judgment seat of Christ my service will be judged not by how much I have done but by how much I could have done. In God's sight my giving is measured not by how much I have given but by how much I could have given and how much I had left after I made my gift. The needs of the world and my total ability to minister to those needs decide the worth of my service.

Not by its size is my gift judged, but by how much of me there is in it. No man gives at all until he has given all. No man gives anything acceptable to God until he has first given himself in love and sacrifice. . . .

In the work of the church the amount one man must do to accomplish a given task is determined by how much or how little the rest of the company is willing to do. It is a rare church whose members all put their shoulder to the wheel. The typical church is composed of the few whose shoulders are bruised by their faithful labors and the many who are unwilling to raise a blister in the service of God and their fellowmen. There may be a bit of wry humor in all this, but it is quite certain that there will be no laughter when each of us gives account to God of the deeds done in the body.

TIC105

Help me to give of myself completely today, Lord. I hold nothing back, even if at the end of the day I'm the only one with a bruised shoulder. Amen.

BE WIDELY READ

For Ezra had prepared his heart to seek the law of the LORD, and to do it, and to teach in Israel statutes and judgments.

—Ezra 7:10

*A*ll else being equal it is desirable that Christians, especially ministers of the gospel, should be widely read. It is a disagreeable experience to present oneself before a teacher for religious instruction and discover in less than three minutes that the said teacher should have changed places with his listeners and learned from them rather than they from him. If he is a humble man and sticks close to the small plot of ground with which he is familiar, he may, if he loves God and men, succeed in ministering to the spiritual needs of his flock. If, however, his ignorance is exceeded by his arrogance, then God help his hearers. If he boasts of his ignorance and scorns learning, show me the nearest exit! I can learn more from a child laughing on the lawn or a cloud passing overhead. SIZ028-029

> *Lord, I'll never be able to be knowledgeable in every field from which my hearers come. But help me to diligently prepare my heart and know Your Word and to declare it humbly, but with authority. Amen.*

READ OR
GET OUT OF
THE MINISTRY

A wise man will hear, and will increase learning; and a man of understanding shall attain unto wise counsels.

—Proverbs 1:5

When a very young minister, I asked the famous holiness preacher, Joseph H. Smith, whether he would recommend that I read widely in the secular field. He replied, "Young man, a bee can find nectar in the weed as well as in the flower." I took his advice (or, to be frank, I sought confirmation of my own instincts rather than advice) and I am not sorry that I did.

John Wesley told the young ministers of the Wesleyan Societies to read or get out of the ministry, and he himself read science and history with a book propped against his saddle pommel as he rode from one engagement to another. Andy Dolbow, the American Indian preacher of considerable note, was a man of little education, but I once heard him exhort his hearers to improve their minds for the honor of God. "When you are chopping wood," he explained, "and you have a dull ax you must work all the harder to cut the log. A sharp ax makes easy work. So sharpen your ax all you can." SIZ033

In the busyness of life, Lord, help me to always guard time to sharpen my ax. Amen.

PUBLIC READING OF SCRIPTURE

Till I come, give attendance to reading, to exhortation, to doctrine.

—1 Timothy 4:13

*O*f course we of this generation cannot know by firsthand experience how the Word of God was read in other times. But it would be hard to conceive of our fathers having done a poorer job than we do when it comes to the public reading of the Scriptures. Most of us read the Scriptures so badly that a good performance draws attention by its rarity.

It could be argued that since everyone these days owns his own copy of the Scriptures, the need for the public reading of the Word is not as great as formerly. If that is true, then let us not bother to read the Scriptures at all in our churches. But if we are going to read the Word publicly, then it is incumbent upon us to read it well. A mumbled, badly articulated and unintelligent reading of the Sacred Scriptures will do more than we think to give the listeners the idea that the Word is not important. . . .

We should by all means read it, and we should make the reading a memorable experience for those who hear. NCA027

Lord, as we read the Scriptures publicly, we are both declaring the very Word of God Himself and drawing people into an experience of worship. Help us never to take that lightly or address it carelessly. Amen.

SOME NEW MYSTERY BAGGED

(For all the Athenians and strangers which were there spent their time in nothing else, but either to tell, or to hear some new thing.)

—Acts 17:21

The temptation to forget the few spiritual essentials and to go wandering off after unimportant things is very strong, especially to Christians of a certain curious type of mind. Such persons find the great majors of the faith of our fathers altogether too tame for them. Their souls loathe that light bread; their appetites crave the gamy tang of fresh-killed meat. They take great pride in their reputation as being mighty hunters before the Lord, and any time we look out we may see them returning from the chase with some new mystery hanging limply over their shoulder.

Usually the game they bring down is something on which there is a biblical closed season. Some vague hint in the Scriptures, some obscure verse about which the translators disagree, some marginal note for which there is not much scholarly authority: these are their favorite meat. They are especially skillful at propounding notions which have never been a part of the Christian heritage of truth. Their enthusiasm mounts with the uncertainty of their position, and their dogmatism grows firmer in proportion to the mystery which surrounds their subject. NCA012-013

Lord, keep me faithful to Your Word, give me understanding of the unfathomable truths contained therein, but deliver me from that danger of seeking some new insight to enhance my reputation as some kind of brilliant scholar. Amen.

JUST A HUCKSTER

He must increase, but I must decrease.

—John 3:30

Some young preacher will study until he has to get thick glasses to take care of his failing eyesight because he has an idea he wants to become a famous preacher. He wants to use Jesus Christ to make him a famous preacher. He's just a huckster buying and selling and getting gain. They will ordain him and he will be known as Reverend and if he writes a book, they will make him a doctor. And he will be known as Doctor; but he's still a huckster buying and selling and getting gain. And when the Lord comes back, He will drive him out of the temple along with the other cattle.

We can use the Lord for anything—or try to use Him. But what I'm preaching and what Paul taught and what was brought down through the years and what gave breath to the modern missionary movement that you and I know about and belong to was just the opposite: "O, God, we don't want anything You have, we want You." That's the cry of a soul on its way up. SAT029

Lord, give us that hunger to know You; deliver us from the pride that makes us want to use You. Let me pray today with John, "He must increase, but I must decrease." Amen.

WHAT A GREAT RESPONSIBILITY!

For the great day of his wrath is come; and who shall be able to stand?

—Revelation 6:17

*W*hat a great responsibility God has laid upon us preachers of His gospel and teachers of His Word. In that future day when God's wrath is poured out, how are we going to answer? How am *I* going to answer? I fear there is much we are doing in the name of the Christian church that is wood, hay and stubble destined to be burned up in God's refining fire. A day is coming when I and my fellow ministers must give account of our stewardship:

What kind of a gospel did we preach?

Did we make it plain that men and women who are apart from Christ Jesus are lost?

Did we counsel them to repent and believe?

Did we tell them of the regenerating power of the Holy Spirit?

Did we warn them of the wrath of the Lamb—the crucified, resurrected, outraged Lamb of God?

With that kind of accounting yet to come, the question John hears from the human objects of God's wrath is especially significant: "Who shall be able to stand?" (6:17). Who indeed?

JIV108

Lord, how am I going to answer?

HUMBLE SERVICE

Thou therefore endure hardness, as a good soldier of Jesus Christ. No man that warreth entangleth himself with the affairs of this life; that he may please him who hath chosen him to be a soldier.

—2 Timothy 2:3-4

Save me from the error of judging a church by its size, its popularity or the amount of its yearly offering. Help me to remember that I am a prophet—not a promoter, not a religious manager, but a prophet. Let me never become a slave to crowds. Heal my soul of carnal ambitions and deliver me from the itch for publicity. Save me from bondage to things. Let me not waste my days puttering around the house. Lay Thy terror upon me, O God, and drive me to the place of prayer where I may wrestle with principalities and powers and the rulers of the darkness of this world. Deliver me from overeating and late sleeping. Teach me self-discipline that I may be a good soldier of Jesus Christ. . . .

And now, O Lord of heaven and earth, I consecrate my remaining days to Thee; let them be many or few, as Thou wilt. Let me stand before the great or minister to the poor and lowly; that choice is not mine, and I would not influence it if I could. I am Thy servant to do Thy will, and that will is sweeter to me than position or riches or fame and I choose it above all things on earth or in heaven. GTM105-106

Enable me by your Holy Spirit to make this prayer genuinely mine. Amen.

PLEASE PRAY FOR ME

I have fought a good fight, I have finished my course, I have kept the faith: Henceforth there is laid up for me a crown of righteousness, which the Lord, the righteous judge, shall give me at that day: and not to me only, but unto all them also that love his appearing.

—2 Timothy 4:7-8

*W*ill you pray for me as a minister of the gospel? I am not asking you to pray for the things people commonly pray for. Pray for me in light of the pressures of our times. Pray that I will not just come to a wearied end—an exhausted, tired, old preacher, interested only in hunting a place to roost. Pray that I will be willing to let my Christian experience and Christian standards cost me something right down to the last gasp! WPJ074

> *Lord, I pray for all of my fellow pastors and Christian leaders. Help us, like Paul, and like Tozer, to finish strong. Amen.*

April

Prayer

To pray successfully is the first lesson the preacher must learn if he is to preach fruitfully; yet prayer is the hardest thing he will ever be called upon to do and, being human, it is the one act he will be tempted to do less frequently than any other. GTM069

THE FIRST LESSON TO LEARN

> *Watch and pray, that ye enter not into temptation: the spirit indeed is willing, but the flesh is weak.*
>
> —Matthew 26:41

*A*lmost anything associated with the ministry may be learned with an average amount of intelligent application. It is not hard to preach or manage church affairs or pay a social call; weddings and funerals may be conducted smoothly with a little help from Emily Post and the Minister's Manual. Sermon making can be learned as easily as shoemaking—introduction, conclusion and all. And so with the whole work of the ministry as it is carried on in the average church today.

But prayer—that is another matter. There Mrs. Post is helpless and the Minister's Manual can offer no assistance. There the lonely man of God must wrestle it out alone, sometimes in fastings and tears and weariness untold. There every man must be an original, for true prayer cannot be imitated nor can it be learned from someone else. GTM069

Lord, I don't want just to learn more about the importance of prayer. I pray that Your Spirit might change me, that I might become more and more genuinely a man of prayer. Amen.

At Home in the Prayer Chamber

Now when Daniel knew that the writing was signed, he went into his house; and his windows being open in his chamber toward Jerusalem, he kneeled upon his knees three times a day, and prayed, and gave thanks before his God, as he did aforetime.

—Daniel 6:10

Thomas à Kempis says that the man of God ought to be more at home in his prayer chamber than before the public. . . .

No man should stand before an audience who has not first stood before God. Many hours of communion should precede one hour in the pulpit. The prayer chamber should be more familiar than the public platform. Prayer should be continuous, preaching but intermittent.

It is significant that the schools teach everything about preaching except the important part, praying. For this weakness the schools are not to be blamed, for the reason that prayer cannot be taught; it can only be done. The best any school or any book (or any article) can do is to recommend prayer and exhort to its practice. Praying itself must be the work of the individual. That it is the one religious work which gets done with the least enthusiasm cannot but be one of the tragedies of our times. GTM070-071

Lord, I pray today that I might more and more be at home in my prayer chamber. Help me to pray with deeper commitment and greater enthusiasm. Amen.

OUR
FIRST
RESPONSIBILITY

I prevented the dawning of the morning, and cried: I hoped in thy word. Mine eyes prevent the night watches, that I might meditate in thy word.

—Psalm 119:147-148

*B*riefly, the way to escape religion as a front is to make it a fount. See to it that we pray more than we preach and we will never preach ourselves out. Stay with God in the secret place longer than we are with men in the public place and the fountain of our wisdom will never dry up. Keep our hearts open to the inflowing Spirit and we will not become exhausted by the outflow. Cultivate the acquaintance of God more than the friendship of men and we will always have abundance of bread to give to the hungry.

Our first responsibility is not to the public but to God and our own souls. . . .

It is by humility, simplicity and constant trustful communion with God that we keep the fountain open with our hearts.

GTM115-116

Lord, why does our first responsibility so easily get crowded out? Quiet me today that this first thing might get the time and attention it deserves. Amen.

LONG
BEFORE
THE LORD

But when Moses went in before the LORD to speak with him, he took the vail off, until he came out. And he came out, and spake unto the children of Israel that which he was commanded.

—Exodus 34:34

*I*t is written of Moses that he "went in before the LORD to speak with him. . . . [a]nd he came out, and spake unto the children of Israel." This is the biblical norm from which we depart to our own undoing and to the everlasting injury of the souls of men. No man has any moral right to go before the people who has not first been long before the Lord. No man has any right to speak to men about God who has not first spoken to God about men. And the prophet of God should spend more time in the secret place praying than he spends in the public place preaching. . . .

One swallow does not make a spring nor one hot day a summer; nor will a few minutes of frantic praying before service bring out the tender buds or make the flowers to appear on the earth. The field must be soaked in sunshine over a long period before it will give forth its treasures. The Christian's heart must be soaked in prayer before the true spiritual fruits begin to grow. ROR105-106

Quiet my heart today, slow me down I pray. Amen.

THE TOP
SIDE OF
OUR SOULS

And he said unto them, Come ye yourselves apart into a desert place, and rest a while: for there were many coming and going, and they had no leisure so much as to eat.

—Mark 6:31

*E*very real Christian, however practical, is in some degree a mystic, his mysticism lying on the upper side of his life. He prays, meditates on spiritual things and communes with God and the invisible world. Also, every Christian, however he may be dedicated to the holy art of prayer and worship, must of necessity descend to work and eat and sleep and pay his taxes and get on somehow with the hard world around him. And if he follows on to know the Lord he must serve in every useful way outlined for him in the Scriptures of truth. To be a Christian it is necessary that he serve his generation as well as his God.

The big problem is to keep the two elements of the Christian life in proper balance. . . .

Today the Christian emphasis falls heavily on the "active" life. . . . The favorite brand of Christianity is that sparked by the man in a hurry, hard hitting, aggressive and ready with the neat quip. We are neglecting the top side of our souls. The light in the tower burns dimly while we hurry about the grounds below, making a great racket and giving the impression of wonderful devotion to our task. PON045-047

Lord, help me to keep the proper balance. Help me especially to cultivate the top side of my soul. Amen.

JUST WAIT ON GOD

Truly my soul waiteth upon God: from him cometh my salvation.

—Psalm 62:1

I think we are the busiest bunch of eager beavers ever seen in the religious world. The idea seems to be that if we are not running in a circle, breathing down the back of our own neck, we are not pleasing God!

When Jesus said, "Go ye into all the world, and preach the gospel to every creature" (Mark 16:15), Peter probably leaped to his feet and, no doubt, scooped up his hat on the way out. He was going to go right then!

But the Lord said, "Peter, come back, and 'tarry ye in the city of Jerusalem, until ye be endued with power from on high' (Luke 24:49)."

I heard a Christian leader warn recently that we are suffering from a rash of amateurism in Christian circles. Christianity has leveled down and down and down. We are as light as butterflies—though we flit, flit, flit around in the sunshine and imagine that we are eagles flapping our broad wings.

Sometimes I think the Church would be better off if we would call a moratorium on activity for about six weeks and just wait on God to see what He is waiting to do for us. That's what they did before Pentecost. COU095

Lord, this morning I'll stop for a while at least to "just wait on God." I know You're wanting to work, and I for one am willing to wait this morning to hear Your voice and discover what You want to do for me today. Amen.

JUST MEDITATE FOR A MONTH

But his delight is in the law of the LORD; and in his law doth he meditate day and night.

—Psalm 1:2

*L*et the old saints be our example. They came to the Word of God and meditated. They laid the Bible on the old-fashioned, handmade chair, got down on the old, scrubbed, board floor and meditated on the Word. As they waited, faith mounted. The Spirit and faith illuminated. They had only a Bible with fine print, narrow margins and poor paper, but they knew their Bible better than some of us do with all of our helps.

Let's practice the art of Bible meditation. . . . Let us open our Bibles, spread them out on a chair and meditate on the Word of God. It will open itself to us, and the Spirit of God will come and brood over it.

I do challenge you to meditate, quietly, reverently, prayerfully, for a month. Put away questions and answers and the filling in of the blank lines in the portions you haven't been able to understand. Put all of the cheap trash away and take the Bible, get on your knees, and in faith, say, "Father, here I am. Begin to teach me!" COU136-137

Guide me, Lord, as I take time to meditate on You. Tozer is stimulating me, but my real desire is to hear from You. I'll get on my knees this morning, Lord, in quiet expectation. Amen.

OVERCOME DISTRACTIONS

But thou, when thou prayest, enter into thy closet, and when thou hast shut thy door, pray to thy Father which is in secret; and thy Father which seeth in secret shall reward thee openly.

—Matthew 6:6

*A*mong the enemies to devotion none is so harmful as distractions. Whatever excites the curiosity, scatters the thoughts, disquiets the heart, absorbs the interests or shifts our life focus from the kingdom of God within us to the world around us—that is a distraction; and the world is full of them. Our science-based civilization has given us many benefits but it has multiplied our distractions and so taken away far more than it has given. . . .

The remedy for distractions is the same now as it was in earlier and simpler times, viz., prayer, meditation and the cultivation of the inner life. The psalmist said "Be still, and know" (Psalm 46:10), and Christ told us to enter into our closet, shut the door and pray unto the Father. It still works. . . .

Distractions *must* be conquered or they will conquer us. So let us cultivate simplicity; let us want fewer things; let us walk in the Spirit; let us fill our minds with the Word of God and our hearts with praise. In that way we can live in peace even in such a distraught world as this. "Peace I leave with you, my peace I give unto you" (John 14:27). SOS130-132

Lord, help me to cultivate simplicity, to be satisfied with fewer things and to find the inner peace that You can give in a life of prayer and meditation. Amen.

MEN WHO DO NOT PRAY

Wherefore, brethren, look ye out among you seven men of honest report, full of the Holy Ghost and wisdom, whom we may appoint over this business.

—Acts 6:3

*L*et us watch that we do not slide imperceptibly to a state where the women do the praying and the men run the churches. Men who do not pray have no right to direct church affairs. We believe in the leadership of men within the spiritual community of the saints, but that leadership should be won by spiritual worth.

Leadership requires vision, and whence will vision come except from hours spent in the presence of God in humble and fervent prayer? All things else being equal, a praying woman will know the will of God for the church far better than a prayerless man.

We do not here advocate the turning of the churches over to the women, but we do advocate a recognition of proper spiritual qualifications for leadership among the men if they are to continue to decide the direction the churches shall take. The accident of being a man is not enough. Spiritual manhood alone qualifies. WTA016

Lord, don't ever let me have leadership that I don't deserve. Don't ever let me become careless in prayer. Don't ever let me rely on the women to pray while I lead. Amen.

THE PRAYER OF FAITH

... The effectual fervent prayer of a righteous man availeth much.

—James 5:16

$\mathcal{A}$ second important requirement if the believing church is to be used in God's ministry is prayer and the response God makes to our prayers uttered in true faith. . . . No matter what our stature or status, we have the authority in the family of God to pray the prayer of faith. The prayer of faith engages the heart of God, meeting God's conditions of spiritual life and victory.

Our consideration of the power and efficacy of prayer enters into the question of why we are part of a Christian congregation and what that congregation is striving to be and do. We have to consider whether we are just going around and around—like a religious merry-go-round. Are we simply holding on to the painted mane of the painted horse, repeating a trip of very insignificant circles to a pleasing musical accompaniment? . . .

All of the advertising we can do will never equal the interest and participation in the things of God resulting from the gracious answers to the prayers of faith generated by the Holy Spirit. TRA007-008

Lord, don't ever let me be satisfied "holding on to the painted mane of the painted horse." I want to be part of a dynamic Body of believers, greatly used of You because we're seeing answers to genuine "prayers of faith generated by the Holy Spirit." Amen.

OH!

Then said I, Ah, Lord GOD!
behold, I cannot speak: for I
am a child.

—Jeremiah 1:6

*T*o be articulate at certain times we are compelled to fall back
upon "Oh!" or "O!"—a primitive exclamatory sound that is
hardly a word at all and that scarcely admits of a definition. . . .
In theology there is no "Oh!" and this is a significant if not an
ominous thing. Theology seeks to reduce what may be known of
God to intellectual terms, and as long as the intellect can comprehend, it can find words to express itself. When God Himself appears before the mind, awesome, vast and incomprehensible, then
the mind sinks into silence and the heart cries out "O Lord God!"
There is the difference between theological knowledge and spiritual experience, the difference between knowing God by hearsay
and knowing Him by acquaintance. And the difference is not ver-
bal merely; it is real and serious and vital.

We Christians should watch lest we lose the "Oh!" from our
hearts. . . . When we become too glib in prayer we are most surely
talking to ourselves. When the calm listing of requests and the
courteous giving of proper thanks take the place of the burdened
prayer that finds utterance difficult we should beware the next
step, for our direction is surely down whether we know it or not.

BAM085-087

Lord, don't ever let me lose the "Oh!" Amen.

NOT ASKING FOR ANYTHING

I love the LORD, because he hath heard my voice and my supplications. Because he hath inclined his ear unto me, therefore will I call upon him as long as I live.

—Psalm 116:1-2

I think that some of the greatest prayer is prayer where you don't say one single word or ask for anything. Now God does answer and He does give us what we ask for. That's plain; nobody can deny that unless he denies the Scriptures. But that's only one aspect of prayer, and it's not even the important aspect. Sometimes I go to God and say, "God, if Thou dost never answer another prayer while I live on this earth I will still worship Thee as long as I live and in the ages to come for what Thou hast done already." God's already put me so far in debt that if I were to live one million millenniums I couldn't pay Him for what He's done for me.

We go to God as we send a boy to a grocery store with a long written list. "God, give me this, give me this, and give me this," and our gracious God often does give us what we want. But I think God is disappointed because we make Him to be no more than a source of what we want. Even our Lord Jesus is presented too often much as "Someone who will meet your need." That's the throbbing heart of modern evangelism. You're in need and Jesus will meet your need. He's the Need-meeter. Well, He is that indeed; but, ah, He's infinitely more than that. WMJ024-025

Father, forgive me for so often just coming to You with my grocery list. You've been so faithful; You've given me so much; You've blessed so richly. I realize my incredible debt to You, and I simply worship at Your feet. Amen.

TAKE TIME TO LISTEN

The entrance of thy words giveth light; it giveth understanding unto the simple. I opened my mouth and panted: for I longed for thy commandments.

—Psalm 119:130-131

*T*he Quakers had many fine ideas about life, and there is a story from them that illustrates the point I am trying to make. It concerns a conversation between Samuel Taylor Coleridge and a Quaker woman he had met. Maybe Coleridge was boasting a bit, but he told the woman how he had arranged the use of time so he would have no wasted hours. He said he memorized Greek while dressing and during breakfast. He went on with his list of other mental activities—making notes, reading, writing, formulating thoughts and ideas—until bedtime.

The Quaker listened unimpressed. When Coleridge was finished with his explanation, she asked him a simple, searching question: "My friend, when dost thee think?"

God is having a difficult time getting through to us because we are a fast-paced generation. We seem to have no time for contemplation. We have no time to answer God when He calls. JAF046

Lord, in this increasingly fast-paced, success-oriented life, slow us down and teach us the value of having time to think. Amen.

TEACH ME TO LISTEN

And the LORD came, and stood, and called as at other times, Samuel, Samuel. Then Samuel answered, Speak; for thy servant heareth.

—1 Samuel 3:10

Lord, teach me to listen. The times are noisy and my ears are weary with the thousand raucous sounds which continuously assault them. Give me the spirit of the boy Samuel when he said to Thee, "Speak, for thy servant heareth." Let me hear Thee speaking in my heart. Let me get used to the sound of Thy voice, that its tones may be familiar when the sounds of earth die away and the only sound will be the music of Thy speaking voice. Amen. POG078

"Speak, for Thy servant heareth." Amen.

A CLOSED MOUTH AND SILENT HEART

My heart was hot within me, while I was musing the fire burned: then spake I with my tongue.

—Psalm 39:3

*P*rayer among evangelical Christians is always in danger of degenerating into a glorified gold rush. Almost every book on prayer deals with the "get" element mainly. How to get things we want from God occupies most of the space. Now, we gladly admit that we may ask for and receive specific gifts and benefits in answer to prayer, but we must never forget that the highest kind of prayer is never the making of requests. Prayer at its holiest moment is the entering into God to a place of such blessed union as makes miracles seem tame and remarkable answers to prayer appear something very far short of wonderful by comparison.

Holy men of soberer and quieter times than ours knew well the power of silence. David said, "I was dumb with silence, I held my peace, even from good; and my sorrow was stirred. My heart was hot within me, while I was musing the fire burned: then spake I with my tongue" (Psalm 39:2-3). There is a tip here for God's modern prophets. The heart seldom gets hot while the mouth is open. A closed mouth before God and a silent heart are indispensable for the reception of certain kinds of truth. No man is qualified to speak who has not first listened.

SOS014-015

> *Lord, teach me to close my mouth. Help me to sit in silence before You, with my mouth closed. Amen.*

THE FILE-CARD MENTALITY

My soul breaketh for the longing that it hath unto thy judgments at all times.... Thy testimonies also are my delight and my counsellors.

—Psalm 119:20, 24

*W*hen religion loses its sovereign character and becomes mere form, this spontaneity is lost also, and in its place come precedent, propriety, system—and the file-card mentality. . . .

The slave to the file card soon finds that his prayers lose their freedom and become less spontaneous, less effective. He finds himself concerned over matters that should give him no concern whatever—how much time he spent in prayer yesterday, whether he did or did not cover his prayer list for the day, whether he gets up as early as he used to do or stays up in prayer as late at night. Inevitably the calendar crowds out the Spirit and the face of the clock hides the face of God. Prayer ceases to be the free breath of a ransomed soul and becomes a duty to be fulfilled. And even if under such circumstances he succeeds in making his prayer amount to something, still he is suffering tragic losses and binding upon his soul a yoke from which Christ died to set him free. OGM079, 081

Oh, Father, I pray that prayer might never become for me "a duty to be fulfilled." Fill me with freedom in my times with You. Amen.

PRAYER CHANGES THE MAN

And whatsoever ye shall ask in my name, that will I do, that the Father may be glorified in the Son. If ye shall ask any thing in my name, I will do it.

—John 14:13-14

*I*n all our praying, however, it is important that we keep in mind that God will not alter His eternal purposes at the word of a man. We do not pray in order to persuade God to change His mind. Prayer is not an assault upon the reluctance of God, nor an effort to secure a suspension of His will for us or for those for whom we pray. Prayer is not intended to overcome God and "move His arm." God will never be other than Himself, no matter how many people pray, nor how long nor how earnestly.

God's love desires the best for all of us, and He desires to give us the best at any cost. He will open rivers in desert places, still turbulent waves, quiet the wind. . . . All these things and a thousand others He has done and will do in answer to prayer, but only because it had been His will to do it from the beginning. No one persuades Him.

What the praying man does is to bring his will into line with the will of God so God can do what He has all along been willing to do. Thus prayer changes the man and enables God to change things in answer to man's prayer. PON051-052

Somehow You have given me the awesome privilege of communing with You, bringing my requests and waiting upon You to bring my will in line with Yours. Then somehow You work in answer to my prayer! Thank You. Amen.

MUCH EVERY WAY

Ah Lord God! behold, thou hast made the heaven and the earth by thy great power and stretched out arm, and there is nothing too hard for thee.

—Jeremiah 32:17

When Tennyson wrote "More things are wrought by prayer than this world dreams of," he probably uttered a truth of vaster significance than even he understood. While it is not always possible to trace an act of God to its prayer-cause, it is yet safe to say that prayer is back of everything that God does for the sons of men here upon earth. One would gather as much from a simple reading of the Scriptures.

What profit is there in prayer? "Much every way." Whatever God can do faith can do, and whatever faith can do prayer can do when it is offered in faith. An invitation to prayer is, therefore, an invitation to omnipotence, for prayer engages the Omnipotent God and brings Him into our human affairs. Nothing is impossible to the man who prays in faith, just as nothing is impossible with God. This generation has yet to prove all that prayer can do for believing men and women. SOS033

Lord, this is a truth with implications too vast for our finite comprehension. Thank You that you use the prayers of believers to engage Your omnipotence. Amen.

ARMED WITH COURAGE

But let him ask in faith, nothing wavering. For he that wavereth is like a wave of the sea driven with the wind and tossed.

—James 1:6

*W*hen entering the prayer chamber, we must come filled with faith and armed with courage. Nowhere else in the whole field of religious thought and activity is courage so necessary as in prayer. The successful prayer must be one without condition. We must believe that God is love and that, being love, He cannot harm us but must ever do us good. Then we must throw ourselves before Him and pray with boldness for whatever we know our good and His glory require, and the cost is no object! Whatever He in His love and wisdom would assess against us, we will accept with delight because it pleased Him. Prayers like that cannot go unanswered. The character and reputation of God guarantee their fulfillment.

We should always keep in mind the infinite loving-kindness of God. No one need fear to put his life in His hands. His yoke is easy; His burden is light. WTA048

Increase my faith; increase my courage. Amen.

CONFIDENCE IN HIM

> *Now unto him that is able to do exceeding abundantly above all that we ask or think, according to the power that worketh in us, unto him be glory in the church by Christ Jesus throughout all ages, world without end. Amen.*
>
> —Ephesians 3:20-21

*Y*ou can have this confidence in God, and you can have this respect for His will. Do not expect God to perform miracles for you so you can write books about them. Do not ever be caught asking God to send you toys like that to play around with.

But if you are in trouble and concerned about your situation and willing to be honest with God, you can have confidence in Him. You can go to Him in the merit of His Son, claiming His promises, and He will not let you down. God will help you, and you will find the way of deliverance.

God will move heaven and earth for you if you will trust Him. FBR049

Thank You, Father, for the majesty of this truth. It certainly is only in the merit of Your Son, but in that merit You've given us a powerful promise. Thank You that You never let us down. Amen.

IF GOD ANSWERS PRAYER

Every good gift and every perfect gift is from above, and cometh down from the Father of lights, with whom is no variableness, neither shadow of turning.

—James 1:17

$\mathcal{W}$hy does God answer prayer? Let's not imagine that it's because somebody was good. We Protestants think we don't believe in saints, but we do. We canonize them: we have Saint George Mueller, Saint C.H. Spurgeon, Saint D.L. Moody and Saint A.B. Simpson. We get the idea that God answered prayer for them because they were really good. They would deny that fervently if they were here.

Nobody ever got anything from God on the grounds that he deserved it. Having fallen, man deserves only punishment and death. So if God answers prayer it's because God is good. From His goodness, His loving-kindness, His good-natured benevolence, God does it! That's the source of everything. AOG046-047

Thank You, God, that You are indeed good, You are faithful, You are gracious, You are full of loving-kindness and benevolence. Thank You that You do in fact answer prayer! Amen.

TWO CONDITIONS MUST BE MET

And this is the confidence that we have in him, that, if we ask any thing according to his will, he heareth us.

—1 John 5:14

*W*hen we go to God with a request that He modify the existing situation for us, that is, that He answer prayer, there are two conditions that we must meet: (1) We must pray in the will of God and (2) we must be on what old-fashioned Christians often call "praying ground"; that is, we must be living lives pleasing to God.

It is futile to beg God to act contrary to His revealed purposes. To pray with confidence the petitioner must be certain that his request falls within the broad will of God for His people.

The second condition is also vitally important. God has not placed Himself under obligation to honor the requests of worldly, carnal or disobedient Christians. He hears and answers the prayers only of those who walk in His way.

The truth is that God always answers the prayer that accords with His will as revealed in the Scriptures, provided the one who prays is obedient and trustful. Further than this we dare not go.

MDP086-087

> *Lord, in the power of Your Holy Spirit, help me to be obedient. May everything I think and do be pleasing in Your sight. Amen.*

WHOLE LIFE PRAYER

If ye abide in me, and my words abide in you, ye shall ask what ye will, and it shall be done unto you.

—John 15:7

$\mathcal{P}$rayer at its best is the expression of the total life. . . .

All things else being equal, our prayers are only as powerful as our lives. In the long pull we pray only as well as we live. . . .

Most of us in moments of stress have wished that we had lived so that prayer would not be so unnatural to us and have regretted that we had not cultivated prayer to the point where it would be as easy and as natural as breathing. . . .

Undoubtedly the redemption in Christ Jesus has sufficient moral power to enable us to live in a state of purity and love where our whole life will be a prayer. Individual acts of prayer that spring out of that kind of total living will have about them a wondrous power not known to the careless or the worldly Christian. ROR081-083

Lord, the real key here is that there is "sufficient moral power" available. In my own strength I fail, but thank You for Your enabling power. Amen.

FAITH GROWS WITH USE

Yet ye have not, because ye ask not.

—James 4:2

$\mathcal{I}$t was a saying of George Mueller that faith grows with use. If we would have great faith we must begin to use the little faith we already have. Put it to work by reverent and faithful praying, and it will grow and become stronger day by day. Dare today to trust God for something small and ordinary and next week or next year you may be able to trust Him for answers bordering on the miraculous. Everyone has some faith, said Mueller; the difference among us is one of degree only, and the man of small faith may be simply the one who has not dared to exercise the little faith he has.

According to the Bible, we have because we ask, or we have not because we ask not. It does not take much wisdom to discover our next move. Is it not to pray, and pray again and again till the answer comes? God waits to be invited to display His power on behalf of His people. The world situation is such that nothing less than God can straighten it out. Let us not fail the world and disappoint God by failing to pray. sos033-034

Lord, I know my faith needs to grow, so please help me to exercise what faith I have and anticipate that growth and stretching. Amen.

PRAY TILL YOU PRAY

Continue in prayer, and watch in the same with thanksgiving.

—Colossians 4:2

*D*r. Moody Stuart, a great praying man of a past generation, once drew up a set of rules to guide him in his prayers. Among these rules is this one: "Pray till you pray.". . .

The habit of breaking off our prayers before we have truly prayed is as common as it is unfortunate. Often the last ten minutes may mean more to us than the first half hour, because we must spend a long time getting into the proper mood to pray effectively. We may need to struggle with our thoughts to draw them in from where they have been scattered through the multitude of distractions that result from the task of living in a disordered world. . . .

If when we come to prayer our hearts feel dull and unspiritual, we should not try to argue ourselves out of it. Rather, we should admit it frankly and pray our way through. Some Christians smile at the thought of "praying through," but something of the same idea is found in the writings of practically every great praying saint from Daniel to the present day. We cannot afford to stop praying till we have actually prayed. TWP069-070

> *Oh Lord, what an important and needed challenge! Help me to wait and "pray through." Amen.*

BE
PATItENT

Rejoicing in hope; patient in tribulation; continuing instant in prayer.

—Romans 12:12

*T*hink of the kernels of grain, the seed, that the farmer plants in the ground in the fall of the year. How patient the farmer must be! Throughout the long, cold winter the seed is dormant. There is no evidence at all that it is there—covered by the cold earth itself. The snows come and go. The ground freezes and thaws. Does the farmer lie awake at night worrying that those seeds he placed in the ground may be ineffective? He does not. He knows that spring will come!

And in due course, the sunshine of March or April warms the air. Spring rains water the ground. The farmer knows then that it will not be long until green shoots suddenly break out from their covering of earth. And in their own time, great waving fields of grain are ready for the harvest. The farmer's faith in the seed he planted is fully justified.

Likewise, God wants us to be patient with every prayer and petition we sincerely send up to that heavenly altar. Our praying done in the Spirit cannot be ineffective. It is as though God is saying to us: "You have planted the seed. You have prayed for My will to be done and for My kingdom to come on earth. . . . The effective prayers of My Son, Jesus, will join with the effective prayers of righteous men and women. Be patient and put your trust in Me, day by day!" JIV122

Lord, give me a patient, steadfast faith, with a willingness to wait for the harvest. Amen.

PRAY WITHOUT CEASING

Pray without ceasing.

—1 Thessalonians 5:17

I knew of an able preacher greatly used of the Lord in evangelism and Bible conferences. He was a busy, busy man. There came the occasion when someone frankly asked him, "Doctor, tell us about your prayer life. How do you pray? How much do you pray?"

The man was embarrassed as he replied, "I must confess to you something I have not confessed before. I do not have the time to pray as I used to. My time alone with God has been neglected."

Not too long afterward, that preacher sustained a serious failure. It brought his ministry to an abrupt end, and he was put on the shelf.

If we want to be honest with God, we will take solemnly the admonition to pray without ceasing. God's work on this earth languishes when God's people give up their ministries of prayer and supplication. I cannot tell you why this is true, but it *is* true.
MMG046-047

> *Deliver me from neglect and keep me faithful in the high priority of prayer. Then guard me from that "serious failure." Amen.*

THE UTILITARIAN CHRIST

I have heard of thee by the hearing of the ear: but now mine eye seeth thee. Wherefore I abhor myself, and repent in dust and ashes.

—Job 42:5-6

*W*ithin the past few years, for instance, Christ has been popularized by some so-called evangelicals as one who, if a proper amount of prayer were made, would help the pious prize fighter to knock another fighter unconscious in the ring. Christ is also said to help the big league pitcher to get the proper hook on his curve. In another instance He assists an athletically-minded parson to win the high jump, and still another not only to come in first in a track meet but to set a new record in the bargain. He is said also to have helped a praying businessman to beat out a competitor in a deal, to underbid a rival and to secure a coveted contract to the discomfiture of someone else who was trying to get it. He is even thought to lend succor to a praying movie actress while she plays a role so lewd as to bring the blood to the face of a professional prostitute.

Thus our Lord becomes the Christ of utility, a kind of Aladdin's lamp to do minor miracles in behalf of anyone who summons Him to do his bidding. ROR024

Lord, help me not to demean the person of Christ or the sovereignty of God with this cheap sham of prayer. Amen.

UNANSWERED PRAYER

Give ear to my words, O LORD, consider my meditation. Hearken unto the voice of my cry, my King, and my God: for unto thee will I pray.

—Psalm 5:1-2

*I*f unanswered prayer continues in a congregation over an extended period of time, the chill of discouragement will settle over the praying people. If we continue to ask and ask and ask, like petulant children, never expecting to get what we ask for but continuing to whine for it, we will become chilled within our beings.

If we continue in our prayers and never get answers, the lack of results will tend to confirm the natural unbelief of our hearts. Remember this: the human heart by nature is filled with unbelief. . . .

Perhaps worst of all is the fact that our failures in prayer leave the enemy in possession of the field. The worst part about the failure of a military drive is not the loss of men or the loss of face but the fact that the enemy is left in possession of the field. In the spiritual sense, this is both a tragedy and a disaster. The devil ought to be on the run, always fighting a rear guard action. Instead, this blasphemous enemy smugly and scornfully holds his position, and the people of God let him have it. No wonder the work of the Lord is greatly retarded. Little wonder the work of God stands still! FBR036-037

Lord, show me Your power today. Increase my faith. Don't ever let the enemy claim any territory because of my doubt and unbelief. Amen.

DON'T LET ME LIVE WRONG

Being confident of this very thing, that he which hath begun a good work in you will perform it until the day of Jesus Christ.

—Philippians 1:6

*F*or years I have made a practice of writing many of my earnest prayers to God in a little book—a book now well worn. I still turn often to the petitions I recorded in that book. I remind God often of what my prayers have been.

One prayer in the book—and God knows it well by this time, for I pray it often—goes like this:

> Oh God, Let me die rather than to go on day by day living wrong. . . . I want to be right so that I can die right. Lord, I do not want my life to be extended if it would mean that I should cease to live right and fail in my mission to glorify You all of my days! . . .

As you will recall from Second Kings 20, the Lord gave Hezekiah a fifteen-year extension of life. Restored to health and vigor, Hezekiah disgraced himself and dishonored God before he died and was buried.

I would not want an extra fifteen years in which to backslide and dishonor my Lord. I would rather go home right now than to live on—if living on was to be a waste of God's time and my own! JIV141-142

Please, Father, help me to finish well. Amen.

Preaching

You may say, "I believe all that. You surely don't think you are telling us anything new!" I don't hope to tell you very much that is new; I only hope to set the table for you, arranging the dishes a little better and a little more attractively so that you will be tempted to partake.
HTB012

LISTEN TO GOD

Then spake Jesus again unto them, saying, I am the light of the world: he that followeth me shall not walk in darkness, but shall have the light of life.

—John 8:12

*I*f while hearing a sermon we can fix on but one real jewel of truth we may consider ourselves well rewarded for the time we have spent.

One such gem was uncovered during a sermon which I heard some time ago. From the sermon I got one worthy sentence and no more, but it was so good that I regret that I cannot remember who the preacher was, that I might give him credit. Here is what he said, "Listen to no man who fails to listen to God." . . .

No man has any right to offer advice who has not first heard God speak. No man has any right to counsel others who is not ready to hear and follow the counsel of the Lord. True moral wisdom must always be an echo of God's voice. The only safe light for our path is the light which is reflected from Christ, the Light of the World. . . .

God has His chosen men still, and they are without exception good listeners. They can hear when the Lord speaks. We may safely listen to such men. But to no others. ROR017-019

Don't ever let me preach my own empty, worthless stuff, Lord. Whenever I enter the pulpit I pray that I might have a fresh word from heaven. Amen.

WHERE I'M GOING TO GRAZE

The same came therefore to Philip, which was of Bethsaida of Galilee, and desired him, saying, Sir, we would see Jesus.

—John 12:21

*T*oward anything like thorough scholarship I make no claim. I am not an authority on any man's teaching; I have never tried to be. I take my help where I find it and set my heart to graze where the pastures are greenest. Only one stipulation do I make: my teacher must know God, as Carlyle said, "otherwise than by hearsay," and Christ must be all in all to him. If a man have only correct doctrine to offer me I am sure to slip out at the first intermission to seek the company of someone who has seen for himself how lovely is the face of Him who is the Rose of Sharon and the Lily of the Valley. Such a man can help me, and no one else can. POMxiv

Forgive me, Lord, and give me a fresh and new vision of You—so that any pasture I spread will be worth grazing in. Amen.

STARVING
AT THE
FATHER'S TABLE

So when they had dined, Jesus saith to Simon Peter, Simon, son of Jonas, lovest thou me more than these? He saith unto him, Yea, Lord; thou knowest that I love thee. He saith unto him, Feed my lambs.

—John 21:15

*T*here is today no lack of Bible teachers to set forth correctly the principles of the doctrines of Christ, but too many of these seem satisfied to teach the fundamentals of the faith year after year, strangely unaware that there is in their ministry no manifest Presence, nor anything unusual in their personal lives. They minister constantly to believers who feel within their breasts a longing which their teaching simply does not satisfy.

I trust I speak in charity, but the lack in our pulpits is real. Milton's terrible sentence applies to our day as accurately as it did to his: "The hungry sheep look up, and are not fed." It is a solemn thing, and no small scandal in the kingdom, to see God's children starving while actually seated at the Father's table. POG008

Lord, send the refreshing of Your Spirit into our midst, that none of those who listen to our teaching may starve at the Father's table. Amen.

A GENUINE GIFT

So being affectionately desirous of you, we were willing to have imparted unto you, not the gospel of God only, but also our own souls, because ye were dear unto us.

—1 Thessalonians 2:8

*L*et me shock you at this point. A naturally bright person can carry on religious activity without a special gift from God. Filling church pulpits every week are some who are using only natural abilities and special training. Some are known as Bible expositors, for it is possible to read and study commentaries and then repeat what has been learned about the Scriptures. Yes, it may shock you, but it is true that anyone able to talk fluently can learn to use religious phrases and can become recognized as a preacher.

But if any person is determined to preach so that his work and ministry will abide in the day of the judgment fire, then he must preach, teach and exhort with the kind of love and concern that comes only through a genuine gift of the Holy Spirit—something beyond his own capabilities. TRA021-022

Lord, grant me that gift as I wait before You. I want to preach with eternal benefit, help me to recognize that only in the power—and love—of the Holy Spirit will that happen. Amen.

GREAT PREACHERS

> *Now we have received, not the spirit of the world, but the spirit which is of God; that we might know the things that are freely given to us of God.*
>
> —1 Corinthians 2:12

I'm against the idea of putting the "big preachers" on tape and playing them back to the congregations that feel they are being starved by listening to "little preachers."

Fallacy, brethren—a thousand times, fallacy!

If we could have the Apostle Paul on tape recordings and let him stand here and preach, he could do no more for you than the Holy Ghost can do, with The Book and the human conscience. . . .

Oh, brethren, I would not detract from God's great men, but I can safely say that that's not what the church needs.

The church needs to listen to the inner voice and do something about it! TTPI, Book 1/108-109

Lord, we're inundated today with "big preachers." And while we appreciate their gifts and ministries, I pray today for all who are "little preachers." Help them not to be discouraged by their seeming smallness but to be faithful servants of Yours, declaring with great passion the message of the Book, in the power of the Holy Spirit. Amen.

A MAJOR PREACHING CHALLENGE

Unto me, who am less than the least of all saints, is this grace given, that I should preach among the Gentiles the unsearchable riches of Christ.

—Ephesians 3:8

$\mathcal{M}$any of us who preach the unsearchable riches of Christ are often pretty dull and hard to listen to.

The freshest thought to visit the human mind should be the thought of God. The story of salvation should put a radiancy in the face and a vibrancy in the voice of him that tells it. Yet it is not uncommon to hear the wondrous message given in a manner that makes it difficult for the hearer to concentrate on what is being said. What is wrong? . . .

It is true that only the Spirit-filled preacher can be morally effective at last; but for the moment we are thinking only of the ability of a speaker to command the attention of his hearers. And if the speaker cannot keep his hearers immediately interested, his message cannot possibly have a long-range effect upon them, no matter how spiritual he may be. WOS067-068

> *Lord, in this media-saturated, video-oriented age, it is increasingly difficult for the preacher to hold the interest of sound-bite listeners. Yet as we give ourselves to the task of preaching, You've promised to bless, and we thank You. Amen.*

A SENSE OF INADEQUACY

But we have this treasure in earthen vessels, that the excellency of the power may be of God, and not of us.

—2 Corinthians 4:7

I believe I had anticipated that it was going to be a pleasure to expound this beautiful and high soaring Gospel of John. However, I must confess that in my preparation and study a sense of inadequacy has come over me—a feeling of inadequacy so stunning, so almost paralyzing that I am not at this juncture able to call it a pleasure to preach.

Perhaps this will be God's way of reducing the flesh to a minimum and giving the Holy Spirit the best possible opportunity to do His eternal work. I fear that sometimes our own eloquence and our own concepts may get in the way, for the unlimited ability to talk endlessly about religion is a questionable blessing. . . .

None of us can approach a serious study and consideration of the eternal nature and person of Jesus Christ without sensing and confessing our complete inadequacy in the face of the divine revelation. CES003, 009

Lord, I've so often been at that place of total inadequacy. I've learned that that is so healthy because then I step aside, I quit relying on my own "eloquence" and I allow the Holy Spirit to take over and do what only He can do anyway! Use me today in my weakness. Amen.

JOHN
3:16

For God so loved the world, that he gave his only begotten Son, that whosoever believeth in him should not perish, but have ever-lasting life.

—John 3:16

I have heard that John 3:16 is a favorite preaching text for young preachers, but I confess that as far as I can recall, I have never had the courage to prepare and preach a sermon with John 3:16 as my text. I suppose I have quoted it as many as 15,000 or 20,000 times in prayer and in testimony, in writing and in preaching, but never as a sermon text. . . .

I think my own hesitation to preach from John 3:16 comes down to this: I appreciate it so profoundly that I am frightened by it—I am overwhelmed by John 3:16 to the point of inadequacy, almost of despair. Along with this is my knowledge that if a minister is to try to preach John 3:16 he must be endowed with great sympathy and a genuine love for God and man. . . .

So, I approach it. I approach it as one who is filled with great fear and yet great fascination. I take off my shoes, my heart shoes, at least, as I come to this declaration that *God so loved the world.*
CES085-086

> *Lord, I take off my "heart shoes" this morning as well as I contemplate this awesome thought. I bow before You in fear and fascination before this text—but also just at the incredible task and privilege of preaching and teaching any portion of Your inspired Word. Amen.*

A SHELL HERE AND A SHELL THERE

And the Word was made flesh, and dwelt among us, (and we beheld his glory, the glory as of the only begotten of the Father,) full of grace and truth.

—John 1:14

$\mathcal{N}$one of us can approach a serious study and consideration of the eternal nature and person of Jesus Christ without sensing and confessing our complete inadequacy in the face of the divine revelation. . . .

Now, I have said all of this because my best faith and my loftiest expectation do not allow me to believe that I can do justice to a text that begins: "And the Word was made flesh, and dwelt among us" (John 1:14) and concludes: "No man hath seen God at any time; the only begotten Son, which is in the bosom of the Father, he hath declared him" (1:18).

This is what we will attempt to do: we will walk along the broad seashore of God and pick up a shell here and a shell there, holding each up to the light to admire its beauty. While we may ultimately have a small store of shells to take with us, they can but remind us of the truth and the fact that there stretches the vastness of the seashore around the great lips of the oceans—and that still buried there is far more than we can ever hope to find or see! CES009, 011

Lord, I glory in the shells I'm looking at this morning— and revel in the vastness of the seashore around me! Amen.

DEADLY RATIONALISM

And my speech and my preaching was not with enticing words of man's wisdom, but in demonstration of the Spirit and of power: that your faith should not stand in the wisdom of men, but in the power of God.

—1 Corinthians 2:4-5

There is today an evangelical rationalism not unlike the rationalism taught by the scribes and Pharisees. They said the truth is in the word, and if you want to know the truth, go to the rabbi and learn the word. If you get the word, you have the truth. . . .

But *revelation is not enough!* There must be illumination before revelation can get to a person's soul. It is not enough that I hold an inspired book in my hands. I must have an inspired heart. There is the difference, in spite of the evangelical rationalist who insists that revelation is enough. . . .

In His day, Christ's conflict was with the theological rationalist. It revealed itself in the Sermon on the Mount and in the whole book of John. Just as Colossians argues against Manichaeism and Galatians argues against Jewish legalism, so the book of John is a long, inspired, passionately outpoured book trying to save us from evangelical rationalism—the doctrine that says the text is enough. Textualism is as deadly as liberalism. FBR021, 023-024

Lord, I believe strongly in the inspiration and authority of the Scriptures; I am committed to expository preaching. I see the danger and pray that You might keep me from this error of textualism. Amen.

THE MESSAGE MUST BE ALIVE

Then the LORD put forth his hand, and touched my mouth. And the LORD said unto me, Behold, I have put my words in thy mouth. See, I have this day set thee over the nations and over the kingdoms, to root out, and to pull down, and to destroy, and to throw down, to build, and to plant.

—Jeremiah 1:9-10

A church can wither as surely under the ministry of soulless Bible exposition as it can where no Bible is given at all. To be effective, the preacher's message must be alive—it must alarm, arouse, challenge; it must be God's present voice to a particular people. Then, and not until then, is it the prophetic word and the man himself, a prophet.

To perfectly fulfill his calling, the prophet must be under the constant sway of the Holy Spirit. Further, he must be alert to moral and spiritual conditions. All spiritual teaching should relate to life. It should intrude into the daily and private living of the hearers. Without being personal, the true prophet will nevertheless pierce the conscience of each listener as if the message had been directed to him or her alone. TWP085-086

Lord, I pray that my preaching and teaching might never become routine. Keep me fresh; keep me under the "constant sway of the Holy Spirit;" keep me alert and alive always. Amen.

ELOQUENCE

And I, brethren, when I came to you, came not with excellency of speech or of wisdom, declaring unto you the testimony of God. For I determined not to know any thing among you, save Jesus Christ, and him crucified.

—1 Corinthians 2:1-2

There are few things in religious circles held in greater esteem than eloquence. Yet there are few things of less actual value or that bring with them greater temptation or more harm.

One qualification everyone expects a preacher to have is the ability to discourse fluently on almost any religious or moral subject. Yet such ability is at best a doubtful asset and unless brought to Christ for cleansing may easily turn out to be the greatest enemy the preacher faces here below. The man who finds that he is able to preach on a moment's notice should accept his ability as an obstacle over which he must try to get victory before he is at his best for God and His kingdom. WTA091

Lord, keep us mindful of our need for humble reliance on the Holy Spirit to accomplish the awesome task to which You have called us. Amen.

PROPHET, NOT ORATOR

> *And I have put my words in thy mouth, and I have covered thee in the shadow of mine hand, that I may plant the heavens, and lay the foundations of the earth, and say unto Zion, Thou art my people.*
>
> —Isaiah 51:16

The Christian minister, as someone has pointed out, is a descendant not of the Greek orator but of the Hebrew prophet.

The differences between the orator and the prophet are many and radical, the chief being that the orator speaks for himself while the prophet speaks for God. The orator originates his message and is responsible to himself for its content. The prophet originates nothing but delivers the message he has received from God who alone is responsible for it, the prophet being responsible to God for its delivery only. The prophet must hear the message clearly and deliver it faithfully, and that is indeed a grave responsibility; but it is to God alone, not to men. GTM085

Lord, please help me never to rely on my own thoughts or message; give me a word from You as I stand before Your people. Amen.

A VOICE
INSTEAD OF
AN ECHO

But Peter and John answered and said unto them, Whether it be right in the sight of God to hearken unto you more than unto God, judge ye. For we cannot but speak the things which we have seen and heard.

—Acts 4:19-20

To escape the snare of artificiality it is necessary that a man enjoy a satisfying personal experience with God. He must be totally committed to Christ and deeply anointed with the Holy Spirit. Further, he must be delivered from the fear of man. The focus of his attention must be God and not men. He must let everything dear to him ride out on each sermon. He must so preach as to jeopardize his future, his ministry, even his life itself. He must make God responsible for the consequences and speak as one who will not have long to speak before he is called to judgment. Then the people will know they are hearing a voice instead of a mere echo. GTM133-134

Lord, I'm going to sit quietly before You this morning and make sure these challenges are indeed the expression of my heart today. Amen.

THE AUTHORITY OF GOD

I do send thee unto them; and thou shalt say unto them, Thus saith the Lord GOD. And they, whether they will hear, or whether they will forbear . . . yet shall know that there hath been a prophet among them.

—Ezekiel 2:4-5

I don't want to be unkind, but I am sure there ought to be a lot more authority in the pulpit than there is now. A preacher should reign from his pulpit as a king from his throne. He should not reign by law nor by regulations and not by board meetings or man's authority. He ought to reign by moral ascendancy.

When a man of God stands to speak, he ought to have the authority of God on him so that he makes the people responsible to listen to him. When they will not listen to him, they are accountable to God for turning away from the divine Word. In place of that needed authority, we have tabby cats with their claws carefully trimmed in the seminary, so they can paw over the congregations and never scratch them at all. They have had their claws trimmed and are just as soft and sweet as can be. . . .

I believe in the authority of God, and I believe if a man doesn't have it, he should go away and pray and wait until he gets the authority and then stand up to speak even if he has to begin on a soapbox on a street corner. Go to a rescue mission and preach with authority! They had it in those days—when they stood up, there was authority! COU150-151

Lord, may I always preach boldly like the apostle Paul, like Ezekiel, like Jeremiah and the prophets. Amen.

PREACH TO MAKE THEM SWEAT

Now when they heard this, they were pricked in their heart, and said unto Peter and to the rest of the apostles, Men and brethren, what shall we do?

—Acts 2:37

$\mathcal{I}$ preach to my congregation week after week. And I pray that I may be able to preach with such convicting power that my people will sweat! I do not want them to leave my services feeling good. The last thing I want to do is to give them some kind of religious tranquilizer—and let them go to hell in their relaxation.

The Christian church was designed to make sinners sweat. I have always believed that, and I still believe it. The messages preached in our churches should make backslidden Christians sweat. And if I achieve that objective when I preach, I thank God with all of my heart, no matter what people think of me. JIV061-062

Lord, help me to preach with boldness—not concerned with "what people think of me." Amen.

OLD-FASHIONED HORSE SENSE

He that hath my command-
ments, and keepeth them, he it is
that loveth me: and he that loveth
me shall be loved of my Father,
and I will love him, and will
manifest myself to him.

—John 14:21

*W*hen they want to get blessed, some people try getting worked up psychologically. . . .

Some people try group dynamics. . . .

What is needed is some old-fashioned, salty horse sense. I am sure there are 189 mules in the state of Missouri that have more sense than a lot of the preachers who are trying to teach people how to get the blessing of God in some way other than by the constituted means. When you get people all broken up, dabbing at their eyes and shaking, what is the result? It does not bring them any closer to God. It does not make them love God any better, in accordance with the first commandment. Nor does it give any greater love for neighbors, which is the second commandment. It does not prepare them to live fruitfully on earth. It does not prepare them to die victoriously, and it does not guarantee that they will be with the Lord at last.

The Lord has constituted means. Jesus said in the Gospel of John, "He that hath my commandments, and keepeth them, he it is that loveth me" (John 14:21). RRR050-052

Father, keep me from the false ways of attempting to secure
Your blessing. Help me to boldly declare the importance of
old-fashioned obedience to Your commands. Amen.

TRUTH DIVORCED FROM LIFE

But be ye doers of the word, and not hearers only, deceiving your own selves.

—James 1:22

*T*here is scarcely anything so dull and meaningless as Bible doctrine taught for its own sake. Truth divorced from life is not truth in its biblical sense, but something else and something less. . . .

No man is better for knowing that God in the beginning created the heaven and the earth. The devil knows that, and so did Ahab and Judas Iscariot. No man is better for knowing that God so loved the world of men that He gave His only begotten Son to die for their redemption. In hell there are millions who know that. Theological truth is useless until it is obeyed. The purpose behind all doctrine is to secure moral action. . . .

Any man with fair pulpit gifts can get on with the average congregation if he just "feeds" them and lets them alone. Give them plenty of objective truth and never hint that they are wrong and should be set right, and they will be content.

On the other hand, the man who preaches truth and applies it to the lives of his hearers will feel the nails and the thorns. He will lead a hard life, but a glorious one. May God raise up many such prophets. The church needs them badly. OGM025-028

Lord, I want to be one of those bold prophets, faithfully declaring Your word, no matter the consequences. Enable me by Your Spirit, I pray in Jesus' name. Amen.

A HIRELING;
NO TRUE
SHEPHERD

Wherefore I put thee in remem-
brance that thou stir up the gift of
God, which is in thee by the put-
ting on of my hands. For God
hath not given us the spirit of fear;
but of power, and of love, and of a
sound mind.

—2 Timothy 1:6-7

*I*t is doubtful whether we can be Christian in anything unless we are Christian in everything. To obey Christ in one or two or ten instances and then in fear of consequences to back away and refuse to obey in another is to cloud our life with the suspicion that we are only fair-weather followers and not true believers at all. To obey when it costs us nothing and refuse when the results are costly is to convict ourselves of moral trifling and gross insincerity. . . .

Again, the pastor when facing his congregation on Sunday morning, dare not think of the effect his sermon may have on his job, his salary or his future relation to the church. Let him but worry about tomorrow and he becomes a hireling and no true shepherd of the sheep. No man is a good preacher who is not willing to lay his future on the line every time he expounds the Word. He must let his job and his reputation ride on each and every sermon or he has no right to think that he stands in the prophetic tradition. SIZ146-147

> *Give me grace to follow, Lord—especially when it re-*
> *ally does cost me something. Amen.*

TOO TIMID
TO TELL
THE TRUTH

Now when they saw the boldness of Peter and John, and perceived that they were unlearned and ignorant men, they marvelled; and they took knowledge of them, that they had been with Jesus.

—Acts 4:13

The contemporary moral climate does not favor a faith as tough and fibrous as that taught by our Lord and His apostles. The delicate, brittle saints being produced in our religious hothouses today are hardly to be compared with the committed, expendable believers who once gave their witness among men. And the fault lies with our leaders. They are too timid to tell the people all the truth. They are now asking men to give to God that which costs them nothing.

Our churches these days are filled (or one-quarter filled) with a soft breed of Christian that must be fed on a diet of harmless fun to keep them interested. About theology they know little. Scarcely any of them have read even one of the great Christian classics, but most of them are familiar with religious fiction and spine-tingling films. No wonder their moral and spiritual constitution is so frail. Such can only be called weak adherents of a faith they never really understood. TIC076

Lord, send the Holy Spirit to renew within us a depth and seriousness in our pulpits. Give us boldness in our preaching. Amen.

MAKING
AN
ACCOMMODATION

*Watch ye and pray, lest ye en-
ter into temptation. The spirit
truly is ready, but the flesh is
weak.*

—Mark 14:38

I am having a hard time trying to comprehend what has happened to sound Bible teaching. What has happened to preaching
on Christian discipleship and on our daily deportment in the spiritual life? We are making an accommodation. We are offering a
take-it-easy, Pollyanna type of approach that does not seem ever to
have heard of total commitment to One who is our Lord and Savior.

I regret that more and more Christian believers are being
drawn into a hazy, fuzzy kind of teaching that assures everyone
who has ever "accepted Christ" that he or she has nothing more
to be concerned about. He is OK and he will always be OK because Christ will be returning before things get too tough.
Then all of us will wear our crowns, and God will see that we
have cities to rule over!

If that concept is accurate, why did our Lord take the stern
and unpopular position that Christian believers should be engaged in watching and praying? MMG031-032

*Lord, help me to watch and pray faithfully. Help me to
boldly accept the challenge of total commitment and
never to make an accommodation to make people comfortable. Amen.*

NIBBLING AT THE TRUTH

Wherefore I take you to record this day, that I am pure from the blood of all men. For I have not shunned to declare unto you all the counsel of God.

—Acts 20:26-27

$\mathcal{T}$his is one of the marks of our modern time—that many are guilty of merely "nibbling" at the truth of the Christian gospel.

I wonder if you realize that in many ways the preaching of the Word of God is being pulled down to the level of the ignorant and spiritually obtuse; that we must tell stories and jokes and entertain and amuse in order to have a few people in the audience? We do these things that we may have some reputation and that there may be money in the treasury to meet the church bills. . . .

In many churches Christianity has been watered down until the solution is so weak that if it were poison it would not hurt anyone, and if it were medicine it would not cure anyone! ITB030-031

Lord, don't ever let me be guilty of watering down the truth or playing to the crowds, concerned about my "reputation" or "money in the treasury." Amen.

MORALLY WRONG TEACHING

Then said Jesus to those Jews which believed on him, If ye continue in my word, then are ye my disciples indeed; and ye shall know the truth, and the truth shall make you free.

—John 8:31-32

*N*o one can know truth except the one who obeys truth. You think you know truth. People memorize the Scriptures by the yard, but that is not a guarantee of knowing the truth. Truth is not a text. Truth is in the text, but it takes the text plus the Holy Spirit to bring truth to a human soul. . . .

Charles G. Finney taught that it was wrong—morally wrong—to teach objective doctrine without a moral application. I have gone to Bible classes and listened to men who were learned in the Word of God. Still I have come away as cold as a pickled fish. There was no help, no lift in my spirit, nothing to warm the inside of my heart. The truth had been given to me just like a proposition in Euclid or a mathematical formula from Pythagoras. And the answer is, "So what? Let's go and have a soda!" Are we aware that we can give people objective truth without moral application? If God's moral Word is true, it means us. And if it means us, we ought to obey it. That is life. That is knowing the truth. FBR064-065

Forgive me, Father, for those times I have been guilty of "morally wrong" teaching. Send Your Spirit both to embolden my preaching and to move the hearts of my hearers to action. Amen.

USE YOUR HEAD!

Of whom we have many things to say, and hard to be uttered, seeing ye are dull of hearing.

—Hebrews 5:11

*M*any a preacher would like to challenge the intellectual and thinking capacity of his congregation, but he has been warned about preaching over the people's heads.

I ask, "What are people's heads for? God Almighty gave them those heads and I think they ought to use them!"

As a preacher, I deny that any of the truths of God which I teach and expound are over the heads of the people. I deny it!

My preaching may go right through their heads if there is nothing in there to stop it, but I do not preach truths which are too much for them to comprehend. We ought to begin using our heads. Brother, you ought to take that head of yours, oil it and rub the rust off and begin to use it as God has always expected you would. God expects you to understand and have a grasp of His truth because you need it from day to day. ICH145

Lord, help me to use my head, to be willing to be stretched intellectually by Your Holy Spirit. Use me to stretch others as well. Amen.

PREACH THE PERSON OF GOD

> *He staggered not at the promise of God through unbelief; but was strong in faith, giving glory to God; and being fully persuaded that, what he had promised, he was able also to perform.*
>
> —Romans 4:20-21

*M*y faith does not rest on God's promises. My faith rests upon God's *character*. Faith must rest in confidence upon the One who made the promises. . . .

When I think of the angels who veil their faces before the God who cannot lie, I wonder why every preacher in North America does not begin preaching about God—and nothing else. What would happen if every preacher just preached about the person and character of God for an entire year—who He is, His attributes, His perfection, His being, the kind of a God He is and why we love Him and why we should trust Him? I tell you, God would soon fill the whole horizon, the entire world. Faith would spring up like grass by the water courses. Then let a man get up and preach the promises of God and the whole congregation would join in chorus: "We can claim the promises; look who made them!" This is the confidence; this is the boldness. FBR042, 045

> *Lord, begin with me. I commit myself today to knowing You more fully and preaching and teaching Your person and character as the foundation of faith. Let confidence and boldness be my testimony. Amen.*

IMPERFECT INTERPRETERS

Being born again . . . by the word of God, which liveth and abideth for ever . . . . This is the word [of the Lord] which by the gospel is preached unto you.

—1 Peter 1:23, 25

*O*ften our missionaries have told us of difficult times they have had with interpreters. The expression of the missionary may go in one way and come out with a different sense to the hearer, and I think when we expound the Scriptures, we are often guilty of being imperfect interpreters. I shall do the best I can to catch the spirit of the man, Peter, and to determine what God is trying to say to us and reduce the interference to a minimum.

Now, I suppose more people would like me if I were to declare that I preach the Bible and nothing but the Bible. I attempt to do that, but honesty compels me to say that the best I can do is to preach the Bible as I understand it. I trust that through your prayers and the Spirit of Christ my understanding may be right. If you pray and if I yield and trust, perhaps what we get from First Peter will indeed be approximately what Peter would say if he were here in person. We will stay as close as we can to the Word of the Living God. ICH017-018

Guide me constantly by Your Spirit so that I may be a faithful mouthpiece. Amen.

MASTER YOUR MEDIUM

Study to shew thyself approved unto God, a workman that needeth not to be ashamed, rightly dividing the word of truth.

—2 Timothy 2:15

*A*mong the countless gifts of God, one of the most precious to us is our beautiful, expressive English tongue. That such a gift should be neglected by busy men and women in their wild race to make a living is at least understandable, if unfortunate; but that it should be neglected as well by the ministers of the sanctuary is not only impossible to understand but completely inexcusable.

For the very reason that God has committed His saving truth to the receptacle of human language, the man who preaches that truth should be more than ordinarily skillful in the use of language. It is necessary that every artist master his medium, every musician his instrument. For a man calling himself a concert pianist to appear before an audience with but a beginner's acquaintance with the keyboard would be no more absurd than for a minister of the gospel to appear before his congregation without a thorough knowledge of the language in which he expects to preach. SIZ041-042

Help me to be a faithful servant, Lord, skilled in the task to which You have called me. Amen.

PREACH THE WORD

Preach the word; be instant in season, out of season; reprove, rebuke, exhort with all longsuffering and doctrine.

—2 Timothy 4:2

I heard of one graduate of a theological school who determined to follow his old professor's advice and preach the Word only. His crowds were average. Then one day a cyclone hit the little town and he yielded to the temptation to preach on the topic "Why God Sent the Cyclone to Centerville." The church was packed. This shook the young preacher and he went back to ask his professor for further advice in the light of what had happened. Should he continue to preach the Word to smaller crowds or try to fill his church by preaching sermons a bit more sensational? The old man did not change his mind. "If you preach the Word," he told the inquirer, "you will always have a text. But if you wait for cyclones you will not have enough to go around." GTM086

Lord, I commit myself again today to avoid the sensational and to faithfully "preach the Word." Amen.

TOO MUCH ORIGINALITY

O Timothy, keep that which is committed to thy trust, avoiding profane and vain babblings, and oppositions of science falsely so called.

—1 Timothy 6:20

Some preachers have such a phobia for repetition and such an unnatural fear of the familiar that they are forever straining after the odd and the startling. The church page of the newspaper almost any Saturday will be sure to announce at least one or two sermon topics so far astray as to be positively grotesque; only by the most daring flight of uncontrolled imagination can any relation be established between the topic and the religion of Christ. We dare not impugn the honesty or the sincerity of the men who thus flap their short wings so rapidly in an effort to take off into the wild blue yonder, but we do deplore their attitudes. No one should try to be more original than an apostle. GTM144

Give me a word from heaven, Father, that will fly without my weak efforts at cute originality! Amen.

OFF-COLOR HUMOR

Let no corrupt communication proceed out of your mouth, but that which is good to the use of edifying, that it may minister grace unto the hearers.... Neither filthiness, nor foolish talking, nor jesting, which are not convenient: but rather giving of thanks.

—Ephesians 4:29, 5:4

*O*ne of the most shocking things in the church is the dirty-mouthed Christian who always walks on the borderline. There is no place for borderline stories that embarrass some people, and there is nothing about sex or the human body that is funny if your mind is clean.

There was once a gathering of officers, and George Washington was present in the room. One of the young officers began to think about a dirty story that he wanted to tell, and he got a smirk on his face. He looked around and said, "I'm thinking of a story. I guess there are no ladies present." Washington straightened up and said, "No, young man, but there are gentlemen." The young officer shut his mouth and kept the dirty story inside his dirty head and heart.

Anything you could not tell with Jesus present, do not tell. Anything you could not laugh at were Jesus present, do not laugh at. RRR067

What an important reminder, Lord! Keep my thoughts pure. Amen.

ALL
IN ONE
SERMON

Now we exhort you, brethren, warn them that are unruly, comfort the feebleminded, support the weak, be patient toward all men.

—1 Thessalonians 5:14

*T*he shepherd of souls is often forced to work at what would appear to be cross purposes with himself.

For instance, he must encourage the timid and warn the self-confident; and these may at any given time be present in his congregation in almost equal numbers. . . .

Another problem he faces is the presence in the normal Christian assembly of believers in every stage of development, from the newly converted who knows almost nothing about the Christian life to the wise and experienced Christian who seems to know almost everything.

Again, the Christian minister must have a word from God for the teen-aged, the middle-aged and the very aged. He must speak to the scholar as well as to the ignorant; he must bring the living Word to the cultured man and woman and to the vulgarian who reads nothing but the sports page and the comic strip. He must speak to the sad and to the happy, to the tender-minded and to the tough-minded, to those eager to live and to some who secretly wish they could die. And he must do this all in one sermon and in a period of time not exceeding forty-five minutes. Surely this requires a Daniel, and Daniels are as scarce in the United States today as in Babylon in 600 B.C. SOS082-083

Lord, I confess myself totally dependent on the Holy Spirit. Enable, I pray, in Jesus' name. Amen.

June

Worship

The whole import and substance of the Bible teaches us that the God who does not need anything nevertheless desires the adoration and worship of His created children. WHT037

GOD'S AWESOMENESS

O the depth of the riches both of the wisdom and knowledge of God! how unsearchable are his judgments, and his ways past finding out!

—Romans 11:33

*W*ebster's Unabridged Dictionary lists 550,000 words. And it is a solemn and beautiful thought that in our worship of God there sometimes rush up from the depths of our souls feelings that all this wealth of words is not sufficient to express. To be articulate at certain times we are compelled to fall back upon "Oh!" or "O!"—a primitive exclamatory sound that is hardly a word at all and that scarcely admits of a definition.

Vocabularies are formed by many minds over long periods and are capable of expressing whatever the mind is capable of entertaining. But when the heart, on its knees, moves into the awesome Presence and hears with fear and wonder things not lawful to utter, then the mind falls flat, and words, previously its faithful servants, become weak and totally incapable of telling what the heart hears and sees. In that awful moment the worshiper can only cry "Oh!" And that simple exclamation becomes more eloquent than learned speech and, I have no doubt, is dearer to God than any oratory. BAM084-085

Today I want to just quietly reflect in unspoken awe. . . . Amen.

THE NORMAL EMPLOYMENT OF MORAL BEINGS

> *The four and twenty elders fall down before him that sat on the throne, and worship him that liveth for ever and ever, and cast their crowns before the throne, saying, Thou art worthy, O Lord, to receive glory and honour and power: for thou hast created all things, and for thy pleasure they are and were created.*
>
> —Revelation 4:10-11

*A*ll of the examples that we have in the Bible illustrate that glad and devoted and reverent worship is the normal employment of moral beings. Every glimpse that is given us of heaven and of God's created beings is always a glimpse of worship and rejoicing and praise because God is who He is.

The apostle John in Revelation 4:10-11 gives us a plain portrayal of created beings around the throne of God. . . .

I can safely say, on the authority of all that is revealed in the Word of God, that any man or woman on this earth who is bored and turned off by worship is not ready for heaven. WHT013

Lord, please don't let me ever become bored with worship!
I pray that You might enhance my vision of Your glory
and draw me into heartfelt worship. Amen.

GOD LISTENS

O come, let us sing unto the LORD: let us make a joyful noise to the rock of our salvation. Let us come before his presence with thanksgiving, and make a joyful noise unto him with psalms.

—Psalm 95:1-2

*W*hat are we going to do about this awesome, beautiful worship that God calls for? I would rather worship God than do any other thing I know of in all this wide world.

I would not even attempt to tell you how many hymnbooks are piled up in my study. I cannot sing a lick, but that is nobody's business. God thinks I am an opera star!

God listens while I sing to Him the old French hymns in translation, the old Latin hymns in translation. God listens while I sing the old Greek hymns from the Eastern church as well as the beautiful psalms done in meter and some of the simpler songs of Watts and Wesley and the rest.

I mean it when I say that I would rather worship God than to do anything else. WHT018

Lord, may that be my testimony as well—"I would rather worship God than do any other thing I know of in all this wide world." Amen.

BEYOND THANKSGIVING

Great is the LORD, and greatly to be praised; and his greatness is unsearchable.

—Psalm 145:3

The dictionary says that to admire is "to regard with wondering esteem accompanied by pleasure and delight; to look at or upon with an elevated feeling of pleasure." According to this definition, God has few admirers among Christians today.

Many are they who are grateful for His goodness in providing salvation. At Thanksgiving time the churches ring with songs of gratitude that "all is safely gathered in." Testimony meetings are mostly devoted to recitations of incidents where someone got into trouble and got out again in answer to prayer. To decry this would be uncharitable and unscriptural, for there is much of the same thing in the Book of Psalms. It is good and right to render unto God thanksgiving for all His mercies to us. But God's admirers, where are they?

The simple truth is that worship is elementary until it begins to take on the quality of admiration. Just as long as the worshiper is engrossed with himself and his good fortune, he is a babe. We begin to grow up when our worship passes from thanksgiving to admiration. As our hearts rise to God in lofty esteem for that which He is ("I AM THAT I AM," Exodus 3:14), we begin to share a little of the selfless pleasure which is the portion of the blessed in heaven. TIC127

Almighty God, I want to be one of Your admirers. Help me to pass beyond thanksgiving to lofty esteem and selfless admiration. Amen.

ASTONISHED REVERENCE

O LORD, our Lord, how excel-
lent is thy name in all the earth!
who hast set thy glory above the
heavens.

—Psalm 8:1

Then there is *admiration*, that is, appreciation of the excellency of God. Man is better qualified to appreciate God than any other creature because he was made in His image and is the only creature who was. This admiration for God grows and grows until it fills the heart with wonder and delight. "In our astonished reverence we confess Thine uncreated loveliness," said the hymn writer. "In our astonished reverence." The God of the modern evangelical rarely astonishes anybody. He manages to stay pretty much within the constitution. Never breaks over our bylaws. He's a very well-behaved God and very denominational and very much one of us, and we ask Him to help us when we're in trouble and look to Him to watch over us when we're asleep. The God of the modern evangelical isn't a God I could have much respect for. But when the Holy Ghost shows us God as He is we admire Him to the point of wonder and delight. WMJ022-023

> *Lord, give me just a taste of "astonished reverence." Let*
> *me see You today as You really are and experience that*
> *"wonder and delight" of which Tozer speaks. Amen.*

REVERENTIAL
FEAR
OF GOD

Let all the earth fear the LORD: let all the inhabitants of the world stand in awe of him.

—Psalm 33:8

*W*hen we come into this sweet relationship, we are beginning to learn astonished reverence, breathless adoration, awesome fascination, lofty admiration of the attributes of God and something of the breathless silence that we know when God is near.

You may never have realized it before, but all of those elements in our perception and consciousness of the divine Presence add up to what the Bible calls "the fear of God.". . .

There are very few unqualified things in our lives, but I believe that the reverential fear of God mixed with love and fascination and astonishment and admiration and devotion is the most enjoyable state and the most purifying emotion the human soul can know. WHT030-031

Oh Lord, let me reach these heights in my worship today—astonished reverence, breathless adoration, awesome fascination, lofty admiration, breathless silence—let me experience that "reverential fear of God" this morning. Amen.

HUMBLED BEFORE GOD

For all those things hath mine hand made, and all those things have been, saith the LORD: but to this man will I look, even to him that is poor and of a contrite spirit, and trembleth at my word.

—Isaiah 66:2

$\mathcal{W}$orship also means to "express in some appropriate manner" what you feel. . . .

And what will be expressed? "A humbling but delightful sense of admiring awe and astonished wonder." It is delightful to worship God, but it is also a humbling thing; and the man who has not been humbled in the presence of God will never be a worshiper of God at all. He may be a church member who keeps the rules and obeys the discipline, and who tithes and goes to conference, but he'll never be a worshiper unless he is deeply humbled. "A humbling but delightful sense of admiring awe." There's an awesomeness about God which is missing in our day altogether; there's little sense of admiring awe in the Church of Christ these days. WMJ004-005

I kneel before You this morning, Lord, with "a humbling but delightful sense of admiring awe and astonished wonder." Use me today, Lord, to stimulate within others some of this much-missing sense of "admiring awe." Amen.

WHY THEY
ACT LIKE
IDIOTS

Who shall not fear thee, O Lord, and glorify thy name? for thou only art holy: for all nations shall come and worship before thee; for thy judgments are made manifest.

—Revelation 15:4

*W*ithout worship we go about miserable; that's why we have all the troubles we have. You wonder why young people act like such idiots. Some young people have a lot of energy and don't know what to do with it, so they go out and act like idiots; and that's why gangsters and communists and sinners of all kinds do what they do. They are endowed by God Almighty with brilliant intelligence and an amazing store of energy, and because they don't know what to do with it they do the wrong thing. That's why I'm not angry with people when I see them go off the deep end, because I know that they have fallen from their first estate along with Adam's brood and all of us together. They haven't been redeemed and so they have energy they don't know what to do with; they have capacity they don't know how to use. They have skills and don't know where to put them, and so they go wild and police have to arrest sixteen-year-olds and put them in jail. If they had been taught that they came into the world in the first place to worship God and to enjoy Him forever and that when they fell Jesus Christ came to redeem them, to make worshipers out of them, they could by the Holy Ghost and the washing of the blood be made into worshiping saints and things would be so different. WMJ008-009

Lord, I pray especially for young people today. Reveal Yourself this morning to some who really need to see You and need to see the purpose for which they came into the world. Amen.

WORSHIPERS FROM REBELS

And not only so, but we also joy in God through our Lord Jesus Christ, by whom we have now received the atonement.

—Romans 5:11

Sometimes evangelical Christians seem to be fuzzy and uncertain about the nature of God and His purposes in creation and redemption. In such instances, the preachers often are to blame. There are still preachers and teachers who say that Christ died so we would not drink and not smoke and not go to the theater.

No wonder people are confused! No wonder they fall into the habit of backsliding when such things are held up as the reason for salvation.

Jesus was born of a virgin, suffered under Pontius Pilate, died on the cross and rose from the grave to make worshipers out of rebels! WHT011

Lord, keep the cross in the forefront of our evangelistic preaching, and fill us with Your longing for sinners to become worshipers. Amen.

OUR REASON FOR EXISTENCE

Give unto the LORD the glory due unto his name; worship the LORD in the beauty of holiness.

—Psalm 29:2

*Y*es, worship of the loving God is man's whole reason for existence. That is why we are born and that is why we are born again from above. That is why we were created and that is why we have been recreated. That is why there was a genesis at the beginning, and that is why there is a re-genesis, called regeneration.

That is also why there is a church. The Christian church exists to worship God first of all. Everything else must come second or third or fourth or fifth. . . .

Sad, sad indeed, are the cries of so many today who have never discovered why they were born. It brings to mind the poet Milton's description of the pathetic lostness and loneliness of our first parents. Driven from the garden, he says, "they took hand in hand and through the valley made their solitary way." WHT056-057

Oh Lord, we live in a world that has so totally lost its way! How few have any concept at all of their reason for existence. How sad to see so many all around us who "took hand in hand and through the valley made their solitary way." Use me today to direct at least one to the right path. Amen.

MADE TO WORSHIP

*The fool hath said in his heart,
There is no God. They are corrupt, they have done abomina-
ble works, there is none that
doeth good.*

—Psalm 14:1

$\mathcal{N}$ow we were made to worship, but the Scriptures tell us something else again. They tell us that man fell and kept not his first estate; that he forfeited the original glory of God and failed to fulfill the creative purpose, so that he is not worshiping now in the way that God meant him to worship. All else fulfills its design; flowers are still fragrant and lilies are still beautiful and the bees still search for nectar amongst the flowers; the birds still sing with their thousand-voice choir on a summer's day, and the sun and the moon and the stars all move on their rounds doing the will of God.

And from what we can learn from the Scriptures we believe that the seraphim and cherubim and powers and dominions are still fulfilling their design—worshiping God who created them and breathed into them the breath of life. Man alone sulks in his cave. Man alone, with all of his brilliant intelligence, with all of his amazing, indescribable and wonderful equipment, still sulks in his cave. He is either silent, or if he opens his mouth at all, it is to boast and threaten and curse; or it's nervous, ill-considered laughter, or it's humor become big business, or it's songs without joy.
WMJ006-007

Oh loving God, bring us out of the cave! Amen.

GOD GAVE MAN A HARP

> *The LORD looked down from heaven upon the children of men, to see if there were any that did understand, and seek God. They are all gone aside, they are all to-gether become filthy: there is none that doeth good, no, not one.*
>
> —Psalm 14:2-3

Man was made to worship God. God gave to man a harp and said, "Here above all the creatures that I have made and created I have given you the largest harp. I put more strings on your instrument and I have given you a wider range than I have given to any other creature. You can worship Me in a manner that no other creature can." And when he sinned man took that instrument and threw it down in the mud and there it has lain for centuries, rusted, broken, unstrung; and man, instead of playing a harp like the angels and seeking to worship God in all of his activities, is ego-centered and turns in on himself and sulks and swears and laughs and sings, but it's all without joy and without worship. . . .

I say that the greatest tragedy in the world today is that God has made man in His image and made him to worship Him, made him to play the harp of worship before the face of God day and night, but he has failed God and dropped the harp. It lies voiceless at his feet. WMJ007-008

> *Lord, what a vivid picture! What a tragedy to see that harp lying in the mud. Do a great work today, Lord, to restore that harp to its rightful use. Amen.*

HONOR THIS PURPOSE

And when Abram was ninety years old and nine, the LORD appeared to Abram, and said unto him, I am the Almighty God; walk before me, and be thou perfect.

—Genesis 17:1

*W*ithout argument, most things are at their best when they are fulfilling their purpose and design.

For instance, a piano is made with a specific purpose: to produce music. However, I happen to know that someone once stood on a piano in order to put a fastener of some kind in the ceiling. Some artistic women have used piano tops as family picture galleries. I have seen piano tops that were cluttered filing cabinets or wide library shelves.

There is an intelligent design in the creation of a piano. The manufacturer did not announce: "This is a good piano. It has at least nineteen uses!" No, the designer had only one thought in mind: "This piano will have the purpose and potential of sounding forth beautiful music!" . . .

Do not miss the application of truth here. God was saying to Abraham, "You may have some other idea about the design and purpose for your life, but you are wrong! You were created in My image to worship Me and to glorify Me. If you do not honor this purpose, your life will degenerate into shallow, selfish, humanistic pursuits." MMG023

Lord, so many lives today have indeed degenerated into "shallow, selfish, humanistic pursuits." Work through me this week to help people with whom I come in contact to see the one purpose for which You created us. Amen.

GOD'S INWARD NECESSITY

So God created man in his own image, in the image of God created he him; male and female created he them.

—Genesis 1:27

$\mathcal{I}$ believe that He created man out of no external necessity. I believe it was an internal necessity. God, being the God He was and is, and being infinitely perfect and infinitely beautiful and infinitely glorious and infinitely admirable and infinitely loving, out of His own inward necessity had to have some creature that was capable of admiring Him and loving Him and knowing Him. So God made man in His own image; in the image and likeness of God made He him; and He made him as near to being like Himself as it was possible for the creature to be like the Creator. The most godlike thing in the universe is the soul of man.

The reason God made man in His image was that he might appreciate God and admire and adore and worship; so that God might not be a picture, so to speak, hanging in a gallery with nobody looking at Him. He might not be a flower that no one could smell; He might not be a star that no one could see. God made somebody to smell that flower, the lily of the valley. He wanted someone to see that glorious image. He wanted someone to see the star, so He made us and in making us He made us to worship Him. WMJ003

Be pleased this morning, Lord, as I do indeed smell the flower and see the star, as I "admire and adore and worship." Amen.

WHAT GOOD IS IT?

And one cried unto another, and said, Holy, holy, holy, is the LORD of hosts: the whole earth is full of his glory.

—Isaiah 6:3

*I*f you want to pray strategically, in a way which would please God, pray that God might raise up men who would see the beauty of the Lord our God and would begin to preach it and hold it out to people, instead of offering peace of mind, deliverance from cigarettes, a better job and nicer cottage. . . .

What good is all our busy religion if God isn't in it? What good is it if we've lost majesty, reverence, worship—an awareness of the divine? What good is it if we've lost a sense of the Presence and the ability to retreat within our own hearts and meet God in the garden? If we've lost that, why build another church? Why make more converts to an effete Christianity? Why bring people to follow after a Savior so far off that He doesn't own them?

We need to improve the quality of our Christianity, and we never will until we raise our concept of God back to that held by apostle, sage, prophet, saint and reformer. When we put God back where He belongs, we will instinctively and automatically move up again; the whole spiral of our religious direction will be upward. AOG194-195

Lord, I do indeed pray that You might "raise up men who would see the beauty of the Lord our God and would begin to preach it and hold it out to people." Amen.

WORSHIP SEVEN DAYS A WEEK

But the LORD is in his holy temple: let all the earth keep silence before him.

—Habakkuk 2:20

So I've got to tell you that if you do not worship God seven days a week, you do not worship Him on one day a week. There is no such thing known in heaven as Sunday worship unless it is accompanied by Monday worship and Tuesday worship and so on. . . .

We come into God's house and say, "The Lord is in His holy temple, let us all kneel before Him." Very nice. I think it's nice to start a service that way once in a while. But when any of you men enter your office Monday morning at 9 o'clock, if you can't walk into that office and say, "The Lord is in my office, let all the world be silent before Him," then you are not worshiping the Lord on Sunday. If you can't worship Him on Monday you didn't worship Him on Sunday. If you don't worship Him on Saturday you are not in very good shape to worship Him on Sunday. TWE009, 024

Lord, permeate my whole life with a spirit of worship every day. Amen.

DISCHARGING OUR OBLIGATION

. . . Walk as children of light: (For the fruit of the Spirit is in all goodness and righteousness and truth;) proving what is acceptable unto the Lord.

—Ephesians 5:8-10

I have to be faithful to what I know to be true, so I must tell you that if you will not worship God seven days a week, you do not worship Him on one day a week. . . .

Too many of us try to discharge our obligations to God Almighty in one day—usually one trip to church. Sometimes, nobly, we make it two trips to church, but it's all on the same day when we have nothing else to do—and that's supposed to be worship. I grant you, sir, that it can be true worship, provided that on Monday and Tuesday and the other days you also experience the blessings of true worship.

I do not say that you must be at church all of the time—how could you be?

You can worship God at your desk, on an elevated train or driving in traffic. You can worship God washing dishes or ironing clothes. . . . You can worship God in whatever is legitimate and right and good. . . .

So that's all right. We can go to church and worship. But if we go to church and worship one day, it is not true worship unless it is followed by continuing worship in the days that follow.

TTPI, Book 1/051-052

Father, I pray that You might give me a sense of Your presence wherever I am, in whatever I'm doing. Direct my heart to worship You throughout the day. Amen.

GOD'S PRESENCE ON MONDAY

Whether therefore ye eat, or drink, or whatsoever ye do, do all to the glory of God.

—1 Corinthians 10:31

*O*n Monday, as we go about our different duties and tasks, are we aware of the Presence of God? The Lord desires still to be in His holy temple, wherever we are. He wants the continuing love and delight and worship of His children, wherever we work.

Is it not a beautiful thing for a businessman to enter his office on Monday morning with an inner call to worship: "The Lord is in my office—let all the world be silent before Him."

If you cannot worship the Lord in the midst of your responsibilities on Monday, it is not very likely that you were worshiping on Sunday! . . .

I guess many people have an idea that they have God in a box. He is just in the church sanctuary, and when we leave and drive toward home, we have a rather faint, homesick feeling that we are leaving God in the big box.

You know that is not true, but what are you doing about it?

WHT122

> *Lord, I expect my whole demeanor, my response to frustrating circumstances, my decisions, my relationships with people—all would be transformed and more pleasing to You if I really grasped this concept and took it with me today. Teach me and change me this morning. Amen.*

WORSHIP WITH A STENCH

Wash you, make you clean; put away the evil of your doings from before mine eyes; cease to do evil.

—Isaiah 1:16

*L*et us suppose we are back in the old days of the high priest, who took incense into the sanctum and went behind the veil and offered it there. And let us suppose that rubber—the worst-smelling thing I can think of when it burns—had been available in those days. Let us suppose that chips of rubber had been mixed with the incense, so that instead of the pure smoke of the spices filling the temple with sweet perfume, there had been the black, angry, rancid smell of rubber mixed with it. How could a priest worship God by mixing with the sweet-smelling ingredients some foul ingredient that would be a stench in the nostrils of priest and people?

So how can we worship God acceptably when there is within our nature something that, when it catches on fire, gives off not a *fragrance* but a *smell*? How can we hope to worship God acceptably when there is something in our nature which is undisciplined, un-corrected, unpurged, unpurified—which is evil and which will not and cannot worship God acceptably? Even granted that a man with evil ingredients in his nature might with some part of him worship God half acceptably, what kind of a way is that to live?

TWE008-009

Purify my heart. Bring to my remembrance anything that might be a stench in Your holy nostrils. Cleanse me, that my worship this morning might be a sweet perfume, pleasing to You in every way. Amen.

WE SEE GOD TOO SMALL

I will praise the name of God with a song, and will magnify him with thanksgiving.

—Psalm 69:30

*W*orship rises or falls in any church altogether depending upon the attitude we take toward God, whether we see God big or whether we see Him little. Most of us see God too small; our God is too little. David said, "O magnify the LORD with me" (Psalm 34:3), and "magnify" doesn't mean to make God big. You can't make God big. But you can *see* Him big.

Worship, I say, rises or falls with our concept of God; that is why I do not believe in these half-converted cowboys who call God the Man Upstairs. I do not think they worship at all because their concept of God is unworthy of God and unworthy of them. And if there is one terrible disease in the Church of Christ, it is that we do not see God as great as He is. We're too familiar with God. WMJ021

> *Sovereign God, expand my vision of You today. Give me some grasp of Your majesty and declare to me Your glory. Then draw me to my knees in awe and reverential worship. Amen.*

WONDER AND AWESOME FEAR

And Moses made haste, and bowed his head toward the earth, and worshipped.

—Exodus 34:8

I have said it before and I will say it again: This low concept of God is our spiritual problem today. Mankind has succeeded quite well in reducing God to a pitiful nothing!

The God of the modern context is no God at all. He is simply a glorified chairman of the board, a kind of big businessman dealing in souls. The God portrayed in much of our church life today commands very little respect.

We must get back to the Bible and to the ministration of God's Spirit to regain a high and holy concept of God. Oh, this awesome, terrible God, the dread of Isaac! This God who made Isaiah cry out, "I am undone!" (Isaiah 6:5). This God who drove Daniel to his knees in honor and respect.

To know the Creator and the God of all the universe is to revere Him. It is to bow down before Him in wonder and awesome fear. MMG079-080

Lord, I'm struck this morning with a sense of awe in Your presence. I bow before You in "wonder and awesome fear." Amen.

WASTED RELIGIOUS ACTIVITY

I was glad when they said unto me, Let us go into the house of the LORD.

—Psalm 122:1

*T*here is probably not another field of human activity where there is so much waste as in the field of religion. . . .

In the average church we hear the same prayers repeated each Sunday year in and year out with, one would suspect, not the remotest expectation that they will be answered. It is enough, it seems, that they have been uttered. The familiar phrase, the religious tone, the emotionally loaded words have their superficial and temporary effect, but the worshiper is no nearer to God, no better morally and no surer of heaven than he was before. Yet every Sunday morning for twenty years he goes through the same routine and, allowing two hours for him to leave his house, sit through a church service and return to his house again, he has wasted more than 170 twelve-hour days with this exercise in futility. . . .

I need only add that all this tragic waste is unnecessary. The believing Christian will relish every moment in church and will profit by it. The instructed, obedient Christian will yield to God as the clay to the potter, and the result will be not waste but glory everlasting. BAM100-101, 103

> *Lord, what an awesome responsibility to come before Your people week after week as Your messenger! I can only do this as Your Holy Spirit feeds my own soul—feed me today, Lord, as I prepare for this Sunday. Amen.*

BUSY, BUSY, BUSY

For thou desirest not sacrifice; else would I give it: thou delightest not in burnt offering. The sacrifices of God are a broken spirit: a broken and a contrite heart, O God, thou wilt not despise.

—Psalm 51:16-17

There is all around us, however, a very evident and continuing substitute for worship. I speak of the compelling temptation among Christian believers to be constantly engaged, during every waking hour, in religious activity.

We cannot deny that it is definitely a churchly idea of service. Many of our sermons and much of our contemporary ecclesiastical teaching lean toward the idea that it is surely God's plan for us to be busy, busy, busy—because it is the best cause in the world in which we are involved.

But if there is any honesty left in us, it persuades us in our quieter moments that true spiritual worship is at a discouragingly low ebb among professing Christians.

Do we dare ask how we have reached this state? . . .

How can our approach to worship be any more vital than it is when so many who lead us, both in the pulpit and in the pew, give little indication that the fellowship of God is delightful beyond telling? WHT026-027

Oh Lord, forgive me for so often falling into the "busy, busy, busy" trap. Help me to demonstrate that "the fellowship of God is delightful beyond telling." Amen.

THE ART OF TRUE WORSHIP

And every creature which is in heaven, and on the earth, and under the earth, and such as are in the sea, and all that are in them, heard I saying, Blessing, and honour, and glory, and power, be unto him that sitteth upon the throne, and unto the Lamb, for ever and ever.

—Revelation 5:13

*I*t remains only to be said that worship as we have described it here is almost (though, thank God, not quite) a forgotten art in our day. For whatever we can say of modern Bible-believing Christians, it can hardly be denied that we are not remarkable for our spirit of worship. The gospel as preached by good men in our times may save souls, but it does not create worshipers. . . .

How few, how pitifully few are the enraptured souls who languish for love of Christ. . . .

If Bible Christianity is to survive the present world upheaval, we shall need to recapture the spirit of worship. We shall need to have a fresh revelation of the greatness of God and the beauty of Jesus. We shall need to put away our phobias and our prejudices against the deeper life and seek again to be filled with the Holy Spirit. He alone can raise our cold hearts to rapture and restore again the art of true worship. TIC130-131

Lord, help us to "raise our cold hearts to rapture and restore again the art of true worship." May it no longer be said that true worship is "a forgotten art." Amen.

NONLITURGICAL WORSHIP

Give unto the Lord the glory due unto his name: bring an offering, and come into his courts. O worship the Lord in the beauty of holiness: fear before him, all the earth.

—Psalm 96:8-9

*W*e of the nonliturgical churches tend to look with some disdain upon those churches that follow a carefully prescribed form of service.... But I have observed that our familiar impromptu service, planned by the leader twenty minutes before, often tends to follow a ragged and tired order almost as standardized as the Mass. The liturgical service is at least beautiful; ours is often ugly. Theirs has been carefully worked out through the centuries to capture as much of beauty as possible and to preserve a spirit of reverence among the worshipers. Ours is often an off-the-cuff makeshift with nothing to recommend it. Its so-called liberty is often not liberty at all but sheer slovenliness. . . .

. . . mostly there is neither order nor Spirit, just a routine prayer that is, except for minor variations, the same week after week, and a few songs that were never much to start with and have long ago lost all significance by meaningless repetition.

In the majority of our meetings there is scarcely a trace of reverent thought, no recognition of the unity of the body, little sense of the divine Presence, no moment of stillness, no solemnity, no wonder, no holy fear. GTM004-005

Lord, thank You for those worship leaders who really are working to restore a sense of genuine worship. May we capture that more and more. Amen.

IN NEED OF WORSHIPERS

But we will give ourselves continually to prayer, and to the ministry of the word.

—Acts 6:4

*W*ell, we have great churches and we have beautiful sanctuaries and we join in the chorus, "We have need of nothing." But there is every indication that we are in need of worshipers.

We have a lot of men willing to sit on our church boards who have no desire for spiritual joy and radiance and who never show up for the church prayer meeting. . . .

They are the fellows who run the church, but you cannot get them to the prayer meeting because they are not worshipers. . . .

It seems to me that it has always been a frightful incongruity that men who do not pray and do not worship are nevertheless actually running many of the churches and ultimately determining the direction they will take.

It hits very close to our own situations, perhaps, but we should confess that in many "good" churches, we let the women do the praying and let the men do the voting.

Because we are not truly worshipers, we spend a lot of time in the churches just spinning our wheels, burning the gasoline, making a noise but not getting anywhere. WHT016-017

> *Lord, make the men in our church, especially the leaders, men of prayer and worship. Please don't allow us to try to lead others where we have not been; don't let us spin our wheels because we are not worshipers. Amen.*

THE PROGRAM

For where two or three are gathered together in my name, there am I in the midst of them.

—Matthew 18:20

$\mathcal{N}$ow, I freely admit that it is impossible to hold a Christian service without an agenda. If order is to be maintained, an order of service must exist somewhere. If two songs are to be sung, someone must know which one is to be sung first, and whether this knowledge is only in someone's head or has been reduced to paper there is indeed a "program," however we may dislike to call it that. The point we make here is that in our times the program has been substituted for the Presence. The program rather than the Lord of glory is the center of attraction. So the most popular gospel church in any city is likely to be the one that offers the most interesting program; that is, the church that can present the most and best features for the enjoyment of the public. . . .

We'll do our churches a lot of good if we each one seek to cultivate the blessed Presence in our services. If we make Christ the supreme and constant object of devotion the program will take its place as a gentle aid to order in the public worship of God. If we fail to do this the program will finally obscure the Light entirely. And no church can afford that. ROR094-096

Lord, I pray that Christ might always be the center of our worship—never the program. Amen.

OMIT
THE THIRD
VERSE

Praise ye the LORD. Praise the
LORD, O my soul. While I live
will I praise the LORD: I will sing
praises unto my God while I have
any being.

—Psalm 146:1-2

$\mathcal{I}$ suppose it is not of vast importance that the third stanza is so often omitted in the singing of a hymn, but just for the record let it be said that the worshipers are deprived of the blessing of the hymn by that omission if, as is often true, the hymn develops a great Christian truth in sermonic outline. To omit a stanza is to lose one link in a golden chain and greatly to reduce the value of the whole hymn.

The significant thing, however, is not what the omission actually does, but what it suggests, viz., a nervous impatience and a desire to get the service over with. We are, for instance, singing "When I Survey the Wondrous Cross." We long to forget the big noisy world and let our hearts go out in reverent worship of that Prince of Glory who died for us, but our sad sweet longing is killed in the bud by the brisk, unemotional voice of the director ordering us to "omit the third verse." . . . Since all standard hymns have been edited to delete inferior stanzas and since any stanza of the average hymn can be sung in less than one minute . . . and since many of our best hymns have already been shortened as much as good taste will allow, we are forced to conclude that the habit of omitting the third stanza reveals religious boredom, pure and simple, and it would do our souls good if we would admit it.

PON123-124

Lord, forgive us of our "desire to get the service over
with," and for our "religious boredom." Amen.

TRUCKLOADS OF GADGETS

Evening, and morning, and at noon, will I pray, and cry aloud: and he shall hear my voice.

—Psalm 55:17

These people who have to have truckloads of gadgets to get their religion going, what will they do when they don't have anything like that? The truck can't get where they're going.

I heard a man boast this afternoon on the radio to come to his place because they were going to bring in equipment from Pennsylvania and Ohio to serve the Lord with. What equipment do you need to serve the Lord with, brother? Why, the dear old camp meeting ladies used to say, "See, this is my harp with ten strings and I praise the Lord!" And they'd clap their little old wrinkled hands with shining faces. What claptrap do you need? Do you need a bushel basket full of stuff to serve the Lord with?

Brother, if you have two knees and even if you're stiffened up with arthritis so you can't get on your knees, you can look up in your heart. For prayer isn't getting on your knees—prayer is the elevation of the heart to God. That's all a man needs. You can pray in a prison, you can pray in an airplane, you can pray in a ship; you can pray anywhere and you can worship God, because it's Himself that we want, Himself. SAT030

Lord, show me Yourself this morning. I don't have any "claptrap" or equipment here; I just want to get on my knees and worship. I meditate on Your works, my soul longs for You, here in the quiet of my study. Amen.

WHAT'S MISSING

*C*hristian churches have come to the dangerous time predicted long ago. It is a time when we can pat one another on the back, congratulate ourselves and join in the glad refrain, "We are rich, and increased with goods, and have need of nothing!"

It certainly is true that hardly anything is missing from our churches these days—except the most important thing. We are missing the genuine and sacred offering of ourselves and our worship to the God and Father of our Lord Jesus Christ. . . .

We have been surging forward. We are building great churches and large congregations. We are boasting about high standards and we are talking a lot about revival.

But I have a question and it is not just rhetoric: *What has happened to our worship? . . .*

I wish that we might get back to worship again. Then when people come into the church they will instantly sense that they have come among holy people, God's people. They can testify, "Of a truth God is in this place." WHT009-010, 020

> *Lord, "I want to be among those who worship." I've been guilty at times of going through the motions, and I pray that today You might fill me with a brand new sense of genuine worship. Amen.*

The Church

The business of the Church is God. She is purest when most engaged with God and she is astray just so far as she follows other interests, no matter how "religious" or humanitarian they may be. SOS080

A MODEL FOR OTHER CHURCHES

> *So that ye were ensamples to all that believe in Macedonia and Achaia. For from you sounded out the word of the Lord not only in Macedonia and Achaia, but also in every place your faith to God-ward is spread abroad; so that we need not to speak any thing.*
>
> —1 Thessalonians 1:7-8

I would like to see a church become so godly, so Spirit-filled that it would have a spiritual influence on all of the churches in the entire area. Paul told some of his people, "ye were ensamples to all that believe" and "in every place your faith to God-ward is spread abroad" (1 Thessalonians 1:7-8).

It is entirely right that I should hope this of you. I could hope that we might become so Spirit-filled, walking with God, learning to worship, living so clean and so separated that everybody would know it, and the other churches in our area would be blessed on account of it. . . .

There is no reason why we could not be a people so filled with the Spirit, so joyfully singing His praises and living so clean in our business and home and school that the people and other churches would know it and recognize it. COU009-010

Please, Lord, enable us to be models of godliness, spirit-filled victory, joy and worship. Amen.

THE MISSING SUPERNATURAL AFFLATUS

And behold, I send the promise of my Father upon you: but tarry ye in the city of Jerusalem, until ye be endued with power from on high.

—Luke 24:49

*W*here adequate power is present almost any means will suffice, but where the power is absent not all the means in the world can secure the desired end. The Spirit of God may use a song, a sermon, a good deed, a text or the mystery and majesty of nature, but always the final work will be done by the pressure of the inliving Spirit upon the human heart.

In the light of this it will be seen how empty and meaningless is the average church service today. All the means are in evidence; the one ominous weakness is the absence of the Spirit's power. The form of godliness is there, and often the form is perfected till it is an aesthetic triumph. Music and poetry, art and oratory, symbolic vesture and solemn tones combine to charm the mind of the worshiper, but too often the supernatural afflatus is not there. The power from on high is neither known nor desired by pastor or people. This is nothing less than tragic, and all the more so because it falls within the field of religion where the eternal destinies of men are involved. POM090-091

Lord, I'm going to set aside some time today to "tarry" in seeking an assurance of the Holy Spirit's work in our church. I'll do my homework in giving good leadership, but again today I affirm my prayer that the Holy Spirit would come in real power in our church. Amen.

LOW MORAL ENTHUSIASM

And in every work that he began in the service of the house of God, and in the law, and in the commandments, to seek his God, he did it with all his heart, and prospered.

—2 Chronicles 31:21

*W*ere some watcher or holy one from the bright world above to come among us for a time with the power to diagnose the spiritual ills of church people, there is one entry which I am quite sure would appear on the vast majority of his reports: *Definite evidence of chronic spiritual lassitude; level of moral enthusiasm extremely low.* . . .

It is true that there is a lot of religious activity among us: interchurch basketball tournaments, religious splash parties followed by devotions, weekend camping trips with a Bible quiz around the fire. Sunday school picnics, building fund drives and ministerial breakfasts are with us in unbelievable numbers, and they are carried on with typical American gusto. It is when we enter the sacred precincts of the heart's personal religion that we suddenly lose all enthusiasm.

So we find this strange and contradictory situation: a world of noisy, headlong religious activity carried on without moral energy or spiritual fervor. OGM003-004

In the busyness of spiritual leadership and church activity, keep me, Lord, from boredom or burn-out. Help me to stay personally fresh in my enthusiasm for You, so that in turn I can pass that genuine enthusiasm on to the people with whom I minister. Amen.

LET'S EAT SOMETHING

Let the word of Christ dwell in you richly in all wisdom; teaching and admonishing one another in psalms and hymns and spiritual songs, singing with grace in your hearts to the Lord.

—Colossians 3:16

*T*imes are bad in the kingdom and getting worse. The tendency is to settle into a rut, and we must get out of it. . . .

When God sends some preacher to say this to a congregation and the congregation is even half ready to listen to him, they say to themselves, "I think the pastor is right about this. We are in a rut, aren't we? No use fighting it. I think we ought to do something about this." Then 99.99 percent of the time the remedy prescribed will be, "Let's come together and eat something. I know we are in a rut. We don't see each other often enough. We ought to get to know each other better, so let's come together and eat something." I have no objection to fellowship, but it is not the answer to what is wrong with us. . . .

I am quite sure that when the man of God thundered, "You have stayed long enough in this place. You are going around in circles. Get you out and take what is given to you by the hand of your God," nobody got up and said, "Mr. Chairman, let's eat something." Eating probably would not have helped. RRR013-015

Thank You for the privilege of Christian fellowship—and of eating together to foster relationships in the Body of Christ. But help us, Lord, to go much deeper. Take us out of the rut through following hard after You, not through surface attempts. Amen.

STAYING IN THE FIRST GRADE

... forgetting those things which are behind, and reaching forth unto those things which are before, I press toward the mark for the prize of the high calling of God in Christ Jesus.

—Philippians 3:13-14

*T*here are Christians who grow up and have no relish for anything spiritually advanced. They're preoccupied with their first lessons. The average church is a school with only one grade and that is the first one. These Christians never expect to get beyond that and they don't want to hear a man very long who wants to take them beyond that. If their pastor insists they do their homework and get ready for the next grade, they begin to pray that the Lord will call "our dear brother" somewhere else. . . . All he's trying to do is prepare them for another grade, but that church is dedicated to the first grade, and the first grade is where it's going to remain.

Paul said some of them went up into the second grade and gave it up, and said, "It's too hard here," and they went back to the first.

"How long have you been in the first grade, Junior?"

"Twelve years.". . .

Paul said, "forgetting those things which are behind . . . I press toward the mark" (Philippians 3:13-14). There was a man not satisfied with the first grade. SAT004-005

> *Father, I do pray that our church might not get stuck in the first grade. Help us not to shrink from the hard lessons that bring us to spiritual maturity. Amen.*

WILDERNESS ENCROACHMENT

Because thou sayest, I am rich, and increased with goods, and have need of nothing; and knowest not that thou art wretched, and miserable, and poor, and blind, and naked.

—Revelation 3:17

*T*he wilderness encroaches on the fruitful field, and unless there is constant fighting off of this encroachment, there will be little or no harvest.

I think it is exactly the same with the church, for as one of the old saints said, "Never think for a minute that there will be a time when you will not be tempted. He is tempted the most effectively who thinks that he isn't being tempted at all."

Just when we think we are not being tempted, that is the time of danger, and so it is with the Church. We lean back on our own laurels and say, "That may be true of some churches, but it is not true of us. We are increased with goods and have need of nothing!" (see Revelation 3:17).

This is to remind us that we must fight for what we have. Our little field of God's planting must have the necessary weapons and plenty of watchmen out there to drive off the crows and all sorts of creatures, to say nothing of the little insects that destroy the crops. We have to keep after them. We must keep our field healthy, and there is only one way to do that, and that is to keep true to the Word of God. We must constantly go back to the grass roots and get the Word into the Church. COU006

Lord, don't ever let us become complacent in Your blessing. Keep us vigilant that our field might stay healthy and the little weeds might never be allowed to take root. Amen.

COMMOTION, NOT DEVOTION

And after the earthquake a fire; but the LORD was not in the fire: and after the fire a still small voice.

—1 Kings 19:12

"The accent in the Church today," says Leonard Ravenhill, the English evangelist, "is not on devotion, but on commotion." Religious extroversion has been carried to such an extreme in evangelical circles that hardly anyone has the desire, to say nothing of the courage, to question the soundness of it. Externalism has taken over. God now speaks by the wind and the earthquake only; the still small voice can be heard no more. The whole religious machine has become a noisemaker. The adolescent taste which loves the loud horn and the thundering exhaust has gotten into the activities of modern Christians. The old question, "What is the chief end of man?" is now answered, "To dash about the world and add to the din thereof.". . .

We must begin the needed reform by challenging the spiritual validity of externalism. What a man is must be shown to be more important than what he does. While the moral quality of any act is imparted by the condition of the heart, there may be a world of religious activity which arises not from within but from without and which would seem to have little or no moral content. Such religious conduct is imitative or reflex. It stems from the current cult of commotion and possesses no sound inner life. ROR078-076

Lord quiet my heart today in the midst of the rush and din of church busyness, that I might be able to hear the "still small voice." Amen.

ACTIVITIES

But speaking the truth in love, may grow up into him in all things, which is the head, even Christ.

—Ephesians 4:15

*I*n an effort to get the work of the Lord done we often lose contact with the Lord of the work and quite literally wear our people out as well. I have heard more than one pastor boast that his church was a "live" one, pointing to the printed calender as a proof—something on every night and several meetings during the day. . . . A great many of these time-consuming activities are useless and others plain ridiculous. "But," say the eager beavers who run the religious squirrel cages, "they provide fellowship and they hold our people together."

To this I reply that what they provide is not fellowship at all, and if that is the best thing the church has to offer to hold the people together it is not a Christian church in the New Testament meaning of that word. The center of attraction in a true church is the Lord Jesus Christ. . . .

If the many activities engaged in by the average church led to the salvation of sinners or the perfecting of believers they would justify themselves easily and triumphantly; but they do not. *My observations have led me to the belief that many, perhaps most, of the activities engaged in by the average church do not contribute in any way to the accomplishing of the true work of Christ on earth.* I hope I am wrong, but I am afraid I am right. TIC136-137

Help us, Lord, to be willing even today to look at our church programs and evaluate what we do in the light of the truth of this challenge. Amen.

THE RIGHT KIND OF LEADERS

Feed the flock of God which is among you, taking the oversight thereof, not by constraint, but willingly; not for filthy lucre, but of a ready mind; neither as being lords over God's heritage, but being ensamples to the flock.

—1 Peter 5:2-3

I believe that it might be accepted as a fairly reliable rule of thumb that the man who is ambitious to lead is disqualified as a leader. The Church of the Firstborn is no place for the demagogue or the petty religious dictator. The true leader will have no wish to lord it over God's heritage, but will be humble, gentle, self-sacrificing and altogether as ready to follow as to lead when the Spirit makes it plain to him that a wiser and more gifted man than himself has appeared.

It is undoubtedly true, as I have said so often, that the church is languishing not for leaders but for the right kind of leaders; for the wrong kind is worse than none at all. Better to stand still than to follow a blind man over a precipice. History will show that the church has prospered most when blessed with strong leaders and suffered the greatest decline when her leaders were weak and time serving. The sheep rarely go much farther than the Shepherd.

WOS191-192

> *Give me the heart of a servant, Lord, that I might be the right kind of leader. Make me Your servant today, I pray in Jesus' name. Amen.*

WHAT DOES GOD SAY?

All scripture is given by inspiration of God, and is profitable for doctrine, for reproof, for correction, for instruction in righteousness.

—2 Timothy 3:16

I knew a man from India who got hold of a New Testament, was converted and started to preach, but he had no background at all. That is, he started from scratch. He did not have a Greek Orthodox or Roman Catholic or Protestant background. He just started from the beginning. He didn't know anything about churches. He testified, "What I did when I had a problem in the church was to go straight to the New Testament and settle it. I let the New Testament tell me what I was to do." The result was that God greatly blessed him and his work in the land of India.

This is what I would like to see in our church—the New Testament order of letting Scripture decide matters. When it comes to a question—any question—what does the Word of God say? All belief and practices should be tested by the Word; no copying unscriptural church methods. We should let the Word of God decide. RRR140

Lord, help us to lead our churches to seek clear direction from Your Word and Your Spirit. Amen.

CHURCH ORGANIZATION

For this cause left I thee in Crete, that thou shouldest set in order the things that are wanting, and ordain elders in every city, as I had appointed thee.

—Titus 1:5

I am and have been for years much distressed about the tendency to over-organize the Christian community, and I have for that reason had it charged against me that I do not believe in organization. The truth is quite otherwise.

The man who would oppose all organization in the church must needs be ignorant of the facts of life. Art is organized beauty; music is organized sound; philosophy is organized thought; science is organized knowledge; government is merely society organized. And what is the true church of Christ but organized mystery? . . .

Many church groups have perished from too much organization, even as others from too little. Wise church leaders will watch out for both extremes. A man may die as a result of having too low blood pressure as certainly as from having too high, and it matters little which takes him off. He is equally dead either way. The important thing in church organization is to discover the scriptural balance between two extremes and avoid both. GTM029, 031

Give us wisdom, Lord, to operate with good organization and wise business practices. But keep us from being so organized that the Holy Spirit has no room to work. Amen.

JUDGING BY THE FINANCIAL REPORT

Charge them that are rich in this world, that they be not highminded, nor trust in uncertain riches, but in the living God, who giveth us richly all things to enjoy.

—1 Timothy 6:17

*W*e in the churches seem unable to rise above the fiscal philosophy which rules the business world; so we introduce into our church finances the psychology of the great secular institutions so familiar to us all and judge a church by its financial report much as we judge a bank or a department store.

A look into history will quickly convince any interested person that the true church has almost always suffered more from prosperity than from poverty. Her times of greatest spiritual power have usually coincided with her periods of indigence and rejection; with wealth came weakness and backsliding. If this cannot be explained, neither apparently can it be escaped. . . .

The point I am trying to make here is that while money has a proper place in the total life of the church militant, the tendency is to attach to it an importance that is far greater than is biblically sound or morally right. The average church has so established itself organizationally and financially that God is simply not necessary to it. So entrenched is its authority and so stable are the religious habits of its members that God could withdraw Himself completely from it and it could run on for years on its own momentum. WOS009-011

Lord, it's hard to ask for You to send us poverty. Keep us mindful that though we have so much our only real wealth is in You. Amen.

PHILIP THE CALCULATOR

Philip answered him, Two hundred pennyworth of bread is not sufficient for them, that every one of them may take a little.

—John 6:7

*H*ere in the New Testament was Philip the Calculator—Philip the Mathematician, Philip the Clerk. There was need for a miracle, and Philip set out to calculate the odds. Probably every Christian group has at least one person with a calculator. I have sat on boards for many years, and rarely is there a board without a Philip the Calculator among its members. When you suggest something, out comes the calculator to prove that it cannot be done. . . .

As I say, I have been sitting on these boards for many years, and there are always two kinds of board members: those who can see the miracle and those who can only see their calculators and their strings of calculations. . . .

The people with the calculators have seen the problem, but they have not seen God. They have figured things out, but they have not figured God in.

Philip the Calculator. He can be a dangerous man in the church of our Lord Jesus Christ. Every suggestion made in the direction of progress gets a negative vote from this man. FBR137-139

Lord, deliver us from the control of the calculator. Increase our faith. Amen.

THE POWER OF CHURCH FINANCES

But if ye have respect to persons, ye commit sin, and are convinced of the law as transgressors.

—James 2:9

$\mathcal{I}$t is an ominous thing in any church when the treasurer begins to exercise power. Since he may be presumed to be a man of God he should have a place equal to that of any other member, and if he is a man of gifts and virtues he will naturally have certain influences among the brethren. This is right and normal as long as he exercises his influences as a man of God and not as a treasurer. The moment he becomes important *because* he is treasurer, the Spirit will be grieved and His manifestations will begin to diminish. . . .

Again, it is a sign and a portent when a member is cultivated for his generosity and given a place of eminence in the church out of proportion to his spiritual gifts and graces. To court a Christian for his financial contributions is as evil a thing as to marry a man for his money. To flatter a man for any reason whatever is to degrade ourselves and imperil his soul. To flatter a man because he is a heavy giver is to offer him a concealed affront as well, for back of the purring and the smirking is the hidden opinion that the man's money is more important than the man and more to be esteemed. wos007-008

Deliver us from the dominance of the dollar. You meet our needs, Lord, and then help us to minister faithfully, with no thought of how the finances might be affected. Amen.

THE GLOOMY VOICE OF UNBELIEF

Now faith is the substance of things hoped for, the evidence of things not seen.

—Hebrews 11:1

The voice of unbelief says, "Yes, I'm a believer. I believe the Bible. I don't like those modernists, liberals and modern scientists who deny the Bible. I would not do that for the world. I believe in God, and I believe that God will bless." That is, He will bless at some other time, in some other place and some other people. Those are three sleepers that bring the work of God to a halt. We are believers and we can quote the creed with approval. We believe it, but we believe that God will bless some other people, some other place, some other time—but not now, not here and not us. . . .

If we allow the gloomy voice of unbelief to whisper to us that God will bless some other time but not now, some other place but not here, some other people but not us, we might as well turn off the lights because nobody will get anywhere. . . .

The average evangelical church lies under a shadow of quiet doubting. The doubt is not the unbelief that argues against Scripture, but worse than that. It is the chronic unbelief that does not know what faith means. RRR152, 157

Lord, today I claim three words to take with me through the day—now, here, us. Thank You that I can claim these and they can change my life. Amen.

A JOYFUL PEOPLE

But whosoever drinketh of the water that I shall give him shall never thirst; but the water that I shall give him shall be in him a well of water springing up into everlasting life.

—John 4:14

*W*e do have many professing Christians in our day who are not joyful, but they spend time trying to work it up. Now, brethren, I say that when we give God His place in the Church, when we recognize Christ as Lord high and lifted up, when we give the Holy Spirit His place, there will be joy that doesn't have to be worked up. It will be a joy that springs like a fountain. Jesus said that it should be a fountain, an artesian well, that springs up from within. That's one characteristic of a Spirit-filled congregation. They will be a joyful people, and it will be easy to distinguish them from the children of the world.

I wonder what the apostle Paul would say if he came down right now and looked us over in our congregations. What if he walked up and down the aisles of our churches, then went to a theater and looked them over, then on to a hockey game, on to the crowds at the shopping center and into the crowded streets? Then when he came back and looked us over again, I wonder if he would see very much difference? COU008

> *Father, I need that artesian well of joy today. The burdens and busyness of leadership sometimes really sap my strength and kill the joy. Help me—and our whole congregation—to demonstrate that real Spirit-inspired joy this week. Amen.*

THE GENUINE JOY OF THE LORD

The he said unto them, Go your way, eat the fat, and drink the sweet, and set portions unto them for whom nothing is prepared: for this day is holy unto our LORD: neither be ye sorry; for the joy of the LORD is your strength.

—Nehemiah 8:10

*W*e are missing the mark about Christian victory and the life of joy in our Savior. We ought to be standing straight and praising our God!

I must agree with the psalmist that the joy of the Lord is the strength of His people. I do believe that the sad world is attracted to spiritual sunshine—the genuine thing, that is.

Some churches train their greeters and ushers to smile, showing as many teeth as possible. But I can sense that kind of display, and when I am greeted by a person who is smiling because he or she has been trained to smile, I know I am shaking the flipper of a trained seal. When the warmth and joy of the Holy Spirit are in a congregation, however, and the folks are spontaneously joyful, the result is a wonderful influence upon others.

I have said it a hundred times: The reason we have to search for so many things to cheer us up is the fact that we are not really joyful and contentedly happy within. . . . But we are Christians, and Christians have every right to be the happiest people in the world. TRA010-011

Lord Jesus, help me today to experience the joy of the Lord. I claim that joy as mine, even in the midst of heavy responsibilities. I'm going to rest in this joy of the Lord as my strength today, and praise You for it! Amen.

AN UNWORTHY CONCEPTION OF GOD

For who in the heaven can be compared unto the LORD? who among the sons of the mighty can be likened unto the LORD? God is greatly to be feared in the assembly of the saints, and to be had in reverence of all them that are about him.

—Psalm 89:6-7

*C*hristianity at any given time is strong or weak depending upon her concept of God. And I insist upon this and I have said it many times, that the basic trouble with the Church today is her unworthy conception of God. I talk with learned and godly people all over the country, and they're all saying the same thing.

Unbelievers say, "Take your cowboy god and go home," and we get angry and say, "They're vile heathen." No, they're not vile heathen—or at least that's not why they say that. They can't respect our "cowboy god." And since evangelicalism has gone overboard to "cowboy religion," its conception of God is unworthy of Him. Our religion is little because our god is little. . . . We do not see God as He is. . . .

A local church will only be as great as its conception of God. An individual Christian will be a success or a failure depending upon what he or she thinks of God. It is critically important that we have a knowledge of the Holy One, that we know what God is like.
AOG041-042

> *O God, help me to capture once again a realization of Your greatness. May the God I represent in my ministry be a God worthy of lavish worship. Amen.*

THE MAJOR DECISION

Hold fast the form of sound words, which thou hast heard of me, in faith and love which is in Christ Jesus. That good thing which was committed unto thee keep by the Holy Ghost which dwelleth in us.

—2 Timothy 1:13-14

There is a great decision that every denomination has to make sometime in the development of its history. Every church also has to make it either at its beginning or a little later—usually a little later. Eventually every board is faced with the decision. . . . Every pastor has to face it and keep renewing his decision on his knees before God. Finally, every church member, every evangelist, every Christian has to make this decision. . . .

The question is this: Shall we modify the truth in doctrine or practice to gain more adherents? Or shall we preserve the truth in doctrine and practice and take the consequences? . . .

A commitment to preserving the truth and practice of the church is what separates me from a great many people who are perhaps far greater than I am in ability. This is my conviction, long held and deeply confirmed by a knowledge of the fact that modern gospel churches, almost without exception, have decided to modify the truth and practice a little in order to have more adherents and get along better. RRR165-167

We're under constant pressure to have more adherents, more members, more numbers, Lord. God help me never to modify or compromise to achieve that, but to tenaciously hold fast to my core beliefs and priorities. Amen.

THE DRY ROT OF NONEXPECTATION

And the word of God increased; and the number of the disciples multiplied in Jerusalem greatly; and a great company of the priests were obedient to the faith.

—Acts 6:7

*T*he church is afflicted by dry rot. This is best explained when the psychology of nonexpectation takes over and spiritual rigidity sets in, which is an inability to visualize anything better, a lack of desire for improvement.

There are many who respond by arguing, "I know lots of evangelical churches that would like to grow, and they do their best to get the crowds in. They want to grow and have contests to make their Sunday school larger." That is true, but they are trying to get people to come and share their rut. They want people to help them celebrate the rote and finally join in the rot. Because the Holy Spirit is not given a chance to work in our services, nobody is repenting, nobody is seeking God, nobody is spending a day in quiet waiting on God with open Bible seeking to mend his or her ways. . . . But more people for what? More people to come and repeat our dead services without feeling, without meaning, without wonder, without surprise? More people to join us in the bondage to the rote? For the most part, spiritual rigidity that cannot bend is too weak to know just how weak it is. RRR008-009

> *Lord, not more people, but more of You. Let me wait upon You, keep me faithful, send Your Holy Spirit. Amen.*

HIGHER EXPECTATIONS

Whom we preach, warning every man, and teaching every man in all wisdom; that we may present every man perfect in Christ Je-sus: whereunto I also labour, striving according to his working, which worketh in me mightily.

—Colossians 1:28-29

The treacherous enemy facing the church of Jesus Christ today is the dictatorship of the routine, when the routine becomes "lord" in the life of the church. Programs are organized and the prevailing conditions are accepted as normal. Anyone can predict next Sunday's service and what will happen. This seems to be the most deadly threat in the church today. When we come to the place where everything can be predicted and nobody expects anything unusual from God, we are in a rut. The routine dictates, and we can tell not only what will happen next Sunday, but what will occur next month and, if things do not improve, what will take place next year. Then we have reached the place where what has been determines what is, and what is determines what will be.

That would be perfectly all right and proper for a cemetery. Nobody expects a cemetery to do anything but conform. . . . But the church is not a cemetery and we should expect much from it, because what has been should not be lord to tell us what is, and what is should not be ruler to tell us what will be. God's people are supposed to grow. RRR005-006

Lord, use me today to help some people to really grow in You. Amen.

THE OLD CROSS
AND THE
NEW CROSS

But God forbid that I should glory, save in the cross of our Lord Jesus Christ, by whom the world is crucified unto me, and I unto the world.

—Galatians 6:14

The old cross slew men; the new cross entertains them. The old cross condemned; the new cross amuses. The old cross destroyed confidence in the flesh; the new cross encourages it. The old cross brought tears and blood; the new cross brings laughter. The flesh, smiling and confident, preaches and sings about the cross; before that cross it bows and toward that cross it points with carefully staged histrionics—but upon that cross it will not die, and the reproach of that cross it stubbornly refuses to bear.

I well know how many smooth arguments can be marshaled in support of the new cross. Does not the new cross win converts and make many followers and so carry the advantage of numerical success? Should we not adjust ourselves to the changing times? Have we not heard the slogan "New days, new ways"? And who but someone very old and very conservative would insist upon death as the appointed way to life? And who today is interested in a gloomy mysticism that would sentence its flesh to a cross and recommend self-effacing humility as a virtue actually to be practiced by modern Christians? These are the arguments, along with many more flippant still, which are brought forward to give an appearance of wisdom to the hollow and meaningless cross of popular Christianity. POM053-054

Help me today to deny myself, to take up my cross and to follow You. Amen.

DIFFERENT FROM THE WORLD

Wherefore come out from among them, and be ye separate, saith the Lord, and touch not the unclean thing; and I will receive you.

—2 Corinthians 6:17

*T*he church's mightiest influence is felt when she is different from the world in which she lives. Her power lies in her being different, rises with the degree in which she differs and sinks as the difference diminishes.

This is so fully and clearly taught in the Scriptures and so well illustrated in Church history that it is hard to see how we can miss it. But miss it we do, for we hear constantly that the Church must try to be as much like the world as possible, excepting, of course, where the world is too, too sinful. . . .

Let us plant ourselves on the hill of Zion and invite the world to come over to us, but never under any circumstances will we go over to them. The cross is the symbol of Christianity, and the cross speaks of death and separation, never of compromise. No one ever compromised with a cross. The cross separated between the dead and the living. The timid and the fearful will cry "Extreme!" and they will be right. The cross is the essence of all that is extreme and final. The message of Christ is a call across a gulf from death to life, from sin to righteousness and from Satan to God. sos035-036

Lord, help me to be willing to be different. Forgive me for the sin of blending in. I pray that our neighbors would see something different in our church and our people and be drawn to the Savior. Amen.

THE STRIPED CANDY TECHNIQUE

And they continued stedfastly in the apostles' doctrine and fellowship, and in the breaking of bread, and in prayers.

—Acts 2:42

*W*ithout biblical authority, or any other right under the sun, carnal religious leaders have introduced a host of attractions that serve no purpose except to provide entertainment for the retarded saints.

It is now common practice in most evangelical churches to offer the people, especially the young people, a maximum of entertainment and a minimum of serious instruction. It is scarcely possible in most places to get anyone to attend a meeting where the only attraction is God. One can only conclude that God's professed children are bored with Him, for they must be wooed to meeting with a stick of striped candy in the form of religious movies, games and refreshments.

This has influenced the whole pattern of church life, and even brought into being a new type of church architecture, designed to house the golden calf.

So we have the strange anomaly of orthodoxy in creed and heterodoxy in practice. The striped-candy technique has been so fully integrated into our present religious thinking that it is simply taken for granted. Its victims never dream that it is not a part of the teachings of Christ and His apostles. MDP135-136

Help me to demonstrate a God so real that no one could ever be bored with Him. Amen.

THE
SELF-EFFACING
SAINT

For I have no man likeminded, who will naturally care for your state. For all seek their own, not the things which are Jesus Christ's.

—Philippians 2:20-21

*I*t is our belief that the evangelical movement will continue to drift farther and farther from the New Testament position unless its leadership passes from the modern religious star to the self-effacing saint who asks for no praise and seeks no place, happy only when the glory is attributed to God and himself forgotten. . . .

Within the last quarter of a century we have actually seen a major shift in the beliefs and practices of the evangelical wing of the church so radical as to amount to a complete sellout; and all this behind the cloak of fervent orthodoxy. With Bibles under their arms and bundles of tracts in their pockets, religious persons now meet to carry on "services" so carnal, so pagan, that they can hardly be distinguished from the old vaudeville shows of earlier days. And for a preacher or a writer to challenge this heresy is to invite ridicule and abuse from every quarter.

Our only hope is that renewed spiritual pressure will be exerted increasingly by self-effacing and courageous men who desire nothing but the glory of God and the purity of the church. May God send us many of them. They are long overdue. OGM016-018

Lord, forgive me for my pride. Give me the humble spirit of the self-effacing saint. Amen.

COMMON PEOPLE

For ye see your calling, brethren, how that not many wise men after the flesh, not many mighty, not many noble, are called: But God hath chosen the foolish things of the world to confound the wise; and God hath chosen the weak things of the world to confound the things which are mighty.

—1 Corinthians 1:26-27

*C*hristian believers and Christian congregations must be thoroughly consecrated to Christ's glory alone. This means absolutely turning their backs on the contemporary insistence on human glory and recognition. I have done everything I can to keep "performers" out of my pulpit. I was not called to recognize "performers." I am confident our Lord never meant for the Christian church to provide a kind of religious stage where performers proudly take their bows, seeking personal recognition. That is not God's way to an eternal work. He has never indicated that proclamation of the gospel is to be dependent on human performances.

Instead, it is important to note how much the Bible has to say about the common people—the plain people. The Word of God speaks with such appreciation of the common people that I am inclined to believe they are especially dear to Him. Jesus was always surrounded by the common people. He had a few "stars," but largely His helpers were from the common people—the good people and, surely, not always the most brilliant. TRA005

In our church, Lord, help us to treat all alike as Your servants. Amen.

GOOD BUT NOT GREAT

Moreover it is required in stewards, that a man be found faithful.

—1 Corinthians 4:2

*T*hen there are the men who are *good but not great*, and we may thank God that there are so many of them, being grateful not that they failed to achieve greatness but that by the grace of God they managed to acquire plain goodness. . . .

Every pastor knows this kind—the plain people who have nothing to recommend them but their deep devotion to their Lord and the fruit of the Spirit which they all unconsciously display. Without these the churches as we know them in city, town and country could not carry on. These are the first to come forward when there is work to be done and the last to go home when there is prayer to be made. They are not known beyond the borders of their own parish because there is nothing dramatic in faithfulness or newsworthy in goodness, but their presence is a benediction wherever they go. They have no greatness to draw to them the admiring eyes of carnal men but are content to be good men and full of the Holy Ghost, waiting in faith for the day that their true worth shall be known. When they die they leave behind them a fragrance of Christ that lingers long after the cheap celebrities of the day are forgotten. GTM099

> *Thank You, Lord, for the host of good people in our church! May each one be richly blessed of You today. Direct me to some today who I could thank for their faithfulness. Amen.*

THE PERFECT CHURCH

> *And above all things have fervent charity among yourselves: for charity shall cover the multitude of sins.*
>
> —1 Peter 4:8

*O*ur lofty idealism would argue that all Christians should be perfect, but a blunt realism forces us to admit that perfection is rare even among the saints. The part of wisdom is to accept our Christian brothers and sisters for what they are rather than for what they should be. . . .

There is much that is imperfect about us, and it is fitting that we recognize it and call upon God for charity to put up with one another. The perfect church is not on this earth. The most spiritual church is sure to have in it some who are still bothered by the flesh.

An old Italian proverb says, "He that will have none but a perfect brother must resign himself to remain brotherless." However earnestly we may desire that our Christian brother go on toward perfection, we must accept him as he is and learn to get along with him. To treat an imperfect brother impatiently is to advertise our own imperfections. WTA055

> *Give me patience and grace today in dealing with others' imperfections. And give them the same grace in dealing with mine! Amen.*

HARMONY AT ANY COST

I beseech Euodias, and beseech Syntyche, that they be of the same mind in the Lord.

—Philippians 4:2

Some misguided Christian leaders feel that they must preserve harmony at any cost, so they do everything possible to reduce friction. They should remember that there is no friction in a machine that has been shut down for the night. Turn off the power, and you will have no problem with moving parts. Also remember that there is a human society where there are no problems—the cemetery. The dead have no differences of opinion. They generate no heat, because they have no energy and no motion. But their penalty is sterility and complete lack of achievement.

What then is the conclusion of the matter? That problems are the price of progress, that friction is the concomitant of motion, that a live and expanding church will have a certain quota of difficulties as a result of its life and activity. A Spirit-filled church will invite the anger of the enemy. TWP112-113

Lord, thank You for the many signs that we are alive! Satan must see real life, and I guess that's a good sign. Give us victory though, that we might not succumb to his attacks. Amen.

100 PIANOS

That they all may be one; as thou, Father, art in me, and I in thee, that they also may be one in us: that the world may believe that thou hast sent me.

—John 17:21

*S*omeone may fear that we are magnifying private religion out of all proportion, that the "us" of the New Testament is being displaced by a selfish "I." Has it ever occurred to you that 100 pianos all tuned to the same fork are automatically tuned to each other? They are of one accord by being tuned, not to each other, but to another standard to which each one must individually bow. So 100 worshipers meeting together, each one looking away to Christ, are in heart nearer to each other than they could possibly be were they to become "unity" conscious and turn their eyes away from God to strive for closer fellowship. Social religion is perfected when private religion is purified. The body becomes stronger as its members become healthier. The whole church of God gains when the members that compose it begin to seek a better and a higher life.

POG090

> *Lord, let this start with me. Give me a closer walk with You today. Then as a leader enable me to encourage others as well, individually, so that all to whom I minister might be in harmony as we individually are close to You. Amen.*

THE CURE FOR DIFFICULTIES

But the LORD said unto Samuel, Look not on his countenance, or on the height of his stature; because I have refused him: for the LORD seeth not as man seeth; for man looketh on the outward appearance, but the LORD looketh on the heart.

—1 Samuel 16:7

*I*ndeed it may be truthfully said that everything of lasting value in the Christian life is unseen and eternal. Things seen are of little real significance in the light of God's presence. He pays small attention to the beauty of a woman or the strength of a man. With Him the heart is all that matters. The rest of the life comes into notice only because it represents the dwelling place of the inner eternal being.

The solution to life's problems is spiritual because the essence of life is spiritual. It is astonishing how many difficulties clear up without any effort when the inner life gets straightened out. . . .

Church difficulties are spiritual also and admit of a spiritual answer. Whatever may be wrong in the life of any church may be cleared up by recognizing the quality of the trouble and dealing with it at the root. Prayer, humility and a generous application of the Spirit of Christ will cure just about any disease in the body of believers. Yet this is usually the last thing we think about when difficulties arise. We often attempt to cure spiritual ills with carnal medicines, and the results are more than disappointing. NCA082-083

Help our church to focus on "prayer, humility and a generous application of the Spirit of Christ." Amen.

August

Evangelism

Every notable advance in the saving work of God among men will, if examined, be found to have two factors present: several converging lines of providential circumstances and a person. LMP050

SPIRITUALLY WORTHY

And, being assembled together with them, [he] commanded them that they should not depart from Jerusalem, but wait for the promise of the Father, which, saith he, ye have heard of me.

—Acts 1:4

*T*he task of the church is twofold: to spread Christianity throughout the world and to make sure that the Christianity she spreads is the pure New Testament kind. . . .

Christianity will always reproduce itself after its kind. A worldly-minded, unspiritual church, when she crosses the ocean to give her witness to peoples of other tongues and other cultures, is sure to bring forth on other shores a Christianity much like her own. . . .

The popular notion that the first obligation of the church is to spread the gospel to the uttermost parts of the earth is false. *Her first obligation is to be spiritually worthy to spread it.* Our Lord said "Go ye," but He also said, "Tarry ye," and the tarrying had to come before the going. Had the disciples gone forth as missionaries before the day of Pentecost it would have been an overwhelming spiritual disaster, for they could have done no more than make converts after their likeness, and this would have altered for the worse the whole history of the Western world and had consequences throughout the ages to come. OGM036-037

Lord, I don't want to be guilty of producing inferior disciples. Send Your Holy Spirit that I might be empowered to produce converts with whom You can be pleased. Amen.

BE PREPARED

And he said unto them, Go ye into all the world, and preach the gospel to every creature.

—Mark 16:15

*R*ecall what happened when Jesus said to the disciples, "Go ye into all the world, and preach the gospel to every creature" (Mark 16:15).

Peter jumped up right away, grabbed his hat and would have been on his way, but Jesus stopped him, and said, "Not yet, Peter! Don't go like that. Tarry until you are endued with power from on high, and then go!"

I believe that our Lord wants us to learn more of Him in worship before we become busy for Him. He wants us to have a gift of the Spirit, an inner experience of the heart, as our first service, and out of that will grow the profound and deep and divine activities which are necessary. ITB139

> *Quiet our hearts, that our evangelistic efforts might spring from a heart of worship. Amen.*

EARLY CHURCH METHODS

*And the multitude of them that be-
lieved were of one heart and of one
soul: neither said any of them that
aught of the things which he possessed was his own; but they had all
things common. And with great
power gave the apostles witness of
the resurrection of the Lord Jesus:
and great grace was upon them all.*

—Acts 4:32-33

A friend of mine went to see a man who was the head of a local communist cell in a local communist headquarters where
they send out literature. The communist said, "Come in, Reverend, and sit down." He went in and sat. "Now, we're communists," he said, "you know that, and you're a minister. Of
course, we're miles apart. But," he said, "I want to tell you
something. We learned our technique from your book of Acts."
And he said, "You who believe the Bible have thrown overboard the methods of the early church and we who don't believe
it have adopted them and they're working."

What was the method? It's a very simple method of the early
church. It was to go witness, give everything to the Lord and
give up all to God and bear your cross, take the consequences.
The result was in the first hundred years of the Christian
church the whole known world was evangelized. SAT010-011

*Lord, we're too selfish, busy doing our own thing. Give us
a spirit of love, of unselfishness, of willingness to pay any
price for the sake of the gospel. Do it for Jesus' sake. Amen.*

SHE HAD TO TELL SOMEONE

Come, see a man, which told me all things that ever I did: is not this the Christ?

—John 4:29

*S*piritual experiences must be shared. It is not possible for very long to enjoy them alone. The very attempt to do so will destroy them.

The reason for this is obvious. The nearer our souls draw to God the larger our love will grow, and the greater our love the more unselfish we shall become and the greater our care for the souls of others. Hence increased spiritual experience, so far as it is genuine, brings with it a strong desire that others may know the same grace that we ourselves enjoy. This leads quite naturally to an increased effort to lead others to a closer and more satisfying fellowship with God. . . .

The impulse to share, to impart, normally accompanies any true encounter with God and spiritual things. The woman at the well, after her soul-inspiring meeting with Jesus, left her waterpots, hurried into the city and tried to persuade her friends to come out and meet Him. "Come, see a man," she said, "which told me all things that ever I did: is not this the Christ?" (John 4:29). Her spiritual excitement could not be contained within her own heart. She had to tell someone. SOS050-051

> *Lord, we have so much more! We've seen Your goodness. We've tasted Your blessing. We've come to love You. Yet how seldom are we that impelled to tell anyone. Direct me even today to someone with whom I can share the glorious news of the gospel. Amen.*

SOVEREIGN OBLIGATION

> *I am debtor both to the Greeks, and to the Barbarians; both to the wise, and to the unwise. So, as much as in me is, I am ready to preach the gospel to you that are at Rome also.*
>
> —Romans 1:14-15

*T*he resurrection of Jesus Christ is something more than making us the happiest people in the Easter parade. Are we to listen to a cantata, join in singing "Up from the Grave He Arose," smell the lilies and go home and forget it? No, certainly not!

The resurrection of Jesus Christ lays hold on us with all the authority of sovereign obligation. It says that the Christian church is to go and make disciples—to go and make disciples of all nations. The moral obligation of the resurrection of Christ is the missionary obligation—the responsibility and privilege of personally carrying the message, of interceding for those who go, of being involved financially in the cause of world evangelization. TRA090

Stimulate me, Lord, with that sense of sovereign obligation. Then lead me to the right person with whom I could share Your grace. Amen.

GOD IS DEPENDING ON US

According as he hath chosen us in him before the foundation of the world, that we should be holy and without blame before him in love.

—Ephesians 1:4

Sin is a disease. It is lawlessness. It is rebellion. It is transgression—but it is also a wasting of the most precious of all treasures on earth. The man who dies out of Christ is said to be lost, and hardly a word in the English tongue expresses his condition with greater accuracy. He has squandered a rare fortune and at the last he stands for a fleeting moment and looks around, a moral fool, a wastrel who has lost in one overwhelming and irrecoverable loss, his soul, his life, his peace, his total mysterious personality, his dear and everlasting all!

Oh, how can we get men and women around us to realize that God Almighty, before the beginning of the world, loved them, and thought about them, planning redemption and salvation and forgiveness?

Christian brethren, why are we not more faithful and serious in proclaiming God's great eternal concerns?

How is this world all around us ever to learn that God is all in all unless we are faithful in our witness?

In a time when everything in the world seems to be vanity, God is depending on us to proclaim that He is the great Reality, and that only He can give meaning to all other realities. CES048

> *Forgive me, Lord. I fear that all too often I have let You down when You were depending on me. Use me today as a faithful servant. Amen.*

NOT WILLING TO TAKE CONTEMPT

And they departed from the presence of the council, rejoicing that they were counted worthy to suffer shame for his name.

—Acts 5:41

*W*e are twentieth-century Christians. Some of us are Christians only because it is convenient and pleasant and because it is not costing us anything. But here is the truth, whether we like it or not: the average evangelical Christian who claims to be born again and have eternal life is not doing as much to propagate his or her faith as the busy adherents of the cults handing out their papers on the street corners and visiting from house to house.

We are not willing to take the spit and the contempt and the abuses those cultists take as they knock on doors and try to persuade everyone to follow them in their mistaken beliefs. The cultists can teach us much about zeal and effort and sacrifice, but most of us do not want to get that serious about our faith—or our Savior. JIV114-115

Lord, let me have the spirit of the early saints. I pour myself out today as Your servant, no matter the cost. Amen.

CALLING US BACK

And the LORD God called unto Adam, and said unto him, Where art thou?

—Genesis 3:9

*A*lthough the human mind stubbornly resists and resents the suggestion that it is a sick, fallen planet upon which we ride, everything within our consciousness, our innermost spirit, confirms that the voice of God is sounding in this world—the voice of God calling, seeking, beckoning to lost men and women! . . .

Sacred revelation declares plainly that the inhabitants of the earth are lost. They are lost by a mighty calamitous visitation of woe which came upon them somewhere in that distant past and is still upon them.

But it also reveals a glorious fact—that this lost race has not been given up!

There is a divine voice that continues to call. It is the voice of the Creator, God, and it is entreating them. Just as the shepherd went everywhere searching for his sheep, just as the woman in the parable went everywhere searching for her coin, so there is a divine search with many variations of the voice that entreats us, calling us back. EFE003, 008

Thank You, Father, for Your grace that continues to call so patiently. Lord, You're calling some today with whom I could have the privilege of sharing the gospel. Give me a sensitivity today to opportunities where I might be Your human voice. Amen.

THE DESPERATE PERSONAL SEARCH

Let your light so shine before men, that they may see your good works, and glorify your Father which is in heaven.

—Matthew 5:16

The average person in the world today, without faith and without God and without hope, is engaged in a desperate personal search throughout his lifetime. He does not really know where he has been. He does not really know what he is doing here and now. He does not know where he is going.

The sad commentary is that he is doing it all on borrowed time and borrowed money and borrowed strength—and he already knows that in the end he will surely die! It boils down to the bewildered confession of many that "we have lost God somewhere along the way.". . .

Man, made more like God than any other creature, has become less like God than any other creature. Created to reflect the glory of God, he has retreated sullenly into his cave—reflecting only his own sinfulness.

Certainly it is a tragedy above all tragedies in this world that man, made with a soul to worship and praise and sing to God's glory, now sulks silently in his cave. Love has gone from his heart. Light has gone from his mind. Having lost God, he blindly stumbles on through this dark world to find only a grave at the end. WHT065-066

Lord, help me to be a light shining in this dark and gloomy cave. Let my light shine today to aid someone struggling blindly through this dark world. Amen.

AT EASE WHILE THE WORLD BURNS

Now then we are ambassadors for Christ, as though God did beseech you by us: we pray you in Christ's stead, be ye reconciled to God.

—2 Corinthians 5:20

*T*he fall of man has created a perpetual crisis. It will last until sin has been put down and Christ reigns over a redeemed and restored world.

Until that time the earth remains a disaster area and its inhabitants live in a state of extraordinary emergency. . . .

To me, it has always been difficult to understand those evangelical Christians who insist upon living in the crisis as if no crisis existed. They say they serve the Lord, but they divide their days so as to leave plenty of time to play and loaf and enjoy the pleasures of the world as well. They are at ease while the world burns. . . .

I wonder whether such Christians actually believe in the Fall of man! RDA, Jan. 17.

> *I'm too often at ease and consumed with my self-interests, Lord. Open my eyes to see the tragedy of friends and acquaintances on their way to a Christless eternity. Do it for Jesus' sake, Amen.*

TIMES OF EXTRAORDINARY CRISIS

Then saith he unto his disciples,
The harvest truly is plenteous, but
the labourers are few: pray ye
therefore the Lord of the harvest,
that he will send forth labourers
into his harvest

—Matthew 9:37-38

et a flood or a fire hit a populous countryside and no able-bodied citizen feels that he has any right to rest till he has done all he can to save as many as he can. While death stalks farmhouse and village no one dares relax; this is the accepted code by which we live. The critical emergency for some becomes an emergency for all, from the highest government official to the local Boy Scout troop. As long as the flood rages or the fire roars on, no one talks of "normal times." No times are normal while helpless people cower in the path of destruction.

In times of extraordinary crisis ordinary measures will not suffice. The world lives in such a time of crisis. Christians alone are in a position to rescue the perishing. We dare not settle down to try to live as if things were "normal." Nothing is normal while sin and lust and death roam the world, pouncing upon one and another till the whole population has been destroyed. BAM030

Lord, help me to respond like Isaiah when he saw the
extraordinary crisis around him, "Lord . . . here am I;
send me" (Isaiah 6:8). Amen.

A CHEAP SALVATION

But have renounced the hidden things of dishonesty, not walking in craftiness, nor handling the word of God deceitfully; but by manifestation of the truth commending ourselves to every man's conscience in the sight of God.

—2 Corinthians 4:2

*H*ere again is seen the glaring discrepancy between biblical Christianity and that of present-day evangelicals, particularly in the United States. . . .

To make converts here we are forced to play down the difficulties and play up the peace of mind and worldly success enjoyed by those who accept Christ. We must assure our hearers that Christianity is now a proper and respectable thing and that Christ has become quite popular with political bigwigs, well-to-do business tycoons and the Hollywood swimming pool set. Thus assured, hell-deserving sinners are coming in droves to "accept" Christ for what they can get out of Him; and though one now and again may drop a tear as proof of his sincerity, it is hard to escape the conclusion that most of them are stooping to patronize the Lord of glory much as a young couple might fawn on a boresome but rich old uncle in order to be mentioned in his will later on. BAM017

Lord, don't let me fall into the trap of offering a cheap salvation. Remind me often that redemption which cost the life of Your Son should never be so cheapened. Amen.

MAN-CENTERED CHRISTIANITY

Thine, O LORD, is the greatness, and the power, and the glory, and the victory, and the majesty: for all that is in the heaven and in the earth is thine; thine is the kingdom, O LORD, and thou art exalted as head above all.

—1 Chronicles 29:11

Christianity today is man-centered, not God-centered. God is made to wait patiently, even respectfully, on the whims of men. The image of God currently popular is that of a distracted Father, struggling in heartbroken desperation to get people to accept a Savior of whom they feel no need and in whom they have very little interest. To persuade these self-sufficient souls to respond to His generous offers God will do almost anything, even using salesmanship methods and talking down to them in the chummiest way imaginable. This view of things is, of course, a kind of religious romanticism which, while it often uses flattering and sometimes embarrassing terms in praise of God, manages nevertheless to make man the star of the show. MDP027

Lord, take me to my knees in worship. Then let me go to share You, our great and majestic God Who deserves our worship. Amen.

TRYING TO DECIDE

(For he saith, I have heard thee in a time accepted, and in the day of salvation have I succoured thee: behold, now is the accepted time; behold, now is the day of salvation.)

—2 Corinthians 6:2

*T*his is so desperately a matter of importance for every human being who comes into the world that I first become indignant, and then I become sad, when I try to give spiritual counsel to a person who looks me in the eye and tells me: "Well, I am trying to make up my mind if I should accept Christ or not."

Such a person gives absolutely no indication that he realizes he is talking about the most important decision he can make in his lifetime—a decision to get right with God, to believe in the eternal Son, the Savior, to become a disciple, an obedient witness to Jesus Christ as Lord.

How can any man or woman, lost and undone, sinful and wretched, alienated from God, stand there and intimate that the death and resurrection of Jesus Christ and God's revealed plan of salvation do not take priority over some of life's other decisions? CES156

Lord, give us boldness to share this vital message with anyone with whom we come in contact who may be facing a Christless eternity. Amen.

GOSPEL IMPLICATIONS

For the grace of God that bringeth salvation hath appeared to all men, teaching us that, denying ungodliness and worldly lusts, we should live soberly, righteously, and godly, in this present world.

—Titus 2:11-12

The fact is that the New Testament message embraces a great deal more than an offer of free pardon. It is a message of pardon, and for that may God be praised; but it is also a message of repentance. It is a message of atonement, but it is also a message of temperance and righteousness and godliness in this present world. It tells us that we must accept a Savior, but it tells us also that we must *deny* ungodliness and worldly lusts. The gospel message includes the idea of amendment, of separation from the world, of cross-carrying and loyalty to the kingdom of God even unto death.

To be strictly technical, these latter truths are corollaries of the gospel, and not the gospel itself; but they are part and parcel of the total message which we are commissioned to declare. . . .

To offer a sinner the gift of salvation based upon the work of Christ, while at the same time allowing him to retain the idea that the gift carries with it no moral implications, is to do him untold injury where it hurts him worst. SOS019-020

Lord, help me to proclaim the truth, the whole truth, and nothing but the truth as I present the gospel today. Amen.

SUCH A SHORT TIME

And he saith unto him, Friend, how camest thou in hither not having a wedding garment? And he was speechless. Then said the king to the servants, Bind him hand and foot, and take him away, and cast him into outer darkness; there shall be weeping and gnashing of teeth.

—Matthew 22:12-13

We have such a short time to prepare for such a long time. By that I mean we have now to prepare for then. We have an hour to prepare for eternity. To fail to prepare is an act of moral folly. For anyone to have a day given to prepare, it is an act of inexcusable folly to let anything hinder that preparation. If we find ourselves in a spiritual rut, nothing in the world should hinder us. Nothing in this world is worth it. If we believe in eternity, if we believe in God, if we believe in the eternal existence of the soul, then there is nothing important enough to cause us to commit such an act of moral folly.

Failing to get ready in time for eternity, and failing to get ready now for the great then that lies out yonder, is a trap in plain sight. There is an odd saying in the Old Testament, "Surely in vain the net is spread in the sight of any bird" (Proverbs 1:17). When the man of God wrote that, he gave the birds a little credit. It would be silly for a bird watching me set the trap to conveniently fly down and get into it. Yet there are people doing that all the time. People who have to live for eternity fall into that trap set for them in plain sight. RRR087-088

Give me a willingness—no, a passion—to do my part in this urgent matter. Amen.

"I GAVE IT ALL UP!"

> *Blessed be the God and Father of our Lord Jesus Christ, who hath blessed us with all spiritual blessings in heavenly places in Christ.*
>
> —Ephesians 1:3

I have been asked more than once what I gave up when I was converted and became a believing child of God. I was a young man, and I well remember that I gave up the hot and smelly rubber factory. I was making tires for an hourly wage, and I gave that up to follow Christ's call into Christian ministry and service.

As a youth I was scared of life and I was scared of death—and I gave that up. I was miserable and glum and unfulfilled—and I gave that up. I had selfish earthly and material ambitions that I could never have achieved—and I gave them up.

That forms the outline of the worthless things that I gave up. And I soon discovered that in Jesus Christ, God had given me everything that is worthwhile.

If God takes away from us the old, wrinkled, beat-up dollar bill we have clutched so desperately, it is only because He wants to exchange it for the whole Federal mint, the entire treasury! He is saying to us, "I have in store for you all the resources of heaven. Help yourself!" JAF049-050

> *Thank You for all we gain through our new life in Christ—in exchange for all the junk we give up! Amen.*

A BOND OF COMPASSION

They that sow in tears shall reap in joy. He that goeth forth and weepeth, bearing precious seed, shall doubtless come again with rejoicing, bringing his sheaves with him.

—Psalm 126:5-6

The testimony of the true follower of Christ might well be something like this: The world's pleasures and the world's treasures henceforth have no appeal for me. I reckon myself crucified to the world and the world crucified to me. But the multitudes that were so dear to Christ shall not be less dear to me. If I cannot prevent their moral suicide, I shall at least baptize them with my human tears. I want no blessing that I cannot share. I seek no spirituality that I must win at the cost of forgetting that men and women are lost and without hope. If in spite of all I can do they will sin against light and bring upon themselves the displeasure of a holy God, then I must not let them go their sad way unwept. I scorn a happiness that I must purchase with ignorance. I reject a heaven that I must enter by shutting my eyes to the sufferings of my fellowmen. I choose a broken heart rather than any happiness that ignores the tragedy of human life and human death. Though I, through the grace of God in Christ, no longer lie under Adam's sin, I would still feel a bond of compassion for all of Adam's tragic race, and I am determined that I shall go down to the grave or up into God's heaven mourning for the lost and the perishing.

And thus and thus will I do as God enables me. Amen. NCA036

Lord Jesus, give me that broken heart as I interact with unsaved people in my ministry today. Amen.

CONVICTION AND PAIN

> *Then said I, Woe is me! for I am undone; because I am a man of unclean lips, and I dwell in the midst of a people of unclean lips: for mine eyes have seen the King, the Lord of hosts.*
>
> —Isaiah 6:5

*W*hen Isaiah cried out, "I am undone!" it was a cry of pain. It was the revealing cry of conscious uncleanness. He was experiencing the undoneness of the creature set over against the holiness of the Creator.

What should happen in genuine conversion? What should a man or woman feel in the transaction of the new birth?

There ought to be that real and genuine cry of pain. That is why I do not like the kind of evangelism that tries to invite people into the fellowship of God by signing a card.

There should be a birth from above and within. There should be the terror of seeing ourselves in violent contrast to the holy, holy, holy God. Unless we come into this place of conviction and pain, I am not sure how deep and real our repentance will ever be. WHT076

Use me today to declare to someone the awesomeness of God. Then let me go to my knees with him in heartfelt repentance. Amen.

SAVED TO WORSHIP

> *Give unto the LORD the glory due unto his name: bring an offering, and come before him: worship the LORD in the beauty of holiness.*
>
> —1 Chronicles 16:29

*T*here is nothing intrinsically wrong with signing a card. It can be a helpful thing so we know who has made inquiry.

But really, my brother or sister, we are brought to God and to faith and to salvation that we might worship and adore Him. We do not come to God that we might be automatic Christians, cookie-cutter Christians, Christians stamped out with a die.

God has provided His salvation that we might be, individually and personally, vibrant children of God, loving God with all our hearts and worshiping Him in the beauty of holiness.

WHT014

> *Lord, I don't need another name in my file, another notch on my belt. But I would like the privilege of bringing someone to the point of salvation so he could become a genuine worshiper of You. Use me, I pray, in Jesus' name. Amen.*

TOO EASILY CONVERTED

But he that received the seed into stony places, the same is he that heareth the word, and anon with joy receiveth it; yet hath he not root in himself, but dureth for a while: for when tribulation or persecution ariseth because of the word, by and by he is offended.

—Matthew 13:20-21

First, we must consider the person who becomes a disciple of Christ on impulse. This is likely to be the person who came in on a wave of enthusiasm, and I am a little bit suspicious of anyone who is too easily converted. I have a feeling that if he or she can be easily converted to Christ, he or she may be very easily flipped back the other way. I am concerned about the person who just yields, who has no sales resistance at all. . . .

Actually, I go along with the man or woman who is thoughtful enough about this decision to say truthfully: "I want a day to think this over," or, "I want a week to read the Bible and to meditate on what this decision means."

I have never considered it a very great compliment to the Christian church that we can generate enthusiasm on such short notice. The less there is in the kettle, the quicker it begins to boil. There are some who get converted on enthusiasm and backslide on principle! FBR055-057

Lord, thank You for this perspective on serious consideration rather than flippant acquiescence. Amen.

THE LONGING AFTER ETERNITY

We take it for granted and we are not surprised at all about the eternal nature of God but the greater wonder is that God has seen fit to put His own everlastingness within the hearts of men and women. . . .

I believe that this is the truth about our troubles and our problems: We are disturbed because God has put everlastingness in our hearts. He has put something within men and women that demands God and heaven—and yet we are too blind and sinful to find Him or even to look for Him! . . .

Men and women need to be told plainly, and again and again, why they are disturbed and why they are upset. They need to be told why they are lost and that if they will not repent they will certainly perish. Doctors and counselors will tell troubled men and women that their problems are psychological, but it is something deeper within the human being that troubles and upsets—it is the longing after eternity! CES052-054

Lord, we long for eternity, but there is so much commotion, activity and noise in our world that that longing is too often drowned out. Help me to break through that madness with the message of Christ today. Amen.

THE RIGHT ROAD TO THE DESIRED DESTINATION

O LORD, I know that the way of man is not in himself: it is not in man that walketh to direct his steps.

—Jeremiah 10:23

*T*he prophet here [in Jeremiah 10:23] turns to a figure of speech, one which appears in the Scriptures so frequently that it is not easy to remember that it is but a figure. Man is seen as a traveler making his difficult way from a past he can but imperfectly recollect into a future about which he knows nothing. And he cannot stay, but must each morning strike his moving tent and journey on toward—and there is the heavy problem—toward what?

It is a simple axiom of the traveler that if he would arrive at the desired destination he must take the right road. How far a man may have traveled is not important; what matters is whether or not he is going the right way, whether the path he is following will bring him out at the right place at last. Sometimes there will be an end to the road, and maybe sooner than he knows; but when he has gone the last step of the way will he find himself in a tomorrow of light and peace, or will the day toward which he journeys be "a day of trouble and distress, a day of wasteness and desolation, a day of darkness and gloominess, a day of clouds and thick darkness"? sos105-106

I look around me, Lord, and everywhere I see aimless wanderers on a course toward eternal destruction. Help me to be more faithful, even today, to point them toward the right destination. Amen.

UNCONVINCING TESTIMONY

For thou shalt be his witness unto all men of what thou hast seen and heard.

—Acts 22:15

*T*here is a large amount of ineffective Christian testimony among us today. Much of it is well-intended, I am sure—honest and sincere. We do the best we can with what we have. But our performance turns out to be something like that of the salesman promoting fountain pens. He tries to make a case for his product, but his would-be customers know he really thinks ballpoints are far more practical.

Too much of our Christian witnessing is unconvincing because *we* have not been convinced. We are ineffectual because we have not yet capitulated to the Lord from glory. It is like the proselyte making proselytes. . . .

Perhaps this is happening because we are trying to plan how everything should happen. Everyone of us reads a little how-to book on witnessing. We try to do it the way we have been taught. But it is perfunctory and without any contagious element. If angels can weep, they must weep salty tears upon seeing a proselyte who has never really met the Lord making another proselyte who will also never meet the Lord. FBR101-102

Out of the abundance of a heart filled with love for You let me speak today. Let me see You this morning in a way that will cause me to leave this prayer time with a renewed passion to minister. Amen.

ONLY THE
SPIRIT CAN
GIVE SIGHT

But if our gospel be hid, it is hid to them that are lost: in whom the god of this world hath blinded the minds of them which believe not, lest the light of the glorious gospel of Christ, who is the image of God, should shine unto them.

—2 Corinthians 4:3-4

$\mathcal{T}$he uncomprehending mind is unaffected by truth. The intellect of the hearer may grasp saving knowledge while yet the heart makes no moral response to it. A classic example of this is seen in the story of Benjamin Franklin and George Whitefield. In his autobiography Franklin recounts in some detail how he listened to the mighty preaching of the great evangelist. He even walked around the square where Whitefield stood to learn for himself how far that golden voice carried. Whitefield talked with Franklin personally about his need of Christ and promised to pray for him. Years later Franklin wrote rather sadly that the evangelist's prayers must not have done any good, for he was still unconverted. . . .

The inward operation of the Holy Spirit is necessary to saving faith. The gospel is light but only the Spirit can give sight. When seeking to bring the lost to Christ we must pray continually that they may receive the gift of seeing. And we must pit our prayer against that dark spirit who blinds the hearts of men. BAM062-063

Lord, I'll do my part today to share the gospel with anyone You'll bring my way. But Holy Spirit, I'll wait for You to open eyes and give sight. I'll leave the results with You. Amen.

SOVEREIGN CALLING

But as many as received him, to them gave he power to become the sons of God, even to them that believe on his name: which were born, not of blood, nor of the will of the flesh, nor of the will of man, but of God.

—John 1:12-13

*T*here is another and worse evil which springs from this basic failure to grasp the radical difference between the natures of the two worlds. It is the habit of languidly "accepting" salvation as if it were a small matter and one wholly in our hands. Men are exhorted to think things over and "decide" for Christ, and in some places one day each year is set aside as "Decision Day," at which time people are expected to condescend to grant Christ the right to save them, a right which they have obviously refused Him up to that time. Christ is thus made to stand again before men's judgment seat; He is made to wait upon the pleasure of the individual, and after long and humble waiting is either turned away or patronizingly admitted. By a complete misunderstanding of the noble and true doctrine of the freedom of the human will, salvation is made to depend perilously upon the will of man instead of upon the will of God.

However deep the mystery, however many the paradoxes involved, it is still true that men become saints not at their own whim but by sovereign calling. POM037-038

Sovereign God, I'm Your servant. I'll share the message, I'll pray for response, but only You can draw an unsaved person to faith in Christ. Thank You for the privilege of having even a small part in Your sovereign work. Amen.

TRUSTING THE LIFEBOAT

And [he] brought them out, and said, Sirs, what must I do to be saved? And they said, Believe on the Lord Jesus Christ, and thou shalt be saved, and thy house.

—Acts 16:30-31

No man has any hope for eternal salvation apart from trusting completely in Jesus Christ and His atonement for men. Simply stated, our Lord Jesus is the lifeboat and we must fully and truly be committed to trusting the lifeboat.

Again, our Lord and Savior is the rope by which it is possible to escape from the burning building. There is no doubt about it—either we trust that rope or we perish.

He is the wonder drug or medication that heals all ills and sicknesses—and if we refuse it, we die.

He is the bridge from hell to heaven—and we take the bridge and cross over by His grace or we stay in hell.

These are simple illustrations, but they get to the point of the necessity of complete trust in Jesus Christ—absolute trust in Him! WPJ063-064

Lord, help me to make this clear as I share the gospel. So many seem to persist in wanting to trust Christ plus their own efforts. Thank You for this free gift of salvation. Amen.

BELIEVE THE RIGHT THINGS

And he said unto them, Ye are from beneath; I am from above: ye are of this world; I am not of this world. I said therefore unto you, that ye shall die in your sins: for if ye believe not that I am he, ye shall die in your sins.

—John 8:23-24

*B*ecause the heart of the Christian life is admittedly faith in a person, Jesus Christ the Lord, it has been relatively easy for some to press this truth out of all proportion and teach that faith in the Person of Christ is all that matters. Who Jesus is matters not, who His Father was, whether Jesus is God or man or both, whether or not He accepted the superstitions and errors of His time as true, whether He actually rose again after His passion or was only thought to have done so by His devoted followers—these things are not important, say the no-creed advocates. What is vital is that we believe on Him and try to follow His teachings.

What is overlooked here is that the conflict of Christ with the Pharisees was over the question of *who He was*. His claim to be God stirred the Pharisees to fury. He could have cooled the fire of their anger by backing away from His claim to equality with God, but He refused to do it. And He further taught that faith in Him embraced a belief that He is very God, and that apart from this there could be no salvation for anyone. . . .

To believe on Christ savingly means to believe the right things about Christ. There is no escaping this. TIC022

Don't let me ever back down from this vital truth of Who You are. Amen.

SALVATION APART FROM OBEDIENCE

For we are his workmanship, created in Christ Jesus unto good works, which God hath before ordained that we should walk in them.

—Ephesians 2:10

Therefore, I must be frank in my feeling that a notable heresy has come into being throughout our evangelical Christian circles—the widely accepted concept that we humans can choose to accept Christ only because we need Him as Savior and we have the right to postpone our obedience to Him as Lord as long as we want to! . . .

I think the following is a fair statement of what I was taught in my early Christian experience and it certainly needs a lot of modifying and a great many qualifiers to save us from being in error.

"We are saved by accepting Christ as our Savior; we are sanctified by accepting Christ as our Lord; we may do the first without doing the second!"

The truth is that salvation apart from obedience is unknown in the sacred Scriptures. Peter makes it plain that we are "elect according to the foreknowledge of God the Father, through sanctification of the Spirit, unto obedience" (1 Peter 1:2).

ICH001-002

Lord, as I rejoice in the free gift of salvation, by grace through faith, remind me regularly that it is a salvation unto good works, that we're saved to serve. Amen.

MODERN SALESMANSHIP

They went out from us, but they were not of us; for if they had been of us, they would no doubt have continued with us: but they went out, that they might be made manifest that they were not all of us.

—1 John 2:19

*I*n our eagerness to make converts I am afraid we have lately been guilty of using the technique of modern salesmanship, which is of course to present only the desirable qualities in a product and ignore the rest. We go to men and offer them a cozy home on the sunny side of the brae. If they will but accept Christ He will give them peace of mind, solve their problems, prosper their business, protect their families and keep them happy all day long. They believe us and come, and the first cold wind sends them shivering to some counselor to find out what has gone wrong; and that is the last we hear of many of them. . . .

By offering our hearers a sweetness-and-light gospel and promising every taker a place on the sunny side of the brae, we not only cruelly deceive them, but we guarantee also a high casualty rate among the converts won on such terms. On certain foreign fields the expression "rice Christians" has been coined to describe those who adopt Christianity for profit. The experienced missionary knows that the convert that must pay a heavy price for his faith in Christ is the one that will persevere to the end. He begins with the wind in his face, and should the storm grow in strength he will not turn back for he has been conditioned to endure it. TIC116-117

Deliver us from the error of producing rice Christians.
Amen.

COMING HOME

And if I go and prepare a place for you, I will come again, and receive you unto myself; that where I am, there ye may be also.

—John 14:3

Some years ago one of our national Christian brothers from the land of Thailand gave his testimony in my hearing. He told what it had meant in his life and for his future when the missionaries came with the good news of the gospel of Christ.

He described the godly life of one of the early missionaries and then said: "He is in the Father's house now."

He told of one of the missionary women and the love of Christ she had displayed, and then said: "She is in the Father's house now."

What a vision for a humble Christian who only a generation before had been a pagan, worshiping idols and spirits—and now because of grace and mercy he talks about the Father's house as though it were just a step away, across the street.

This is the gospel of Christ—the kind of Christianity I believe in. What joy to discover that God is not mad at us and that we are His children. . . . What a hope that makes it possible for the Lord's people to lie down quietly when the time comes and whisper, "Father, I am coming home!" EFE050-051

Thank You, Lord, for this incredible truth! And this is the message of hope that we share as we proclaim the gospel! Let us do it joyfully today. Amen.

*S*eptember

Revival

If we surrender our hearts to God we may expect a wondrous enlargement. And who knows what He can do if we take our hands off and let Him work? ROR115

BORN AFTER MIDNIGHT

And I say unto you, Ask, and it shall be given you; seek, and ye shall find; knock, and it shall be opened unto you. For every one that asketh receiveth; and he that seeketh findeth; and to him that knocketh it shall be opened.

—Luke 11:9-10

*A*mong revival-minded Christians I have heard the saying, "Revivals are born after midnight."

This is one of those proverbs which, while not quite literally true, yet points to something very true.

If we understand the saying to mean that God does not hear our prayer for revival made in the daytime, it is of course not true. If we take it to mean that prayer offered when we are tired and worn-out has greater power than prayer made when we are rested and fresh, again it is not true. . . .

Yet there is considerable truth in the idea that revivals are born after midnight, for revivals (or any other spiritual gifts and graces) come only to those who want them badly enough. . . .

No, there is no merit in late hour prayers, but it requires a serious mind and a determined heart to pray past the ordinary into the unusual. Most Christians never do. And it is more than possible that the rare soul who presses on into the unusual experience reaches there after midnight. BAM007-008, 010

Lord, give me this kind of longing after revival. Help me to give myself to this serious prayer for revival. Amen.

A
PURIFIED
CHURCH

But what things were gain to me, those I counted loss for Christ. Yea doubtless, and I count all things but loss for the excellency of the knowledge of Christ Jesus my Lord: for whom I have suffered the loss of all things, and do count them but dung, that I may win Christ.

—Philippians 3:7-8

*O*ur most pressing obligation today is to do all in our power to obtain a revival that will result in a reformed, revitalized, purified church. It is of far greater importance that we have better Christians than that we have more of them. Each generation of Christians is the seed of the next, and degenerate seed is sure to produce a degenerate harvest not a little better than but a little worse than the seed from which it sprang. Thus the direction will be down until vigorous, effective means are taken to improve the seed. . . .

To carry on these activities [evangelism, missions] scripturally the church should be walking in fullness of power, separated, purified and ready at any moment to give up everything, even life itself, for the greater glory of Christ. For a worldly, weak, decadent church to make converts is but to bring forth after her own kind and extend her weakness and decadence a bit further out. . . .

So vitally important is spiritual quality that it is hardly too much to suggest that attempts to grow larger might well be suspended until we have become better. SOS154-156

Help us not to water down the message and make our teaching so shallow that we don't challenge our people to holy living. Amen.

THE CURSE OF SELF-RIGHTEOUSNESS

But grow in grace, and in the knowledge of our Lord and Saviour Jesus Christ. To him be glory both now and for ever. Amen.

—2 Peter 3:18

Self-righteousness is terrible among God's people. If we feel that we are what we ought to be, then we will remain what we are. We will not look for any change or improvement in our lives. This will quite naturally lead us to judge everyone by what we are. This is the judgment of which we must be careful. To judge others by ourselves is to create havoc in the local assembly.

Self-righteousness also leads to complacency. Complacency is a great sin. . . . Some have the attitude, "Lord, I'm satisfied with my spiritual condition. I hope one of these days You will come, I will be taken up to meet You in the air and I will rule over five cities." These people cannot rule over their own houses and families, but they expect to rule over five cities. They pray spottily and sparsely, rarely attending prayer meeting, but they read their Bibles and expect to go zooming off into the blue yonder and join the Lord in the triumph of the victorious saints. RRR010-011

Lord, keep me from the curse of self-righteousness. Show me my sin and need for continued growth. If revival is to come, it needs to start with me, and it won't start unless I'm constantly reminded of my need. Amen.

LIVING AT A FEVER PITCH

And whatsoever ye do, do it heartily, as to the Lord, and not unto men.

—Colossians 3:23

*W*e live at a fever pitch, and whether we are erecting buildings, laying highways, promoting athletic events, celebrating special days or welcoming returning heroes, we always do it with an exaggerated flourish. Our building will be taller, our highway broader, our athletic contest more colorful, our celebration more elaborate and more expensive than would be true anywhere else on earth. We walk faster, drive faster, earn more, spend more and run higher blood pressure than any other people in the world.

In only one field of human interest are we slow and apathetic: that is the field of personal religion. There for some strange reason our enthusiasm lags. Church people habitually approach the matter of their personal relation to God in a dull, half-hearted way which is altogether out of keeping with their general temperament and wholly inconsistent with the importance of the subject. OGM003-004

> *Lord, revive my zeal for things of God. I get caught up in the fever pitch of so many things. Help me to set my priorities right and give myself more completely to enhancing my relationship with You. Amen.*

THE ARROW OF INFINITE DESIRE

Blessed are they which do hunger and thirst after righteousness: for they shall be filled.

—Matthew 5:6

$\mathscr{T}$hese words are addressed to those of God's children who have been pierced with the arrow of infinite desire, who yearn for God with a yearning that has overcome them, who long with a longing that has become pain.

"Blessed are they which do hunger and thirst after righteousness, for they shall be filled" (Matthew 5:6). . . .

A dead body feels no hunger and the dead soul knows not the pangs of holy desire. "If you want God," said the old saint, "you have already found Him." Our desire for fuller life is proof that some life must be there already. . . .

In nature everything moves in the direction of its hungers. In the spiritual world it is not otherwise. We gravitate toward our inward longings, provided of course that those longings are strong enough to move us. Impotent dreaming will not do. The religious urge that is not followed by a corresponding act of the will in the direction of that urge is a waste of emotion. SIZ017-018

> *Oh, God, I have that longing to know You, that hunger and thirst for righteousness, that "desire for fuller life." Move me along in the direction of that hunger, Lord, and give me the strength to follow "in the direction of that urge." Amen.*

REVIVAL ON OUR TERMS

I am the Lord: that is my name: and my glory will I not give to another, neither my praise to graven images.

—Isaiah 42:8

*T*here seems to be a notion abroad that if we talk enough and pray enough, revival will set in like a stock market boom or a winning streak on a baseball club. We appear to be waiting for some sweet chariot to swing low and carry us into the Big Rock Candy Mountain of religious experience.

Well, it is a pretty good rule that if everyone is saying something it is not likely to be true; or, if it has truth at the bottom, it has been so distorted by wrong emphasis as to have the effect of error in its practical outworking. And such, I believe, is much of the revival talk we hear today. . . .

Our mistake is that we want God to send revival on our terms. We want to get the power of God into our hands, to call it to us that it may work for us in promoting and furthering our kind of Christianity. We want still to be in charge, guiding the chariot through the religious sky in the direction we want it to go, shouting "Glory to God," it is true, but modestly accepting a share of the glory for ourselves in a nice inoffensive sort of way. We are calling on God to send fire on our altars, completely ignoring the fact that they are *our* altars and not God's. SIZ008-009

Forgive me, Lord, for wanting any of the credit or any of the control as I call on You to do a work among my people. Work today in Your way, on Your terms, only for Your glory. Amen.

BLESSING ON OUR TERMS

Then said Jesus unto his disciples, If any man will come after me, let him deny himself, and take up his cross, and follow me.

—Matthew 16:24

*H*ere is what grieves me, and I believe this also grieves the Holy Spirit: My hearers rise to this call emotionally, but they will not confirm it by a corresponding change in their way of life. Their goodness is like the morning clouds—by 9 o'clock the sun has burnt off the fog. This is what happens to many people's good intentions.

They rise emotionally to an urgent message that we become a New Testament church, that we become a model church, that we have the order of the New Testament and the power of the Holy Spirit in order that we might worship, work and witness. Emotionally they rise to it, but they will not confirm their emotions by corresponding changes in their way of life.

They want to be blessed by God, but they want God to bless them on their terms. They look pensively to God for victory, but they will not bring their giving into line. They will not practice family prayer, rushing off without it. They will not take time for secret prayer and will not forgive those who have wronged them. They will not seek to be reconciled to those with whom they have quarreled. They will not pick up their crosses and say, "Jesus, I my cross have taken, All to leave, and follow Thee." RRR146-147

Lord, may my desire for You rise above emotions. I do want to be blessed of You, both personally and in my ministry. I commit myself this morning to a willingness to take my cross and follow You—and to take the necessary action to come on Your terms. Amen.

GOD IN OUR MIDST

And he said, My presence shall go with thee, and I will give thee rest. And he said unto him, If thy presence go not with me, carry us not up hence.

—Exodus 33:14-15

*I*n what I have to say I may not be joined by any ground swell of public opinion, but I have a charge to make against the church. We are not consciously aware of God in our midst. We do not seem to sense the tragedy of having almost completely lost the awareness of His presence. . . .

Revival and blessing come to the church when we stop looking at a picture of God and look at God Himself. Revival comes when, no longer satisfied just to know about a God in history, we meet the conditions of finding Him in living, personal experience. . . .

Modern mankind can go everywhere, do everything and be completely curious about the universe. But only a rare person now and then is curious enough to want to know God. MMG121-122, 127

Oh Lord, show me Your glory. I don't want to be satisfied with just a second-hand picture of You; I want to sense Your living presence with me. I long to know You. Amen.

A DIVINE VISITATION

And I, brethren, could not speak unto you as unto spiritual [people], but as unto carnal, even as unto babes in Christ.

—1 Corinthians 3:1

I believe that it might be well for us if we just stopped all of our business and got quiet and worshiped God and waited on Him. It doesn't make me popular when I remind you that we are a carnal bunch, but it is true, nevertheless, that the body of Christians is carnal. The Lord's people ought to be a sanctified, pure, clean people, but we are a carnal crowd. We are carnal in our attitudes, in our tastes and carnal in many things. Our young people often are not reverent in our Christian services. We have so degraded our religious tastes that our Christian service is largely exhibitionism. We desperately need a divine visitation—for our situation will never be cured by sermons! It will never be cured until the Church of Christ has suddenly been confronted with what one man called the *mysterium tremendium*—the fearful mystery that is God, the fearful majesty that is God. This is what the Holy Spirit does. He brings the wonderful mystery that is God to us, and presents Him to the human spirit. COU066-067

Oh Lord, deliver me from carnal attitudes, actions and desires. Give me this morning a divine visitation to purify and cleanse me. Let me sense today the majesty and awesomeness of the "mysterium tremendium" as I wait upon You. Amen.

WE NEED A REVIVAL!

And I will say to my soul, Soul, thou hast much goods laid up for many years; take thine ease, eat, drink, and be merry. But God said unto him, Thou fool, this night thy soul shall be required of thee: then whose shall those things be, which thou hast provided? So is he that layeth up treasure for himself, and is not rich toward God.

—Luke 12:19-21

We need a revival! We need a revival of consecration to death, a revival of happy abandonment to the will of God that will laugh at sacrifice and count it a privilege to bear the cross through the heat and burden of the day. We are too much influenced by the world and too little controlled by the Spirit. We of the deeper life persuasion are not immune to the temptations of ease and we are in grave danger of becoming a generation of pleasure lovers.

Any who disagree with these conclusions are within their rights, and I would be the last to deny them the privilege. But in the name of a thousand struggling churches and disheartened pastors, may I not plead for a little more loyalty to the local church during this season of difficulty?

May God raise up a people who will consult their pleasures less and the great need more. GTM159-160

Lord, make me today one of those "who will consult their pleasures less and the great need more." Amen.

HOW MUCH DOES REVIVAL COST?

And I will set my tabernacle among you: and my soul shall not abhor you. And I will walk among you, and will be your God, and ye shall be my people.

—Leviticus 26:11-12

So we sit down to have a board meeting. What are we going to do to stir ourselves up? Who can we get? Where will we look? We forget that all the time Jehovah is present. "I am *Jehovah-shammah*; I am in the midst of you. Why don't you talk to me?" No, we don't ask Him.

"I am your banner of victory." But we say, "I just wonder how much it will cost?" How much does a revival cost? Absolutely nothing and absolutely everything—that is how much it will cost. It will cost not one dime, and it will cost everything we have. You cannot import it by flying someone in from New Zealand. How many of these blessed preachers have come in from Ireland and England? They did some big things over there, we heard, so we flew them in and they never got anywhere. I never saw anything result from trying to import God. He does not fly over in a jet. He says, "I am Jehovah; I am with you. I am where you are; I am here now. Call on Me." RRR158-159

I call upon You, Jehovah, to work a mighty work in and through me. Amen.

TIME IS RUNNING OUT

> *The night is far spent, the day is at hand: let us therefore cast off the works of darkness, and let us put on the armour of light.*
>
> —Romans 13:12

The absence of spiritual devotion today is an omen and a portent. The modern church is all but contemptuous of the sober virtues—meekness, modesty, humility, quietness, obedience, self effacement, patience. To be accepted now, religion must be in the popular mood. Consequently, much religious activity reeks with pride, display, self-assertion, self-promotion, love of gain and devotion to trivial pleasures.

It behooves us to take all this seriously. Time is running out for all of us. What is done must be done quickly. We have no right to lie idly by and let things take their course. A farmer who neglects his farm will soon lose it; a shepherd who fails to look after his flock will find the wolves looking after it for him. A misbegotten charity that allows the wolves to destroy the flock is not charity at all but indifference, rather, and should be known for what it is and dealt with accordingly.

It is time for Bible-believing Christians to begin to cultivate the sober graces and to live among men like sons of God and heirs of the ages. And this will take more than a bit of doing, for the whole world and a large part of the church is set to prevent it. But "if God be for us, who can be against us?" (Romans 8:31). WTA050-051

Lord, speak to me as I pray slowly through that list of "sober virtues"—and also that list of attitudes with which much religious activity reeks. Convict me; change me; cultivate within me the "sober graces." Amen.

GIVE ME THYSELF

Be merciful unto me, O Lord:
for I cry unto thee daily. Rejoice
the soul of thy servant: for unto
thee, O Lord, do I lift up my soul.

—Psalm 86:3-4

*A*nd here's a little prayer that was made by Lady Julian:

> *O God, of Thy goodness give me Thyself, for Thou art*
> *enough for me, and I may ask nothing that is less and*
> *find any full honors to Thee. God give me Thyself!*

We make out that a revival is everybody running around falling on everybody else's neck and saying, "Forgive me for thinking a bad thought about you. Forgive me for that nickel that I forgot to pay back." Or we say a revival consists of people getting very loud and noisy. Well, that might happen in a revival, but the only kind of revival that would be here when the worlds are on fire is the revival that begins by saying, "Oh God, give me Thyself! For nothing less than Thee will do."

"Anything less than God," Julian said, "ever me wanteth." I like that little expression. Translated into modern English it means, "It won't be enough." AOG032

Oh, God, "of Thy goodness give me Thyself." Amen.

A Growing Hunger after God

My soul longeth, yea, even fainteth for the courts of the LORD: my heart and my flesh crieth out for the living God.

—Psalm 84:2

*I*n this hour of all-but-universal darkness one cheering gleam appears: Within the fold of conservative Christianity there are to be found increasing numbers of persons whose religious lives are marked by a growing hunger after God Himself. They are eager for spiritual realities and will not be put off with words, nor will they be content with correct "interpretations" of truth. They are athirst for God, and they will not be satisfied till they have drunk deep at the Fountain of Living Water.

This is the only real harbinger of revival which I have been able to detect anywhere on the religious horizon. It may be the cloud the size of a man's hand for which a few saints here and there have been looking. It can result in a resurrection of life for many souls and a recapture of that radiant wonder which should accompany faith in Christ, that wonder which has all but fled the Church of God in our day. POG007

O Father, may their numbers increase more and more— those who "are athirst for God, and [who] will not be satisfied till they have drunk deep at the Fountain of Living Water." Amen.

TO THE INDIVIDUAL ONLY

For we must all appear before the judgment seat of Christ; that every one may receive the things done in his body, according to that he hath done, whether it be good or bad.

—2 Corinthians 5:10

No church is any better or worse than the individual Christians who compose it. . . .

One consequence of our failure to see clearly the true nature of revival is that we wait for years for some supernatural manifestation that never comes, overlooking completely our own individual place in the desired awakening. Whatever God may do for a church must be done in the single unit, the one certain man or woman. Some things can happen only to the isolated, single person; they cannot be experienced en masse. Statistics show, for instance, that 100 babies are born in a certain city on a given day. Yet the birth of each baby is for that baby a unique experience, an isolated, personal thing. . . .

Three thousand persons were converted at Pentecost, but each one met his sin and his Savior alone. The spiritual birth, like the natural one, is for each one a unique, separate experience shared in by no one. And so with that uprush of resurgent life we call revival. It can come to the individual only. SIZ014-015

Lord, make me sensitive this morning to my "own individual place in the desired awakening." Whatever work needs to be done to this "isolated, single person"—do it today, I pray. Amen.

MEET GOD ALONE FIRST

. . . immediately I conferred not with flesh and blood: neither went I up to Jerusalem to them which were apostles before me; but I went into Arabia, and returned again unto Damascus.

—Galatians 1:16-17

Nothing can prevent the spiritual rejuvenation of the soul that insists upon having it. Though that solitary man must live and walk among persons religiously dead, he may experience the great transformation as certainly and as quickly as if he were in the most spiritual church in the world.

The man that *will* have God's best becomes at once the object of the personal attention of the Holy Spirit. Such a man will not be required to wait for the rest of the church to come alive. He will not be penalized for the failures of his fellow Christians, nor be asked to forego the blessing till his sleepy brethren catch up. God deals with the individual heart as exclusively as if only one existed. . . .

Every prophet, every reformer, every revivalist had to meet God alone before he could help the multitudes. The great leaders who went on to turn thousands to Christ had to begin with God and their own soul. The plain Christian of today must experience personal revival before he can hope to bring renewed spiritual life to his church. SIZ015-016

Lord, send revival to Your church today; begin the work in me and then let it spread one person at a time. Amen.

LET ANYONE SEEK HIS FACE

Let the wicked forsake his way, and the unrighteous man his thoughts: and let him return unto the LORD; and he will have mercy upon him; and to our God, for he will abundantly pardon.

—Isaiah 55:7

*I*t will require a determined heart and more than a little courage to wrench ourselves loose from the grip of our times and return to biblical ways. But it can be done. Every now and then in the past Christians have had to do it. History has recorded several large-scale returns led by such men as St. Francis, Martin Luther and George Fox. Unfortunately, there seems to be no Luther or Fox on the horizon at present. Whether or not another such return may be expected before the coming of Christ is a question upon which Christians are not fully agreed, but that is not of too great importance to us now.

What God in His sovereignty may yet do on a world-scale I do not claim to know. But what He will do for the plain man or woman who seeks His face I believe I do know and can tell others. Let any man turn to God in earnest, let him begin to exercise himself unto godliness, let him seek to develop his powers of spiritual receptivity by trust and obedience and humility, and the results will exceed anything he may have hoped in his leaner and weaker days. POG066

> *Lord, today I commit myself to "turn to God in earnest," to "begin to exercise [myself] unto godliness," and to "seek to develop [my] powers of spiritual receptivity by trust and obedience and humility." Amen.*

DELIVERANCE COMES BY DELIVERERS

> *Now therefore, behold, the cry of the children of Israel is come unto me: and I have also seen the oppression wherewith the Egyptians oppress them. Come now therefore, and I will send thee unto Pharaoh, that thou mayest bring forth my people the children of Israel out of Egypt.*
>
> —Exodus 3:9-10

*Y*es, if evangelical Christianity is to stay alive, it must have men again—the right kind of men. It must repudiate the weaklings who dare not speak out, and it must seek in prayer and much humility the coming again of men of the stuff of which prophets and martyrs are made. God will hear the cries of His people as He heard the cries of Israel in Egypt, and He will send deliverance by sending deliverers. It is His way.

And when the deliverers come—reformers, revivalists, prophets—they will be men of God and men of courage. They will have God on their side because they are careful to stay on God's side. They will be coworkers with Christ and instruments in the hands of the Holy Spirit. Such men will be baptized with the Spirit indeed and through their labors He will baptize others and send the long-delayed revival. TWP020

> *Lord, send those men to the Church soon. Raise up a mighty army even among young people today who will become that kind of man. We need a great movement of the Spirit of God that would bring the much-needed revival. Amen.*

POURED-OUT DEVOTION

Receive him therefore in the Lord with all gladness; and hold such in reputation: because for the work of Christ he was nigh unto death, not regarding his life, to supply your lack of service toward me.

—Philippians 2:29-30

*T*hat many Christians in our day are lukewarm and somnolent will not be denied by anyone with an anointed eye, but the cure is not to stir them up to a frenzy of activity. That would be but to take them out of one error and into another. What we need is a zealous hunger for God, an avid thirst after righteousness, a pain-filled longing to be Christlike and holy. We need a zeal that is loving, self-effacing and lowly. No other kind will do.

That pure love for God and men which expresses itself in a burning desire to advance God's glory and leads to poured-out devotion to the temporal and eternal welfare of our fellowmen is certainly approved of God; but the nervous, squirrel-cage activity of self-centered and ambitious religious leaders is just as certainly offensive to Him and will prove at last to have been injurious to the souls of countless millions of human beings. SIZ081-082

Lord, give me that "zealous hunger for God," that "avid thirst after righteousness," that "painfilled longing to be Christlike and holy." I want to give myself in "poured-out devotion" for Your glory. Use me as Your servant, for Jesus' sake, Amen.

THE URGENCY OF GOD'S WILL

And one of the elders answered, saying unto me, What are these which are arrayed in white robes? and whence came they? And I said unto him, Sir, thou knowest. And he said to me, These are they which came out of great tribulation, and have washed their robes, and made them white in the blood of the Lamb.

—Revelation 7:13-14

*I*f we are serious about our Christian witness, the day may be near when we may be persecuted—even killed—for our faith. We should be stirred, as John was stirred, as we witness this vast company of God's saints in heaven who have come through earth's great tribulation.

I am not saying we are not Christians. I am only trying to find out why we are so far from revival and refreshing and renewal. I am only trying to determine why we are so far from recognizing the urgency of God's will laid upon us by the Holy Spirit.

If we belong to Jesus Christ, we should never compromise our spiritual decisions on the basis of "What is this going to cost me?" We ought only to ask, "What is my spiritual duty and my spiritual privilege before God?" JIV115

Please, Lord, give me this kind of commitment. Amen.

ONENESS OF MIND

Behold, how good and how pleasant it is for brethren to dwell together in unity!

—Psalm 133:1

*G*od always works where His people meet His conditions, but only when and as they do. Any spiritual visitation will be limited or extensive, depending how well and how widely conditions are met.

The first condition is oneness of mind among the persons who are seeking the visitation. . . .

Historically, revivals have been mainly the achieving of a oneness of mind among a number of Christian believers. In the second chapter of Acts it is recorded that they were "all with one accord in one place" (2:1) when the Spirit came upon them. He did not come to bring them into oneness of accord; He came because they were already so. The Spirit never comes to *give* unity (though His presence certainly aids and perfects such unity as may exist). He comes to that company who have, through repentance and faith, brought their hearts into one accord. . . .

Every church should strive for unity among its members, not languidly, but earnestly and optimistically. Every pastor should show his people the possibilities for power that lie in this fusion of many souls into one. PTP059, 061, 064

Lord, give us that unity in our church today. Give us a oneness of mind that we might experience Your full blessing in our midst. Amen.

UNITY PRECEDES BLESSING

With all lowliness and meekness, with longsuffering, forbearing one another in love; endeavouring to keep the unity of the Spirit in the bond of peace.

—Ephesians 4:2-3

*U*nity of mind on the part of the people of God precedes the blessing. I have often heard people pray, "Oh Lord, send the Holy Spirit that we may become a united people." That is all right except it is precisely backward. The Holy Spirit comes because we are a united people; He does not come to make us a united people. Our prayer should be more like, "Lord, help us to get united in order that the blessing might flow and there might be an outpouring of oil and dew and life." . . .

This teaches us that unity is necessary to the outpouring of the Spirit of God. If you have 120 volts of electricity coming into your house but you have broken wiring, you may turn the switch, but nothing works—no lights come on, the stove doesn't warm, your radio doesn't turn on. Why? Because you have broken wiring. The power is ready to do its work with all the appliances in your home, but where there is broken wiring, you have no power. Unity is necessary among the children of God if we are going to know the flow of power. SAT086-087

Lord, help us to get united in order that the blessings might flow. Amen.

DON'T SUBSTITUTE PRAYING FOR OBEYING

And Samuel said, Hath the LORD as great delight in burnt offerings and sacrifices, as in obeying the voice of the LORD? Behold, to obey is better than sacrifice, and to hearken than the fat of rams.

—1 Samuel 15:22

*H*ave you noticed how much praying for revival has been going on of late—and how little revival has resulted?

Considering the volume of prayer that is ascending these days, rivers of revival should be flowing in blessing throughout the land. That no such results are in evidence should not discourage us; rather it should stir us to find out why our prayers are not answered. . . .

I believe our problem is that we have been trying to substitute praying for obeying; and it simply will not work. . . .

Prayer is never an acceptable substitute for obedience. The sovereign Lord accepts no offering from His creatures that is not accompanied by obedience. To pray for revival while ignoring or actually flouting the plain precept laid down in the Scriptures is to waste a lot of words and get nothing for our trouble. OGM055-057

Search me, O God, and know my heart; show me any wicked way that needs to be corrected in my own life before revival can come. I'm praying for revival; help me to also be obeying. Amen.

NOT JUST INTENSITY OF PRAYER

Beloved, if our heart condemn us not, then have we confidence toward God. And whatsoever we ask, we receive of him, because we keep his commandments, and do those things that are pleasing in his sight.

—1 John 3:21-22

*I*ntensity of prayer is no criterion of its effectiveness. A man may throw himself on his face and sob out his troubles to the Lord and yet have no intention to obey the commandments of Christ. Strong emotion and tears may be no more than the outcropping of a vexed spirit, evidence of stubborn resistance to God's known will. . . .

No matter what I write here, thousands of pastors will continue to call their people to prayer in the forlorn hope that God will finally relent and send revival if only His people wear themselves out in intercession. To such people God must indeed appear to be a hard taskmaster, for the years pass and the young get old and the aged die and still no help comes. The prayer meeting room becomes a wailing wall and the lights burn long, and still the rains tarry.

Has God forgotten to be gracious? Let any reader begin to obey and he will have the answer. SIZ020-021

Lord, help me to obey Your commandments. Help me to live in obedience, so I may know the Father's love. Amen.

IT REQUIRES OBEDIENCE

And why call ye me, Lord, Lord, and do not the things which I say?

—Luke 6:46

*I*t is my conviction that much, very much, prayer for and talk about revival these days is wasted energy. Ignoring the confusion of figures, I might say that it is hunger that appears to have no object; it is dreamy wishing that is too weak to produce moral action. It is fanaticism on a high level for, according to John Wesley, "a fanatic is one who seeks desired ends while ignoring the constituted means to reach those ends.". . .

The correction of this error is extremely difficult for it entails more than a mere adjustment of our doctrinal beliefs; it strikes at the whole Adam-life and requires self-abnegation, humility and cross carrying. In short it requires *obedience*. And that we will do anything to escape.

It is almost unbelievable how far we will go to avoid obeying God. We call Jesus "Lord" and beg Him to rejuvenate our souls, but we are careful to do not the things He says. When faced with a sin, a confession or a moral alteration in our life, we find it much easier to pray half a night than to obey God. SIZ018-020

May this never be true of my life, Lord! I see the futility; I'm convinced of the need. Now enable me by Your Spirit to live this obedience. Amen.

MORE THAN TALK AND PRAYER

Only be thou strong and very courageous, that thou mayest observe to do according to all the law, which Moses my servant commanded thee: turn not from it to the right hand or to the left, that thou mayest prosper whithersoever thou goest.

—Joshua 1:7

$\mathcal{I}$t will take more than talk and prayer to bring revival. There must be a return to the Lord *in practice* before our prayers will be heard in heaven. We dare not continue to trouble God's way if we want Him to bless ours. . . .

If we are foolish enough to do it, we may spend the new year vainly begging God to send revival, while we blindly overlook His requirements and continue to break His laws. Or we can begin now to obey and learn the blessedness of obedience. The Word of God is before us. We have only to read and do what is written there and revival is assured. It will come as naturally as the harvest comes after the plowing and the planting.

Yes, this could be the year the revival comes. It's strictly up to us. SIZ010-011

Lord, I pray that this would be the year when Your people will get serious about heart-felt obedience to Your commands. Then send the great revival among us! Amen.

DOING
THE WILL
OF GOD

By this we know that we love the children of God, when we love God, and keep his commandments. For this is the love of God, that we keep his commandments: and his commandments are not grievous.

*W*e urgently need a new kind of reformation throughout our Christian churches—a reformation that will cause us not only to accept the will of God but to actively seek it and adore it! ...

The reformation we need now can best be described in terms of spiritual perfection—which reduced to its simplest form is no more and no less than doing the will of God! This would expose us all at the point of our need, no matter how sound we think we are in doctrine and no matter how great our reputations.

I long for the positive and genuine renewal which would come if the will of God could be totally accomplished in our lives. Everything that is unspiritual would flee, and all that is not Christlike would vanish, and all that is not according to the New Testament would be rejected. ...

Do we voluntarily and actively observe God's commandments, making positive changes in our lives as God may indicate in order to bring the entire life into accord with the New Testament? ITB089-090

Oh, Lord, "I long for the positive and genuine renewal which would come if the will of God could be totally accomplished in our lives." Let it begin in me . . . today. Amen.

THE
FIRE
FALLS

For as the body without the spirit is dead, so faith without works is dead also.

—James 2:26

*F*or a long time I have believed that truth, to be understood, must be lived; that Bible doctrine is wholly ineffective until it has been digested and assimilated by the total life. . . .

We must be willing to obey if we would know the true inner meaning of the teachings of Christ and the apostles. I believe this view prevailed in every revival that ever came to the church during her long history. Indeed a revived church may be distinguished from a dead one by the attitude of its members toward the truth. The dead church holds to the shell of truth without surrendering the will to it, while the church that wills to do God's will is immediately blessed with a visitation of spiritual powers.

Theological facts are like the altar of Elijah on Carmel before the fire came, correct, properly laid out, but altogether cold. When the heart makes the ultimate surrender, the fire falls and true facts are transmuted into spiritual truth that transforms, enlightens, sanctifies. The church or the individual that is Bible taught without being Spirit taught (and there are many of them) has simply failed to see that truth lies deeper than the theological statement of it. TIC092-094

Lord, send the fire today. Amen.

A REVIVAL OF REPENTANCE

If my people, which are called by my name, shall humble themselves, and pray, and seek my face, and turn from their wicked ways; then will I hear from heaven, and will forgive their sin, and will heal their land.

—2 Chronicles 7:14

$\mathcal{I}$ have little fear that any nation or combination of nations could bring down the United States and Canada by military action from without. But this I do fear—we sin and sin and do nothing about it. There is so little sense of the need of repentance—so little burden for the will of God to be wrought in our national life. I fear that the voice of blood will become so eloquent that God Almighty will have no choice but to speak the word that will bring us down.

I do pray often: "Oh God, send a revival of repentance and the fear of God that will sweep through the continent that we may be spared and that we may honor Thee!" EFE044

Lord, I pray for our country today. Our morality has deteriorated so horribly since Tozer's day. I too pray, "Oh, God, send a revival of repentance and the fear of God that will sweep through the continent that we may be spared and that we may honor Thee!" Amen.

NO LIMIT TO WHAT GOD COULD DO

And when they found them not, they drew Jason and certain brethren unto the rulers of the city, crying, These that have turned the world upside down are come hither also.

—Acts 17:6

*T*here is no limit to what God could do in our world if we would dare to surrender before Him with a commitment like this:

> Oh God, I hereby give myself to You. I give my family. I give my business. I give all I possess. Take all of it, Lord—and take me! I give myself in such measure that if it is necessary that I lose everything for Your sake, let me lose it. I will not ask what the price is. I will ask only that I may be all that I ought to be as a follower and disciple of Jesus Christ, my Lord. Amen.

If even 300 of God's people became that serious, our world would never hear the last of it! They would influence the news. Their message would go everywhere like birds on the wing. They would set off a great revival of New Testament faith and witness.

God wants to deliver us from the easygoing, smooth and silky, fat and comfortable Christianity so fashionable today. I hope we are willing to let the truth get hold of us, even at the cost of rejection or embarrassment.

The faith of the heavenly overcomers cost them everything and gained them everything. What of our faith? JIV116-117

> *Oh God, I hereby give myself to You "in such measure that if it is necessary that I lose everything for Your sake, let me lose it." Amen.*

October

Failure and Success

No man is worthy to succeed until he is willing to fail. No man is morally worthy of success in religious activities until he is willing that the honor of succeeding should go to another if God so wills. BAM058

PARALYSIS FROM PAST MISTAKES

For as the heaven is high above the earth, so great is his mercy toward them that fear him. As far as the east is from the west, so far hath he removed our transgressions from us.

—Psalm 103:11-12

*D*o not let any of the things of the world or past mistakes paralyze your hearts. I believe there are Christians who have allowed some of their past mistakes to paralyze them. You were so bright and cheerful in your spiritual life once, and then you made some tragic mistake or had something happen to you. You got out of it somehow, and prayed and wept your way out of it. But it did something to you, and now you cannot lick it.

Past wrongs that have been done to you, past failures, times you thought you were going to win and did not, or present sins or discouragement—these things are not mental at all. They are deeper than that; they are subconscious, and they prevent us from believing.

I most urgently exhort you, and I trust God Almighty to deliver you; to sponge that out of your spirit; to sponge that out of your heart so you are not hindered by unbelief. RRR162-163

I pray for all of my fellow servants who need deliverance, who need to have the past sponged out of their spirits and hearts. Amen.

IF A MAN FALLS

If we confess our sins, he is faithful and just to forgive us our sins, and to cleanse us from all unrighteousness.

—1 John 1:9

*A*re you allowing Satan to magnify the memories of your spiritual failures? He will always keep them before you unless you take your stand and move up in faith.

The devil will whisper, "You didn't get very far along toward the deeper life, did you?"

He will say, "You made a big 'to-do' about wanting to be filled with the Spirit and you really flopped, didn't you?"

He will taunt you with the fact that you may have stumbled in the faith—and perhaps more than once! The devil wants you to live in a state of discouraged chagrin and remorse.

Remember, the Bible does not teach that if a man falls down, he can never rise again. The fact that he falls is not the most important thing—but rather that he is forgiven and allows God to lift him up! ITB007

Father, I worship You this morning and thank You for the wonderful truth of First John 1:9. Amen.

THE SCHOOL OF FAILURE

Like as a father pitieth his children, so the LORD pitieth them that fear him. For he knoweth our frame; he remembereth that we are dust.

—Psalm 103:13-14

*F*or some of us last year was one in which we did not acquit ourselves very nobly as Christians, considering the infinite power available to us through the indwelling Spirit. But through the goodness of God we may go to school to our failures. The man of illuminated mind will learn from his mistakes, yes even from his sins. If his heart is trusting and penitent, he can be a better man next year for last year's fault—but let him not return again to folly. Repentance should be radical and thorough, and the best repentance for a wrong act, as Fenelon said, is not to do it again. . . .

Brother Lawrence expressed the highest moral wisdom when he testified that if he stumbled and fell he turned at once to God and said, "O Lord, this is what You may expect of me if You leave me to myself." He then accepted forgiveness, thanked God and gave himself no further concern about the matter. WOS102-104

Oh Lord, some of us have graduate degrees from this school! Help us to learn well from our failures, to accept Christ's forgiveness and to move on. Give victory for today, I pray, in Jesus' name. Amen.

TUNE THE STRINGS

Neglect not the gift that is in thee, which was given thee by prophecy, with the laying on of the hands of the presbytery. Meditate upon these things; give thyself wholly to them; that thy profiting may appear to all.

—1 Timothy 4:14-15

I have been forced to admit that one of the things hardest for me to understand and try to reconcile is the complete aimlessness of so many Christians' lives. . . .

Probably the worst part of this situation among us is the fact that so many of our Christian brothers and sisters have unusual gifts and talents and capacities—yet they have not exercised this discipline of girding up the mind and spiritual potential in order to make the necessary progress in the Christian life.

Why should a pastor have to confess total failure from year to year? Why should he have to go from one church to another, starting something, trying something—only to admit failure again?

I don't think he has ever really girded himself. He has abilities but they are not disciplined. He has a fine mind but it is not girded up. He is like a man with a treasured Stradivarius violin that has never been put in tune. He has never taken time to sit down and tune that priceless instrument, therefore he gets no melody and harmony from it. ICH142-143

Lord, help me today to gird myself in the Holy Spirit's power; to discipline myself to faithful service; to gird my mind to excellence. Amen.

NO PAST AT ALL!

Therefore if any man be in Christ, he is a new creature: old things are passed away; behold, all things are become new.

—2 Corinthians 5:17

$\mathcal{I}$n our churches we often sing, "Arise, my soul, arise! Shake off thy guilty fears." But nothing happens and we keep our fears. Why do we claim on one hand that our sins are gone and on the other act just as though they are not gone?

Brethren, we have been declared "Not Guilty!" by the highest court in all the universe. Still there are honest Christians, earnestly seeking the face of God, who cannot seem to break loose and find real freedom. The grave clothes trip them up every time they try to move on a little faster. Satan uses their past sins to terrify them.

Now, on the basis of grace as taught in the Word of God, when God forgives a man, He trusts him as though he had never sinned. God did not have mental reservations about any of us when we became His children by faith. When God forgives a man, He doesn't think, *I will have to watch this fellow because he has a bad record.* No, He starts with him again as though he had just been created and as if there had been no past at all! That is the basis of our Christian assurance—and God wants us to be happy in it. ITB006-007

Thank You, Father, for that glorious freedom of forgiveness. Thank You for Your marvelous grace. No past at all! What a wonderful, incomprehensible truth! I humbly and joyfully worship You this morning. Amen.

STOP TINKERING

And she called the name of the LORD that spake unto her, Thou God seest me: for she said, Have I also here looked after him that seeth me?

—Genesis 16:13

$\mathcal{F}$aith is the least self-regarding of the virtues. It is by its very nature scarcely conscious of its own existence. Like the eye which sees everything in front of it and never sees itself, faith is occupied with the Object upon which it rests and pays no attention to itself at all. While we are looking at God we do not see ourselves—blessed riddance. The man who has struggled to purify himself and has had nothing but repeated failures will experience real relief when he stops tinkering with his soul and looks away to the perfect One. While he looks at Christ, the very things he has so long been trying to do will be getting done within him. It will be God working in him to will and to do. . . .

When we lift our inward eyes to gaze upon God we are sure to meet friendly eyes gazing back at us, for it is written that the eyes of the Lord run to and fro throughout all the earth. The sweet language of experience is "Thou God seest me" (Genesis 16:13). When the eyes of the soul looking out meet the eyes of God looking in, heaven has begun right here on this earth.

POG084-086

Keep my eyes fixed on You, Lord. Help me to stop tinkering and realize my total inability to change. I look to You to change me and give me victory as I focus on Your friendly eyes looking lovingly at me. Amen.

QUIET
HEROES

*Blessed are the meek: for they
shall inherit the earth. . . .
Blessed are the pure in heart:
for they shall see God.*

—Matthew 5:5, 8

*W*e have but to become acquainted with, or even listen to, the big names of our times to discover how wretchedly inferior most of them are. Many appear to have arrived at their present eminence by pull, brass, nerve, gall and lucky accident. We turn away from them sick to our stomach and wonder for a discouraged moment if this is the best the human race can produce. But we gain our self-possession again by the simple expedient of recalling some of the plain men we know, who live unheralded and unsung, and who are made of stuff infinitely finer than the hoarse-voiced braggarts who occupy too many of the highest offices in the land. . . .

The church also suffers from this evil notion. Christians have fallen into the habit of accepting the noisiest and most notorious among them as the best and the greatest. They too have learned to equate popularity with excellence, and in open defiance of the Sermon on the Mount they have given their approval not to the meek but to the self-assertive; not to the mourner but to the self-assured; not to the pure in heart who see God but to the publicity hunter who seeks headlines. MDP096-097

Lord, I thank You for all the unknown but faithful pastors serving churches in quiet places. Thank You for the "quiet heroes" and their faithful service; give them great encouragement today. Amen.

THE CARNAL DESIRE TO MAKE GOOD

For we preach not ourselves, but Christ Jesus the Lord; and ourselves your servants for Jesus' sake.

—2 Corinthians 4:5

*O*ur Lord died an apparent failure, discredited by the leaders of established religion, rejected by society and forsaken by His friends. The man who ordered Him to the cross was the successful statesman whose hand the ambitious hack politician kissed. It took the resurrection to demonstrate how gloriously Christ had triumphed and how tragically the governor had failed.

Yet today the professed church seems to have learned nothing. We are still seeing as men see and judging after the manner of man's judgment. How much eager-beaver religious work is done out of a carnal desire to make good. How many hours of prayer are wasted beseeching God to bless projects that are geared to the glorification of little men. How much sacred money is poured out upon men who, in spite of their tear-in-the-voice appeals, nevertheless seek only to make a fair show in the flesh.

The true Christian should turn away from all this. Especially should ministers of the gospel search their own hearts and look deep into their inner motives. No man is worthy to succeed until he is willing to fail. No man is morally worthy of success in religious activities until he is willing that the honor of succeeding should go to another if God so wills. BAM058

Lord, deliver us from pride. For Jesus' sake, Amen.

THE PASSION FOR PUBLICITY

For neither at any time used we flattering words, as ye know, nor a cloke of covetousness; God is witness: nor of men sought we glory, neither of you, nor yet of others, when we might have been burdensome, as the apostles of Christ.

—1 Thessalonians 2:5-6

*I*f this is a fairly accurate view of things, what can we say then when Christian men vie with one another for place and position? What can we answer when we see them hungrily seeking for praise and honor? How can we excuse the passion for publicity which is so glaringly evident among Christian leaders? What about political ambition in Church circles? What about the fevered palm that is stretched out for more and bigger "love offerings"? What about the shameless egotism among Christians? How can we explain the gross man-worship that habitually blows up one and another popular leader to the size of a colossus? What about the obsequious hand kissing of moneyed men by those purporting to be sound preachers of the gospel?

There is only one answer to these questions; it is simply that in these manifestations we see the world and nothing but the world. No passionate profession of love for "souls" can change evil into good. These are the very sins that crucified Jesus. POM126

Deliver me, O God, from this insidious trap. Give me a humble spirit, willing to serve You faithfully, however obscure might be my service. Amen.

THE SCRAMBLE FOR POPULARITY

Blessed are ye, when men shall revile you, and persecute you, and shall say all manner of evil against you falsely, for my sake. Rejoice, and be exceeding glad: for great is your reward in heaven: for so persecuted they the prophets which were before you.

—Matthew 5:11-12

*P*opular Judaism slew the prophets and crucified Christ. Popular Christianity killed the Reformers, jailed the Quakers and drove John Wesley into the streets. When it comes to religion, the crowds are always wrong. At any time there are a few who see, and the rest are blinded. To stand by the truth of God against the current religious vogue is always unpopular and may be downright dangerous. . . .

Christianity's scramble for popularity today is an unconscious acknowledgment of spiritual decline. Her eager fawning at the feet of the world's great is a grief to the Holy Spirit and an embarrassment to the sons of God. . . .

Lot was a popular believer. . . . But when trouble struck, he had to send quick for Abraham to get him out of the jam. And where did they find Abraham? Out on the hillside, far away from the fashionable crowds. It has always been so. . . . For every Noah there is always a vast multitude who will not believe it is going to rain.

We are sent to bless the world, but never are we told to compromise with it. NCA020-021

Deliver me from the scramble for popularity and strengthen me to serve alone, oblivious to the roar of the crowds. Amen.

THE SMALL AND THE GREAT

Yea, all of you be subject one to another, and be clothed with humility: for God resisteth the proud, and giveth grace to the humble.

—1 Peter 5:5

$\mathcal{S}$ ome time ago we heard a short address by a young preacher during which he quoted the following, "If you are too big for a little place, you are too little for a big place."

It is an odd rule of the kingdom of God that when we try to get big, we always get smaller by the moment. God is jealous of His glory and will not allow anyone to share it with Him. The effort to appear great will bring the displeasure of God upon us and effectively prevent us from achieving the greatness after which we pant.

Humility pleases God wherever it is found, and the humble person will have God for his or her friend and helper always. Only the humble are completely sane, for they are the only ones who see clearly their own size and limitations. Egotists see things out of focus. To themselves they are large and God is correspondingly small, and that is a kind of moral insanity. TWP034

> *Lord, help me never to be too big for a little place. In humility let me serve and revel in You as my "friend and helper always." Amen.*

TRUE SERVICE

. . . not with eyeservice, as men-pleasers; but in singleness of heart, fearing God: and whatsoever ye do, do it heartily, as to the Lord, and not unto men; knowing that of the Lord ye shall receive the reward of the inheritance: for ye serve the Lord Christ.

—Colossians 3:22-24

*A*ny serious-minded Christian may at some time find himself wondering whether the service he is giving to God is the best it could be. He may even have times of doubting, and fear that his toil is fruitless and his life empty. . . .

The church has marked out certain work and approved it as service acceptable to God, and for the most part the church has been right. But it should be kept in mind that it is not the kind or quantity of work that makes it true service—it is the *quality*.

Before the judgment seat of Christ, very little will be heard of numbers or size; moral quality is about all that will matter then. . . .

It would be a shock to most of us to learn just what God thinks of our breathless activity, and a greater shock to many to find out the true quality of our service as God sees it. For not all religious activity is accepted of God, not even when it appears to produce results and get things done. The Lord seeth not as man seeth. . . .

In Christian service *motive* is everything, for it is motive that gives to every moral act its final quality. NCA069-070

> *Lord, remind me that "Before the judgment seat of Christ, very little will be heard of numbers or size; moral quality is about all that will matter then." Amen.*

TRUE GREATNESS

But it shall not be so among you: but whosoever will be great among you, let him be your minister; and whosoever will be chief among you, let him be your servant.

—Matthew 20:26-27

$\mathcal{T}$he essence of [God's] teaching is that true greatness lies in character, not in ability or position. Men in their blindness had always thought that superior talents made a man great, and so the vast majority believe today. To be endowed with unusual abilities in the field of art or literature or music or statecraft, for instance, is thought to be in itself an evidence of greatness, and the man thus endowed is hailed as a great man. Christ taught, and by His life demonstrated, that greatness lies deeper. . . .

While a few philosophers and religionists of pre-Christian times had seen the fallacy in man's idea of greatness and had exposed it, it was Christ who located true greatness and showed how it could be attained. "Whosoever will be great among you, let him be your minister; and whosoever will be chief among you, let him be your servant" (Matthew 20:26-27). It is that simple and that easy—and that difficult. BAM050

Lord, this truth is indeed contrary to the philosophy of the world. Stimulate my heart this morning to desire this true greatness for Your glory. Amen.

SIZE MATTERS LITTLE

And he said unto them, Ye are they which justify yourselves before men; but God knoweth your hearts: for that which is highly esteemed among men is abomination in the sight of God.

—Luke 16:15

To God quality is vastly important and size matters little. When set in opposition to size, quality is everything and size nothing. . . .

Man's moral fall has clouded his vision, confused his thinking and rendered him subject to delusion. One evidence of this is his all but incurable proneness to confuse values and put size before quality in his appraisal of things. The Christian faith reverses this order, but even Christians tend to judge things by the old Adamic rule. How big? How much? and How many? are the questions oftenest asked by religious persons when trying to evaluate Christian things. . . .

The Church is dedicated to things that matter. Quality matters. Let's not be led astray by the size of things. BAM072-073, 075

Encourage all those pastors who are discouraged today because they don't match up to the "success" of the big churches. Amen.

QUANTITY RATHER THAN QUALITY

From that time many of his disciples went back, and walked no more with him.

—John 6:66

*T*ime may show that one of the greatest weaknesses in our modern civilization has been the acceptance of quantity rather than quality as the goal after which to strive. . . .

Christianity is resting under the blight of degraded values. And it all stems from a too-eager desire to impress, to gain fleeting attention, to appear well in comparison with some world-beater who happens for the time to have the ear or the eye of the public.

This is so foreign to the Scriptures that we wonder how Bible-loving Christians can be deceived by it. The Word of God ignores size and quantity and lays all its stress upon quality. Christ, more than any other man, was followed by the crowds, yet after giving them such help as they were able to receive, He quietly turned from them and deposited His enduring truths in the breasts of His chosen twelve. . . .

Pastors and churches in our hectic times are harassed by the temptation to seek size at any cost and to secure by inflation what they cannot gain by legitimate growth. . . . Many a man of God is being subjected to cruel pressure by the ill-taught members of his flock who scorn his slow methods and demand quick results and a popular following regardless of quality. NCA007-008

Open our eyes, Lord, to evaluate our success or failure by Your standards, and be encouraged. Amen.

ONE TEST TODAY: SUCCESS

For we are not as many, which corrupt the word of God: but as of sincerity, but as of God, in the sight of God speak we in Christ.

—2 Corinthians 2:17

*M*uch that passes for Christianity today is the brief bright effort of the severed branch to bring forth its fruit in its season. But the deep laws of life are against it. Preoccupation with appearances and a corresponding neglect of the out-of-sight root of the true spiritual life are prophetic signs which go unheeded. Immediate "results" are all that matter, quick proofs of present success without a thought of next week or next year. Religious pragmatism is running wild among the orthodox. Truth is whatever works. If it gets results it is good. There is but one test for the religious leader: success. Everything is forgiven him except failure.

A tree can weather almost any storm if its root is sound, but when the fig tree which our Lord cursed "dried up from the roots" it immediately "withered away" (Mark 11:20-21). A church that is soundly rooted cannot be destroyed, but nothing can save a church whose root is dried up. No stimulation, no advertising campaigns, no gifts of money and no beautiful edifice can bring back life to the rootless tree. ROR008-009

Lord, give us solid roots. Forgive us for our preoccupation with success and move in Your church today to restore to us a proper perspective. Amen.

OUR DOWRY OF EVERLASTINGNESS

As for man, his days are as grass: as a flower of the field, so he flourisheth. For the wind passeth over it, and it is gone; and the place thereof shall know it no more. But the mercy of the LORD is from everlasting to everlasting upon them that fear him, and his righteousness unto children's children.

—Psalm 103:15-17

*W*e who follow Christ are men and women of eternity. We must put no confidence in the passing scenes of the disappearing world. We must resist every attempt of Satan to palm off upon us the values that belong to mortality. Nothing less than forever is long enough for us. We view with amused sadness the frenetic scramble of the world to gain a brief moment in the sun. . . .

The church must claim again her ancient dowry of everlastingness. She must begin again to deal with ages and millenniums rather than with days and years. She must not count numbers but test foundations. She must work for permanence rather than for appearance. Her children must seek those enduring things that have been touched with immortality. The shallow brook of popular religion chatters on its nervous way and thinks the ocean too quiet and dull because it lies deep in its mighty bed and is unaffected by the latest shower. NCA009

Oh Lord, remind me constantly of this eternal perspective. Amen.

GREATNESS HAS ITS PRICE

For ye remember, brethren, our labour and travail: for labouring night and day, because we would not be chargeable unto any of you, we preached unto you the gospel of God.

—1 Thessalonians 2:9

The laws of success operate also in the higher field of the soul—spiritual greatness has its price. Eminence in the things of the Spirit demands a devotion to these things more complete than most of us are willing to give. But the law cannot be escaped. If we would be holy we know the way; the law of holy living is before us. The prophets of the Old Testament, the apostles of the New and, more than all, the sublime teachings of Christ are there to tell us how to succeed. . . .

The amount of loafing practiced by the average Christian in spiritual things would ruin a concert pianist if he allowed himself to do the same thing in the field of music. The idle puttering around that we see in church circles would end the career of a big league pitcher in one week. No scientist could solve his exacting problem if he took as little interest in it as the rank and file of Christians take in the art of being holy. The nation whose soldiers were as soft and undisciplined as the soldiers of the churches would be conquered by the first enemy that attacked it. Triumphs are not won by men in easy chairs. Success is costly. WTA025-026

Give me a willingness to pay any cost which You may exact in my service for You. Amen.

FAITH DARES TO FAIL

Therefore judge nothing before the time, until the Lord come, who both will bring to light the hidden things of darkness, and will make manifest the counsels of the hearts: and then shall every man have praise of God.

—1 Corinthians 4:5

God may allow His servant to succeed when He has disciplined him to a point where he does not need to succeed to be happy. The man who is elated by success and cast down by failure is still a carnal man. At best his fruit will have a worm in it.

God will allow His servant to succeed when he has learned that success does not make him dearer to God nor more valuable in the total scheme of things. We cannot buy God's favor with crowds or converts or new missionaries sent out or Bibles distributed. All these things can be accomplished without the help of the Holy Spirit. A good personality and a shrewd knowledge of human nature is all that any man needs to be a success in religious circles today. . . .

We can afford to follow Him to failure. Faith dares to fail. The resurrection and the judgment will demonstrate before all worlds who won and who lost. We can wait. BAM059

Father, keep me faithful today. I don't need to succeed in the world's eyes; I'll wait. Amen.

GODLINESS IS NOT VALUED

His lord said unto him, Well done, thou good and faithful ser-vant: thou hast been faithful over a few things, I will make thee ruler over many things: enter thou into the joy of thy lord.

—Matthew 25:21

*A*fter more than thirty years of observing the religious scene I have been forced to conclude that saintliness and church leadership are not often synonymous. . . .

Were the church a pure and Spirit-filled body, wholly led and directed by spiritual considerations, certainly the purest and the saintliest men and women would be the ones most appreciated and most honored; but the opposite is true. Godliness is no longer valued, except for the very old or the very dead. . . . The Christlike, the self-forgetting, the other-worldly are jostled aside to make room for the latest converted playboy who is usually not too well converted and still very much of a playboy. . . .

The wise Christian will be content to wait for that day. In the meantime, he will serve his generation in the will of God. If he should be overlooked in the religious popularity contests he will give it but small attention. He knows whom he is trying to please and he is willing to let the world think what it will of him. He will not be around much longer anyway, and where he is going men will be known not by their Hooper rating but by the holiness of their character. MDP097-099

Help me to focus on "holiness of . . . character" whether I'm valued by people or not. Amen.

No Little Failures

> And Jabez called on the God of Israel, saying, Oh thou that wouldest bless me indeed, and enlarge my coast, and that thine hand might be with me, and that thou wouldest keep me from evil, that it may not grieve me! And God granted him that which he requested.
>
> —1 Chronicles 4:10

When Simpson succeeded it was in a big way. When he failed he made great failures. It had to be so. Men of his caliber do not make little mistakes. They fly too high and too far to steer their courses by city maps. They ask not, "What street is that?" but "What continent?" And when they get off of the course for a moment they will be sure to pull up a long way from their goal. Their range and speed make this inevitable. Little men who never get outside of their own yards point to these mistakes with great satisfaction. But history has a way of disposing of these critics by filing them away in quiet anonymity. She cannot be bothered to preserve their names. She is too busy chalking up the great successes and huge failures of her favorites. WNG108-109

Lord, give me the boldness to attempt big things for You—so that whether I succeed or fail it will be in a big way! Amen.

OUR GOD IS TOO SMALL

O magnify the LORD with me,
and let us exalt his name together.

—Psalm 34:3

I am positively sure after many years of observation and prayer that the basis of all of our trouble today, in religious circles, is that our God is too small.

When [the psalmist] says magnify the Lord, he doesn't mean that you are to make God big, but you are to see Him big. When we take a telescope and look at a star, we don't make the star bigger, we only see it big. Likewise you cannot make God bigger, but you are only to see Him bigger. . . .

My brethren, God calls us to magnify Him, to see Him big. A meeting is not big because a lot of people are present. A meeting is big because a number of people see a big God in the meeting. And the bigger God is seen, the greater the meeting. A friend of mine has a little saying, "I would rather have a big, little meeting than a little, big meeting." There are a lot of big meetings that are little because the God in them is a small God. And there are a lot of little meetings that are big because God is big in the midst of them. . . .

That is the first thing—magnify God. Your ministry will be little, and you will live and die little unless you have a bigger God. SAT036-037, 040-042

> *Lord, help me always to not only be satisfied with, but*
> *in fact to strive for, that "big, little meeting" rather than*
> *a "little, big meeting." Amen.*

JUST A SMALL CHURCH UPCOUNTRY

How precious also are thy thoughts unto me, O God! how great is the sum of them! If I should count them, they are more in number than the sand: when I awake, I am still with thee.

—Psalm 139:17-18

No matter how insignificant he may have been before, a man becomes significant the moment he has had an encounter with the Son of God. When the Lord lays His hand upon a man, that man ceases at once to be ordinary. He immediately becomes extraordinary, and his life takes on cosmic significance. The angels in heaven take notice of him and go forth to become his ministers (Hebrews 1:14). Though the man had before been only one of the faceless multitude, a mere cipher in the universe, an invisible dust grain blown across endless wastes—now he gets a face and a name and a place in the scheme of meaningful things. Christ knows His own sheep "by name."

A young preacher introduced himself to the pastor of a great metropolitan church with the words, "I am just the pastor of a small church upcountry." "Son," replied the wise minister, "there are no small churches." And there are no unknown Christians, no insignificant sons of God. Each one signifies, each is a "sign" drawing the attention of the Triune God day and night upon him. The faceless man has a face, the nameless man a name, when Jesus picks him out of the multitude and calls him to Himself. WTA019

Lord, I pray for the pastors of small churches. Let them see how much You care for them, and how significant You see their ministry to be. Amen.

COWORKERS, NOT COMPETITORS

> *And he is the head of the body, the church: who is the beginning, the firstborn from the dead; that in all things he might have the preeminence.*
>
> —Colossians 1:18

*G*od's servants are not to be competitors, but coworkers. . . .

A local church, as long as it is indwelt by the Holy Spirit, cannot entertain the psychology of competition. When it begins to compete with another church, it is a true church of God no longer; it has voided its character and gone down onto a lower level. The Spirit that indwells it is no longer divine; it is human merely, and its activities are pitched on the plane of the natural. . . .

The Holy Spirit always cooperates with Himself in His members. The Spirit-directed body does not tear itself apart by competition. The ambitions of the various members are submerged in the glory of the Head, and whatever brings honor to the Head meets with the most eager approval of the members.

We should cultivate the idea that we are coworkers rather than competitors. We should ask God to give us the psychology of cooperation. We should learn to think of ourselves as being members in particular of one and the same body, and we should reject with indignation every suggestion of the enemy designed to divide our efforts. NCA056-057

> *Lord, forgive us for the sin of comparison and competition. Replace it in our hearts with a spirit of cooperation as coworkers. May the glory all go to the Head. Amen.*

THE GREAT GODDESS NUMBERS

Now if any man build upon this foundation gold, silver, precious stones, wood, hay, stubble; every man's work shall be made manifest: for the day shall declare it, because it shall be revealed by fire; and the fire shall try every man's work of what sort it is.

—1 Corinthians 3:12-13

The emphasis today in Christian circles appears to be on quantity, with a corresponding lack of emphasis on quality. Numbers, size and amount seem to be very nearly all that matters even among evangelicals. . . . The church that can show an impressive quantitative growth is frankly envied and imitated by other ambitious churches.

This is the age of the Laodiceans. The great goddess Numbers is worshiped with fervent devotion and all things religious are brought before her for examination. Her Old Testament is the financial report and her New Testament is the membership roll. To these she appeals as arbiters of all questions, the test of spiritual growth and the proof of success or failure in every Christian endeavor.

A little acquaintance with the Bible should show this up for the heresy it is. To judge anything spiritual by statistics is to judge by other than scriptural judgment. It is to admit the validity of externalism and to deny the value our Lord places upon the soul as over against the body. . . . Yet it is being done every day by ministers, church boards and denominational leaders. And hardly anyone notices the deep and dangerous error. SOS153

Oh Lord, convict us! Forgive us! Deliver us! Amen.

CROWDS AT ANY PRICE

As it is written, There is none righteous, no, not one.... They are all gone out of the way, they are together become unprofitable; there is none that doeth good, no, not one.

—Romans 3:10, 12

The crowds-at-any-price mania has taken a firm grip on American Christianity and is the motivating power back of a shockingly high percentage of all religious activity. . . .

Our constant effort should be to reach as many persons as possible with the Christian message, and for that reason numbers are critically important. But our first responsibility is not to make converts but to uphold the honor of God in a world given over to the glory of fallen man. No matter how many persons we touch with the gospel we have failed unless, along with the message of invitation, we have boldly declared the exceeding sinfulness of man and the transcendent holiness of the Most High God. They who degrade or compromise the truth in order to reach larger numbers, dishonor God and deeply injure the souls of men.

The temptation to modify the teachings of Christ with the hope that larger numbers may "accept" Him is cruelly strong in this day of speed, size, noise and crowds. But if we know what is good for us, we'll resist it with every power at our command. SIZ117-119

Lord, give me a deep, unshakable commitment "to uphold the honor of God in a world given over to the glory of fallen men"—whether I achieve crowds and success or not. Amen.

STATUS SYMBOLS

And I turned to see the voice that spake with me. And being turned, I saw seven golden candlesticks; and in the midst of the seven candlesticks one like unto the Son of man.

—Revelation 1:12-13

In our time we have all kinds of status symbols in the Christian church—membership, attendance, pastoral staff, missionary offerings. But there is only one status symbol that should make a Christian congregation genuinely glad. That is to know that our Lord is present, walking in our midst! . . .

No matter the size of the assembly or its other attributes, our Lord wants it to be known by His presence in the midst. I would rather have His presence in the church than anything else in all the wide world. . . .

The Christian church dares not settle for anything less than the illumination of the Holy Spirit and the presence of our divine Prophet, Priest and King in our midst. Let us never be led into the mistake that so many are making—sighing and saying, "Oh, if we only had bigger, wiser men in our pulpits! Oh, if we only had more important men in places of Christian leadership!" JIV059-060, 063

Lord, I pray that I might never deviate from that significant thought: "I would rather have His presence in the church than anything else in all the wide world." Amen.

THE THINGS THAT MATTER

That ye may approve things that are excellent; that ye may be sincere and without offence till the day of Christ; being filled with the fruits of righteousness, which are by Jesus Christ, unto the glory and praise of God.

—Philippians 1:10-11

*I*n life there will be found certain great fundamentals, like pillars bearing up the weight of some mighty building. . . .

The wise man will simplify his life by going to the center of it. He will look well to the foundations and, having done that, he will not worry about the rest.

Life as we know it in our painfully intricate civilization can be deadly unless we learn to distinguish the things that matter from those that do not. It is never the major things that destroy us, but invariably the multitude of trifling things which are mistakenly thought to be of major importance. These are so many that, unless we get out from under them, they will crush us body and soul. . . .

Every believer as well as every minister of Christ must decide whether he will put his emphasis upon the majors or the minors. He must decide whether he will stay by the sober truths which constitute the beating heart of the Scriptures or turn his attention to those marginal doctrines which always bring division and which, at their best, could not help us much on our way to the Celestial City. NCA011, 014

Deliver us today from the trifling things and help us to spend every minute of the day on "the things that matter." Amen.

NOT MEASURING UP

Therefore, my beloved brethren, be ye steadfast, unmoveable, always abounding in the work of the Lord, forasmuch as ye know that your labour is not in vain in the Lord.

—1 Corinthians 15:58

$\mathcal{I}$t is good to come to the understanding that while God wants us to be holy and Spirit-filled, He does not expect us to look like Abraham or to play the harp like David or to have the same spiritual insight given to Paul.

All of those former heroes of the faith are dead. You are alive in your generation. A Bible proverb says that it is better to be a living dog than a dead lion. You may wish to be Abraham or Isaac or Jacob, but remember that they have been asleep for long centuries, and you are still around! You can witness for your Lord today. You can still pray. You can still give of your substance to help those in need. You can still encourage the depressed.

I hope you have not missed something good from God's hand because you felt you did not measure up to Gideon or Isaiah. In this your generation, give God all of your attention! Give Him all of your love! Give Him all of your devotion and faithful service! You do not know what holy, happy secret God may want to whisper to your responsive heart. JAF072

Father, I commit myself to faithfulness today. You have given me life today; You have given me the gifts You want me to have and use; You have called me by Your grace to serve You. I give it all to You today. Amen.

UNSUNG BUT SINGING

But in all things approving ourselves as the ministers of God, in much patience, in afflictions, in necessities, in distresses . . . as unknown, and yet well known.

—2 Corinthians 6:4, 9

*U*nsung but singing: this is the short and simple story of many today whose names are not known beyond the small circle of their own small company. Their gifts are not many nor great, but their song is sweet and clear. . . .

Well, the world is big and tangled and dark, and we are never sure where a true Christian may be found. One thing we do know: the more like Christ he is the less likely it will be that a newspaper reporter will be seeking him out. However much he may value the esteem of his fellowmen, he may for the time be forced to stand under the shadow of their displeasure. Or the busy world may actually not even know he is there—except that they hear him singing. BAM054-055

Father, may my song today be a sweet sound in Your ears—even if in Yours alone. Amen.

I REFUSE TO COMPETE

So then neither is he that planteth any thing, neither he that watereth; but God that giveth the increase. Now he that planteth and he that watereth are one: and every man shall receive his own reward according to his own labour.

—1 Corinthians 3:7-8

"Dear Lord, I refuse henceforth to compete with any of Thy servants. They have congregations larger than mine. So be it. I rejoice in their success. They have greater gifts. Very well. That is not in their power nor in mine. I am humbly grateful for their greater gifts and my smaller ones. I only pray that I may use to Thy glory such modest gifts as I possess. I will not compare myself with any, nor try to build up my self-esteem by noting where I may excel one or another in Thy holy work. I herewith make a blanket disavowal of all intrinsic worth. I am but an unprofitable servant. I gladly go to the foot of the class and own myself the least of Thy people. If I err in my self judgment and actually underestimate myself I do not want to know it. I purpose to pray for others and to rejoice in their prosperity as if it were my own. And indeed it is my own if it is Thine own, for what is Thine is mine, and while one plants and another waters it is Thou alone that giveth the increase." PON104-105

Amen.

November

Spiritual Warfare and Sin

To be entirely safe from the devil's snares the man of God must be completely obedient to the Word of the Lord. The driver on the highway is safe, not when he reads the signs but when he obeys them. TIC051

ETERNAL ENMITY

Beloved, think it not strange concerning the fiery trial which is to try you ... but rejoice, inasmuch as ye are partakers of Christ's sufferings; that, when his glory shall be revealed, ye may be glad also with exceeding joy.

—1 Peter 4:12-13

There are two spirits in the earth, the Spirit of God and the spirit of Satan, and these are at eternal enmity. The ostensible cause of religious hatred may be almost anything; the true cause is nearly always the same: the ancient animosity which Satan, since the time of his inglorious fall, has ever felt toward God and His kingdom. Satan is aflame with desire for unlimited dominion over the human family; and whenever that evil ambition is challenged by the Spirit of God, he invariably retaliates with savage fury. . . .

It is possible within the provisions of redemptive grace to enter into a state of union with Christ so perfect that the world will instinctively react toward us exactly as it did toward Him in the days of His flesh. . . .

It is the Spirit of Christ in us that will draw Satan's fire. The people of the world will not much care what we believe and they will stare vacantly at our religious forms, but there is one thing they will never forgive us—the presence of God's Spirit in our hearts. . . . Satan will never cease to make war on the Man-child, and the soul in which dwells the Spirit of Christ will continue to be the target for his attacks. WOS003-004

Lord, thank You for victory through Jesus Christ. Amen.

IRRECONCILABLE HOSTILITY

> *For we wrestle not against flesh and blood, but against principalities, against powers, against the rulers of the darkness of this world, against spiritual wickedness in high places.*
>
> —Ephesians 6:12

*I*n the early days, when Christianity exercised a dominant influence over American thinking, men and women conceived the world to be a battleground. Our fathers believed in sin and the devil and hell as constituting one force, and they believed in God and righteousness and heaven as the other. By their very nature, these forces were opposed to each other forever in deep, grave, irreconcilable hostility. Humans, our fathers held, had to choose sides—they could not be neutral. For them it must be life or death, heaven or hell, and if they chose to come out on God's side they could expect open war with God's enemies. The fight would be real and deadly and would last as long as life continued here below. . . .

How different today. The fact remains the same, but the interpretation has changed completely. People think of the world, not as a battleground, but as a playground. We are not here to fight; we are here to frolic. We are not in a foreign land; we are at home. We are not getting ready to live, but we are already living, and the best we can do is rid ourselves of our inhibitions and our frustrations and live this life to the full. TWP004-005

Help me to be willing to take a stand for righteousness, to choose clearly to be on Your side against the enemy, to pay any price—and then to look forward to laying down my sword later in heaven. Amen.

SATAN'S STRATEGY

Wherefore take unto you the whole armour of God, that ye may be able to withstand in the evil day, and having done all, to stand.

—Ephesians 6:13

Now I do not think that Satan much cares to destroy us Christians physically. The soldier dead in battle who died performing some deed of heroism is not a great loss to the army but may rather be an object of pride to his country. On the other hand the soldier who cannot or will not fight but runs away at the sound of the first enemy gun is a shame to his family and a disgrace to his nation. So a Christian who dies in the faith represents no irreparable loss to the forces of righteousness on earth and certainly no victory for the devil. But when whole regiments of professed believers are too timid to fight and too smug to be ashamed, surely it must bring an astringent smile to the face of the enemy; and it should bring a blush to the cheeks of the whole Church of Christ.

The devil's master strategy for us Christians then is not to kill us physically (though there may be some special situations where physical death fits into his plan better), but to destroy our power to wage spiritual warfare. And how well he has succeeded. The average Christian these days is a harmless enough thing. God knows. He is a child wearing with considerable self-consciousness the harness of the warrior; he is a sick eaglet that can never mount up with wings; he is a spent pilgrim who has given up the journey and sits with a waxy smile trying to get what pleasure he can from sniffing the wilted flowers he has plucked by the way. TIC072

Oh, God, give me grace to fight valiantly. Amen.

THROW OFF HINDRANCES

Wherefore seeing we also are compassed about with so great a cloud of witnesses, let us lay aside every weight, and the sin which doth so easily beset us, and let us run with patience the race that is set before us, looking unto Jesus the author and finisher of our faith.

—Hebrews 12:1-2

Is Satan giving you a hard time in your life of faith—in the Christian race you are running? Expect it if you are a believing child of God!

Satan hates your God. He hates Jesus Christ. He hates your faith. You should be aware of the devil's evil intentions. He wants you to lose the victor's crown in the race you have entered by faith through grace. . . .

When by faith we have entered this lifelong spiritual course, the Holy Spirit whispers, "Do you truly want to be among the victors in this discipline?" When we breathe our "Yes! Yes!" He whispers of ways that will aid us and carry us to certain victory.

The Spirit tells us to throw off everything that would hinder us in the race. He tells us to be aware of the little sins and errors that could divert us from the will of God as we run. But here is the important thing: He tells us to keep our eyes on Jesus, because He alone is our pacesetter and victorious example. JAF075-077

Father, let me see Jesus this morning. Then go with me today and help me to keep my eyes fixed on Him. Amen.

Don't
Suffer
Shipwreck

This charge I commit unto thee, son Timothy, according to the prophecies which went before on thee, that thou by them mightest war a good warfare; holding faith, and a good conscience; which some having put away concerning faith have made shipwreck.

—1 Timothy 1:18-19

*Y*et the ministry is one of the most perilous of professions. The devil hates the Spirit-filled minister with an intensity second only to that which he feels for Christ Himself. The source of this hatred is not difficult to discover. An effective, Christlike minister is a constant embarrassment to the devil, a threat to his dominion, a rebuttal of his best arguments and a dogged reminder of his coming overthrow. No wonder he hates him.

Satan knows that the downfall of a prophet of God is a strategic victory for him, so he rests not day or night devising hidden snares and deadfalls for the ministry. Perhaps a better figure would be the poison dart that only paralyzes its victim, for I think that Satan has little interest in killing the preacher outright. An ineffective, half-alive minister is a better advertisement for hell than a good man dead. So the preacher's dangers are likely to be spiritual rather than physical, though sometimes the enemy works through bodily weaknesses to get to the preacher's soul. GTM090-091

I pray for every one of my fellow servants, especially those who may be close to succumbing. Give Your great grace and victory today. Amen.

A SAINT IN EMBRYO

For I delight in the law of God after the inward man: but I see another law in my members, warring against the law of my mind, and bringing me into captivity to the law of sin which is in my members.

—Romans 7:22-23

The regenerate man often has a more difficult time of it than the unregenerate, for he is not one man but two. He feels within him a power that tends toward holiness and God, while at the same time he is still a child of Adam's flesh and a son of the red clay. This moral dualism is to him a source of distress and struggle wholly unknown to the once-born man. Of course the classic critique upon this is Paul's testimony in the seventh chapter of his Roman epistle.

The true Christian is a saint in embryo. The heavenly genes are in him and the Holy Spirit is working to bring him on into a spiritual development that accords with the nature of the heavenly Father from whom he received the deposit of divine life. Yet he is here in this mortal body subject to weakness and temptation, and his warfare with the flesh sometimes leads him to do extreme things. "For the flesh lusteth against the Spirit, and the Spirit against the flesh: and these are contrary the one to the other: so that ye cannot do the things that ye would" (Galatians 5:17). TIC053-054

Lord, sometimes I could wish I were not "still a child of Adam's flesh and a son of the red clay." But I live in this flesh and realize constantly my total dependence on You for spiritual victory. Grant it today, for Jesus' sake. Amen.

OUR OLD NATURE

Mortify therefore your members which are upon the earth; fornication, uncleanness, inordinate affection, evil concupiscence, and covetousness, which is idolatry.

—Colossians 3:5

There are a lot of people trying to get away with the old man. What do I mean by the old man? I mean your pride, your bossiness, your nastiness, your temper, your mean disposition, your lustfulness and your quarrelsomeness. What do I mean, Reverend? I mean your study, your hunting for a bigger church, being dissatisfied with the offering and blaming the superintendent because you cannot get called. . . .

Deacons, what do I mean? I mean sitting around in board meetings wearing your poor pastor out, because you are too stubborn to humble yourself and admit you are wrong.

What do I mean, musicians? I mean that demeanor that makes you hate somebody that can sing a little better than you can. I mean that jealousy that makes you want to play the violin when everybody knows you can't, especially the choir director. You hate him, wish he were dead, and secretly pray that he would get called to Punxsutawney. That is what I mean. All of this may be under the guise of spirituality and we may have learned to put our head over on one side, fold our hands gently and put on a beatific smile like St. Francis of Assisi, and still be just as carnal as they come. SAT043-044

May Your Holy Spirit bring the proper conviction and repentance to my heart and give me victory over any carnal thoughts that might be mine. Amen.

INCREASED HOSTILITY

Be sober, be vigilant; because your adversary the devil, as a roaring lion, walketh about, seeking whom he may devour.

—1 Peter 5:8

*A*s we move farther on and mount higher up in the Christian life we may expect to encounter greater difficulties in the way and meet increased hostility from the enemy of our souls. . . .

Satan hates the true Christian for several reasons. One is that God loves him, and whatever is loved by God is sure to be hated by the devil. Another is that the Christian, being a child of God, bears a family resemblance to the Father and to the household of faith. Satan's ancient jealousy has not abated nor his hatred for God diminished in the slightest. Whatever reminds him of God is without other reason the object of his malignant hate.

A third reason is that a true Christian is a former slave who has escaped from the galley, and Satan cannot forgive him for this affront. A fourth reason is that a praying Christian is a constant threat to the stability of Satan's government. The Christian is a holy rebel loose in the world with access to the throne of God. Satan never knows from what direction the danger will come. TIC071

Lord, it's not hard to see why Satan attacks. May I continue to be enough of a threat to him to merit his attention! Don't ever let me become so anemic in my Christian walk that he doesn't need to bother with me. Amen.

THE COST OF QUITTING

For consider him that endured such contradiction of sinners against himself, lest ye be wearied and faint in your minds. Ye have not yet resisted unto blood, striving against sin.

—Hebrews 12:3-4

*I*f Satan opposes the new convert he opposes still more bitterly the Christian who is pressing on toward a higher life in Christ. The Spirit-filled life is not, as many suppose, a life of peace and quiet pleasure. It is likely to be something quite the opposite.

Viewed one way it is a pilgrimage through a robber-infested forest; viewed another, it is a grim warfare with the devil. Always there is struggle, and sometimes there is a pitched battle with our own nature where the lines are so confused that it is all but impossible to locate the enemy or to tell which impulse is of the Spirit and which of the flesh. . . .

My point here is that if we want to escape the struggle we have but to draw back and accept the currently accepted low-keyed Christian life as the normal one. That is all Satan wants. That will ground our power, stunt our growth and render us harmless to the kingdom of darkness.

Compromise will take the pressure off. Satan will not bother a man who has quit fighting. But the cost of quitting will be a life of peaceful stagnation. We sons of eternity just cannot afford such a thing. TIC073

> *Oh God, don't ever let me compromise to take the pressure off! Don't ever let me settle for "peaceful stagnation" as long as I have breath to serve You. Amen.*

PREPARATION IS VITAL

David said moreover, The LORD that delivered me out of the paw of the lion, and out of the paw of the bear, he will deliver me out of the hand of this Philistine.

—1 Samuel 17:37

The whole Bible and all past history unite to teach that battles are always won before the armies take the field. The critical moment for any army is not the day it engages the foe in actual combat; it is the day before or the month before or the year before. . . .

Preparation is vital. The rule is, prepare or fail. Luck and bluster will do for a while, but the law will catch up with us sooner or later, usually sooner. . . .

It did not take Moses long to lead the children of Israel out through the Red Sea to deliverance and freedom; but his fittedness to lead them out was the result of years of hard discipline. It took David only a few minutes to dispose of Goliath; but he had beaten the giant long before in the person of the lion and the bear. . . .

Preparation is vital. Let this be noted by everyone. We can seek God today and get prepared to meet temptation tomorrow; but if we meet the enemy without first having met God, the outcome is not conjectural; the issue is already decided. We can only lose. NCA077-079

Lord, quiet my heart this morning and feed me from Your Word. I can't enter the battle of today without this vital preparation. Help me even in the busiest of days to maintain this discipline of preparation. Amen.

FIGHT
OR
DIE

For all that is in the world, the lust of the flesh, and the lust of the eyes, and the pride of life, is not of the Father, but is of the world. And the world passeth away, and the lust thereof: but he that doeth the will of God abideth for ever.

—1 John 2:16-17

$\mathcal{S}$omeday the church can relax her guard, call her watchmen down from the wall and live in safety and peace; but not yet, not yet. . . .

The healthiest man has enough lethal bacteria in him to kill him within twenty-four hours except for one thing—the amazing power of the human organism to resist bacterial attack. Every mortal body must fight its internal enemies day and night. Once it surrenders its hours are numbered. Quite literally it must fight or die. . . .

The church lives in a hostile world. Within and around her are enemies that not only could destroy her, but are meant to and will unless she resists force with yet greater force. The Christian would collapse from sheer external pressure were there not within him a counterpressure sufficiently great to prevent it. The power of the Holy Spirit is, therefore, not optional but necessary. Without it the children of God simply cannot live the life of heaven on earth. The hindrances are too many and too effective. TIC086-087

Thank You for the power of the Holy Spirit within me to wage this constant warfare for me. Give Your strength today. Amen.

BE
YE
HOLY

And the LORD spake unto Moses, saying, Speak unto all the congregation of the children of Israel, and say unto them: Ye shall be holy: for I the LORD your God am holy.

—Leviticus 19:1-2

$\mathcal{N}$o one whose senses have been exercised to know good and evil but must grieve over the sight of zealous souls seeking to be filled with the Holy Spirit while they are yet living in a state of moral carelessness or borderline sin. Such a thing is a moral contradiction. Whoever would be filled and indwelt by the Spirit should first judge his life for any hidden iniquities; he should courageously expel from his heart everything which is out of accord with the character of God as revealed by the Holy Scriptures.

At the base of all true Christian experience must lie a sound and sane morality. No joys are valid, no delights legitimate where sin is allowed to live in life or conduct. No transgression of pure righteousness dare excuse itself on the ground of superior religious experience. To seek high emotional states while living in sin is to throw our whole life open to self-deception and the judgment of God. "Be ye holy" is not a mere motto to be framed and hung on the wall. It is a serious commandment from the Lord of the whole earth. POM102

Father, deliver me from "moral carelessness" and "borderline sin." I commit myself today, in the power of the Holy Spirit, to a holiness of life that will be pleasing to You. Amen.

WRONG JUDGMENT

Be not deceived; God is not mocked: for whatsoever a man soweth, that shall he also reap.

—Galatians 6:7

 Sin, I repeat, in addition to anything else it may be, is always an act of wrong judgment. To commit a sin a man must for the moment believe that things are different from what they really are; he must confound values; he must see the moral universe out of focus; he must accept a lie as truth and see truth as a lie; he must ignore the signs on the highway and drive with his eyes shut; he must act as if he had no soul, and was not accountable for his moral choices.

Sin is never a thing to be proud of. No act is wise that ignores remote consequences, and sin always does. Sin sees only today, or at most tomorrow; never the day after tomorrow, next month or next year. Death and judgment are pushed aside as if they did not exist and the sinner becomes for the time a practical atheist who by his act denies not only the existence of God but the concept of life after death. . . .

The notion that the careless sinner is the smart fellow and the serious-minded Christian, though well-intentioned, is a stupid dolt altogether out of touch with life will not stand up under scrutiny. Sin is basically an act of moral folly, and the greater the folly the greater the fool. MDP047-048

Keep me from sin today. Deliver me from "moral folly," again in the power of Your Holy Spirit. Amen.

DISPOSITIONAL SINS

Let all bitterness, and wrath, and anger, and clamour, and evil speaking, be put away from you, with all malice.

—Ephesians 4:31

$\mathcal{D}$ ispositional sins are fully as injurious to the Christian cause as the more overt acts of wickedness. These sins are as many as the various facets of human nature. Just so there may be no misunderstanding let us list a few of them: sensitiveness, irritability, churlishness, faultfinding, peevishness, temper, resentfulness, cruelty, uncharitable attitudes; and of course there are many more. These kill the spirit of the church and slow down any progress which the gospel may be making in the community. Many persons who had been secretly longing to find Christ have been turned away and embittered by manifestations of ugly dispositional flaws in the lives of the very persons who were trying to win them. . . .

Unsaintly saints are the tragedy of Christianity. People of the world usually pass through the circle of disciples to reach Christ, and if they find those disciples severe and sharp-tongued they can hardly be blamed if they sigh and turn away from Him. . . .

The low state of religion in our day is largely due to the lack of public confidence in religious people. OGM084-085

Oh Lord, may I never be an "unsaintly saint!" Give me a pleasant disposition today, not that people would be attracted to me, but that through me they may be irresistibly drawn to Christ. Amen.

SELF-SINS

I am crucified with Christ: nevertheless I live; yet not I, but Christ liveth in me: and the life which I now live in the flesh I live by the faith of the Son of God, who loved me, and gave himself for me.

—Galatians 2:20

To be specific, the self-sins are self-righteousness, self-pity, self-confidence, self-sufficiency, self-admiration, self-love and a host of others like them. They dwell too deep within us and are too much a part of our natures to come to our attention till the light of God is focused upon them. The grosser manifestations of these sins—egotism, exhibitionism, self-promotion—are strangely tolerated in Christian leaders, even in circles of impeccable orthodoxy. They are so much in evidence as actually, for many people, to become identified with the gospel. I trust it is not a cynical observation to say that they appear these days to be a requisite for popularity in some sections of the church visible. Promoting self under the guise of promoting Christ is currently so common as to excite little notice. . . .

Self is the opaque veil that hides the face of God from us. It can be removed only in spiritual experience, never by mere instruction. We may as well try to instruct leprosy out of our system. There must be a work of God in destruction before we are free. We must invite the cross to do its deadly work within us. We must bring our self-sins to the cross for judgement. POG043-044

I pray that the cross would obliterate the self-sins in my life and let me live only for Jesus Christ and His glory. Amen.

He Lost His Temper

He that hath no rule over his own spirit is like a city that is broken down, and without walls.

—Proverbs 25:28

*S*ome people have a temper. We blame it on our Irish grandfather or on something else; but it's a plague spot. I remember a man who had a very high spiritual testimony and became a leading pastor in his denomination. One night at a board meeting, he lost his temper like a mule driver and after that, nobody believed in him.

One time, a man I thought was a fine Christian had a new car and somebody came along and dented his fender. He blew like a little bomb. I never believed in him again. Whenever I see a man blow his top, I never believe in that man unless I know he has gone to the Fountain that cleanses and gotten delivered. No man has any more right to go around with an uncleaned temper than he has to hold a rattlesnake in his jacket pocket. He has no more right to do that than he has to leave untreated a cancer on his tongue, because it will destroy his ministry. He can pray and testify, give and labor, but if one day he blows up, nobody will believe in him after that. SAT060

Lord, deliver me from any tendency to an uncontrolled temper. Keep me from the loss of credibility that can do irreparable harm to my ministry. Make me a pure vessel. Amen.

RESENTMENT

Looking diligently lest any man fail of the grace of God; lest any root of bitterness springing up trouble you, and thereby many be defiled.

—Hebrews 12:15

*I*n the course of scores of conferences and hundreds of conversations, I have many times heard people say, "I resent that." But I repeat: I have never heard the words used by a victorious man. Resentment simply cannot dwell in a loving heart. Before resentfulness can enter, love must take its flight and bitterness take over. The bitter soul will compile a list of slights at which it takes offense and will watch over itself like a mother bear over her cubs. And the figure is apt, for the resentful heart is always surly and suspicious like a she-bear.

Few sights are more depressing than that of a professed Christian defending his supposed rights and bitterly resisting any attempt to violate them. Such a Christian has never accepted the way of the cross. The sweet graces of meekness and humility are unknown to him. He grows every day harder and more acrimonious as he defends his reputation, his rights, his ministry, against his imagined foes.

The only cure for this sort of thing is to die to self and rise with Christ into newness of life. OGM105-106

Keep me, I pray, in the way of the cross, the way of meekness and humility. Amen.

THE EROTIC AGE

> *It is reported commonly that there is fornication among you, and such fornication as is not so much as named among the Gentiles, that one should have his father's wife.*
>
> —1 Corinthians 5:1

The period in which we now live may well go down in history as the Erotic Age. Sex love has been elevated into a cult. Eros has more worshipers among civilized men today than any other god. For millions the erotic has completely displaced the spiritual. . . .

Now if this god would let us Christians alone I for one would let his cult alone. The whole spongy, fetid mess will sink some day under its own weight and become excellent fuel for the fires of hell, a just recompense which is meet, and it becomes us to feel compassion for those who have been caught in its tragic collapse. Tears and silence might be better than words if things were slightly otherwise than they are. But the cult of Eros is seriously affecting the Church. The pure religion of Christ that flows like a crystal river from the heart of God is being polluted by the unclean waters that trickle from behind the altars of abomination that appear on every high hill and under every green tree from New York to Los Angeles. BAM036-037

> *Lord, I pray for any of Your servants who are caught in the trap of immorality or pornography. This "whole spongy, fetid mess" has so many in its clutches—give victory today, I pray, in Jesus' name. Amen.*

NO PRIVATE SIN

Your glorying is not good. Know ye not that a little leaven leaveneth the whole lump? Purge out therefore the old leaven, that ye may be a new lump, as ye are unleavened.

—1 Corinthians 5:6-7

$\mathcal{N}$o sin is private. It may be secret but it is not private.

It is a great error to hold, as some do, that each man's conduct is his own business unless his acts infringe on the rights of others. "My liberty ends where yours begins," is true, but that is not all the truth. No one ever has the right to commit an evil act, no matter how secret. God wills that men should be free, but not that they be free to commit sin. . . .

Coming still closer, we Christians should know that our unchristian conduct cannot be kept in our own backyard. The evil birds of sin fly far and influence many to their everlasting loss. The sin committed in the privacy of the home will have its effect in the assembly of the saints. The minister, the deacon, the teacher who yields to temptation in secret becomes a carrier of moral disease whether he knows it or not. The church will be worse because one member sins. The polluted stream flows out and on, growing wider and darker as it affects more and more persons day after day and year after year. SIZ074, 077

Lord, this is especially true of us who are leaders in the church. Show to me and my fellow servants this morning the horror of the consequences of our sin. Keep us pure and faithful, for Your glory. Amen.

EXAMINE YOURSELF

Search me, O God, and know my heart: try me, and know my thoughts: and see if there be any wicked way in me, and lead me in the way everlasting.

—Psalm 139:23-24

The philosopher Socrates said, "An unexamined life is not worth living." If a common philosopher could think that, how much more we Christians ought to listen to the Holy Spirit when He says, "Examine yourself." An unexamined Christian lies like an unattended garden. Let your garden go unattended for a few months, and you will not have roses and tomatoes but weeds. An unexamined Christian life is like an unkempt house. Lock your house up as tight as you will and leave it long enough, and when you come back you will not believe the dirt that got in from somewhere. An unexamined Christian is like an untaught child. A child that is not taught will be a little savage. It takes examination, teaching, instruction, discipline, caring, tending, weeding and cultivating to keep the life right. RRR043

Search me, O God, and know my heart; try me, and know my anxieties; and see if there is any wicked way in me, and lead me in the way everlasting. Amen.

THE SEARED CONSCIENCE

Unto the pure all things are pure: but unto them that are defiled and unbelieving is nothing pure; but even their mind and conscience is defiled.

—Titus 1:15

*B*ut when a conscience has become seared, when a man has played with the fire and burned his conscience and calloused it until he can handle the hot iron of sin without shrinking, there is no longer any safety for him.

Titus wrote in his epistle about those to whom nothing is pure any longer, "but even their mind and conscience is defiled" (Titus 1:15).

Here Titus speaks of an inward corruption, revealed in impure thoughts and soiled language. I am just as afraid of people with soiled tongues as I am of those with a communicable disease.

Actually, a foul tongue is evidence of a deeper spiritual disease and Titus goes on to tell us that those with defiled consciences become reprobates, something just washed up on the shore, a moral shipwreck. EFE064-065

Oh Lord, deliver me from that "inward corruption." Guard my mind and my tongue; convict me of any carelessness or straying. Keep my conscience alive and active. Lord, I really don't want to end up a dirty old man, "washed up on the shore, a moral shipwreck." Amen.

DISTRACTIONS

And Jesus answered and said unto her, Martha, Martha, thou art careful and troubled about many things: but one thing is needful: and Mary hath chosen that good part, which shall not be taken away from her.

—Luke 10:41-42

*F*ailing in his frontal attacks upon the child of God, Satan often turns to more subtle means of achieving his evil purpose. He resorts to devious methods in his attempt to divert the Christian from carrying out the task God has committed to him. He often succeeds by involving the saint in some other lesser occupation and so distracting him. . . .

Satan's distracting words often come from the most unexpected quarters. Martha would call Mary away from sitting at the feet of the Master. Sometimes, if we are not careful, our best friend may distract us. Or it might be some very legitimate activity. This day's bustle and hurly-burly would too often and too soon call us away from Jesus' feet. These distractions must be immediately dismissed, or we shall know only the "barrenness of busyness." WTA028-029

> *Father, keep me today from the myriad distractions that would keep me from the main thing. I long to stay at Jesus' feet. Deliver me today from the "barrenness of busyness." Amen.*

MEDIOCRE CHRISTIANITY

> *Let not sin therefore reign in your mortal body, that ye should obey it in the lusts thereof. Neither yield ye your members as instruments of unrighteousness unto sin: but yield yourselves unto God, as those that are alive from the dead, and your members as instruments of righteousness unto God.*
>
> —Romans 6:12-13

It is disheartening to those who care, and surely a great grief to the Spirit, to see how many Christians are content to settle for less than the best. Personally I have for years carried a burden of sorrow as I have moved among evangelical Christians who somewhere in their past have managed to strike a base compromise with their heart's holier longings and have settled down to a lukewarm, mediocre kind of Christianity utterly unworthy of themselves and of the Lord they claim to serve. And such are found everywhere. . . .

Every man is as close to God as he wants to be; he is as holy and as full of the Spirit as he wills to be. . . .

Yet we must distinguish wanting from wishing. By "want" I mean wholehearted desire. Certainly there are many who wish they were holy or victorious or joyful but are not willing to meet God's conditions to obtain. TIC064

> *Oh Lord, give me that "wholehearted desire" that keeps me from being satisfied with mediocre Christianity. Amen.*

SEEK GOD'S REMEDY

My little children, these things write I unto you, that ye sin not. And if any man sin, we have an advocate with the Father, Jesus Christ the righteous.

—1 John 2:1

$\mathcal{I}$ wish it were possible to anoint the head of every Christian preacher so that he would never sin again while the world stands. Perhaps some would consider that a happy way to deal with the subject. But, in fact, if any person can be removed from the possibility of sin, he or she can only be some kind of a robot run by pulleys, wheels and push buttons. A person morally incapable of doing evil would be, by the same token, morally incapable of doing good. A free human will is necessary to the concept of morality. I repeat: If our wills are not free to do evil, neither are they free to do good. . . .

But what was the sinning priest to do? Should he give up to discouragement? Should he resign himself to failure? No! There was a remedy. And what about ministers and all of God's servants today? In a time of temptation and failure, should they simply quit? Should they write a letter of resignation and walk out, saying, "I am not an Augustine or a Wesley; therefore, I give up"? No, if they are aware of what the Word of God says, they will seek God's remedy. TRA074-076

> *Thank You, God, for Your glorious remedy! Thank You for Your love; thank You for Your grace; thank You for constant forgiveness in Jesus Christ. Amen.*

MY KINGDOM GO

Thy kingdom come. Thy will be done in earth, as it is in heaven.

—Matthew 6:10

*I*t may surprise you that Aldous Huxley, often a critic of orthodox and evangelical Christianity, has been quoted as saying: "*My kingdom go* is the necessary corollary to *Thy* kingdom *come*." . . .

Certainly His kingdom can never be realized in my life until my own selfish kingdom is deposed. It is when I resign, when I am no longer king of my domain that Jesus Christ will become king of my life.

Now, in confession, may I assure you that a Christian clergyman cannot follow any other route to spiritual victory and daily blessing than that which is prescribed so plainly in the Word of God. It is one thing for a minister to choose a powerful text, expound it and preach from it—it is quite something else for the minister to honestly and genuinely live forth the meaning of the Word from day to day. A clergyman is a man—and often he has a proud little kingdom of his own, a kingdom of position and often of pride and sometimes with power. Clergymen must wrestle with the spiritual implications of the crucified life just like everyone else, and to be thoroughgoing men of God and spiritual examples to the flock of God, they must die daily to the allurements of their own little kingdoms of position and prestige. WPJ173-174

Lord, I quit, I resign, I'm no longer "king of my domain." I die to "my own little kingdom of position and prestige." Rule in my life today. Amen.

THE
DEVIL'S
TAUNTS

There is therefore now no condemnation to them which are in Christ Jesus, who walk not after the flesh, but after the Spirit.

—Romans 8:1

$\mathcal{G}$od knows that sin is a terrible thing—and the devil knows it, too. So he follows us around and as long as we will permit it, he will taunt us about our past sins.

As for myself, I have learned to talk back to him on this score. I say, "Yes, Devil, sin is terrible—but I remind you that I got it from you! And I remind you, Devil, that everything good—forgiveness and cleansing and blessing—everything that is good I have freely received from Jesus Christ!"

Everything that is bad and that is against me I got from the devil—so why should he have the effrontery and the brass to argue with me about it? Yet he will do it because he is the devil, and he is committed to keeping God's children shut up in a little cage, their wings clipped so that they can never fly! ITB006

Thank You again this morning, Father, for Your marvelous "forgiveness and cleansing and blessing." Thank You for Your grace that completely silences the devil. Amen.

VICTORY ASSURED

And Jacob was left alone; and there wrestled a man with him until the breaking of the day. And when he saw that he prevailed not against him, he touched the hollow of his thigh; and the hollow of Jacob's thigh was out of joint, as he wrestled with him.

—Genesis 32:24-25

The enemy never quite knows how to deal with a humble man; he is so used to dealing with proud, stubborn people that a meek man upsets his timetable. And furthermore, the man of true humility has God fighting on his side—who can win against God?

Strange as it may seem, we often win over our enemies only after we have first been soundly defeated by the Lord Himself. God often conquers our enemies by conquering us. . . . When God foresees that we must meet a deadly opponent, he assures our victory by bringing us down in humbleness at His own feet. After that, everything is easy. We have put ourselves in a position where God can fight for us, and in a situation like that, the outcome is decided from eternity. WTA014

Lord, help me to submit willingly to You, in complete humility, without struggle or wrestling. Then You fight for me against my strong enemy. I'll rest—and revel—in Your victory. Amen.

GRACE AND FORGIVENESS

And such were some of you: but ye are washed, but ye are sanctified, but ye are justified in the name of the Lord Jesus, and by the Spirit of our God.

—1 Corinthians 6:11

I do not know all of the Savior's reasons for choosing the woman at the well. I know that His revelation of Himself to her constituted an everlasting rebuke to human self-righteousness. I know that every smug woman who walks down the street in pride and status ought to be ashamed of herself. I know that every self-righteous man who looks into his mirror each morning to shave what he believes to be an honest face ought to be ashamed of himself. . . .

Jesus was able to see potential in the woman at the well that we could never have sensed. What a gracious thing for us that Jesus Christ never thinks about what we have been! He always thinks about what we are going to be. You and I are slaves to time and space and records and reputations and publicity and the past—all that we call the case history. Jesus Christ cares absolutely nothing about anyone's moral case history. He forgives it and starts from there as though the person had been born one minute before. FBR103-104

Again I worship You today, great God, for Your matchless grace. No matter what my past, thank You, thank You, thank You, thank You, that "Jesus Christ cares absolutely nothing about anyone's moral case history." Amen.

WHAT PAST?

I, even I, am he that blotteth out thy transgressions for mine own sake, and will not remember thy sins.

—Isaiah 43:25

O ne of the old German devotional philosophers took the position that God loves to forgive big sins more than He does little sins because the bigger the sin, the more glory accrues to Him for His forgiveness. I remember the writer went on to say that not only does God forgive sins and enjoy doing it, but as soon as He has forgiven them, He forgets them and trusts the person just as if he or she had never sinned. I share his view that God not only forgives great sins as readily as little ones, but once He has forgiven them He starts anew right there and never brings up the old sins again. . . .

When a person makes a mistake and has to be forgiven, the shadow may hang over him or her because it is hard for other people to forget. But when God forgives, He begins the new page right there, and then the devil runs up and says, "What about this person's past?" God replies: "What past? There is no past. We started out fresh when he came to Me and I forgave him!" FBR112

Lord, this concept is so foreign to our human understanding and our human way of doing things. Your grace in forgiving—and forgetting—is beyond our comprehension. But I worship You for it today. Amen.

THE CLEANSED CONSCIENCE

Let us draw near with a true heart in full assurance of faith, having our hearts sprinkled from an evil conscience, and our bodies washed with pure water.

—Hebrews 10:22

What a relief to find the writer to the Hebrews encouraging us to "draw near with a true heart in full assurance of faith, having our hearts sprinkled from an evil conscience" (Hebrews 10:22).

A sprinkled conscience—surely this is a gracious thing for men and women in the world to know!

One of the most relieving, enriching, wholesome, wondrous things we can know is that sudden sense of the lifting of the burden as the conscience goes free—God giving freedom to that conscience which has been evil, diseased and protesting.

Peter wrote about this and called it "the answer of a good conscience toward God, [saves us] by the resurrection of Jesus Christ" (1 Peter 3:21).

This is the kind of conversion I believe in—when your sins are cleansed and forgiven through the blood of the Lamb, you will know it! . . .

A transaction has taken place within the human spirit. The heart suddenly knows itself clean and the burden lifts from the mind and there is a true sense that heaven is pleased and God is smiling and the sins are gone. EFE065-066

Lord, I fall on my face before You in heartfelt worship. Amen.

Trials and Pain

The devil, things and people being what they are, it is necessary for God to use the hammer, the file and the furnace in His holy work of preparing a saint for true sainthood. It is doubtful whether God can bless a man greatly until He has hurt him deeply. ROR137

THE DARK NIGHT OF THE SOUL

How long wilt thou forget me, O LORD? for ever? how long wilt thou hide thy face from me?

—Psalm 13:1

Some of you know something of that which has been called "the dark night of the soul." Some of you have spiritual desire and deep longing for victory but it seems to you that your efforts to go on with God have only brought you more bumps and more testings and more discouragement. You are tempted to ask, "How long can this go on?" . . .

Yes, there is a dark night of the soul. There are few Christians willing to go into this dark night and that is why there are so few who enter into the light. It is impossible for them ever to know the morning because they will not endure the night.

ITB080-081

I pray for any who are suffering and struggling today. Bring Your deep-seated peace and the assurance that the morning is coming. Thank You that Your grace is sufficient. Amen.

PILES OF ASHES

Now no chastening for the present seemeth to be joyous, but grievous: nevertheless afterward it yieldeth the peaceable fruit of righteousness unto them which are exercised thereby.

—Hebrews 12:11

$\mathcal{I}$f God has singled you out to be a special object of His grace you may expect Him to honor you with stricter discipline and greater suffering than less favored ones are called upon to endure. . . .

If God sets out to make you an unusual Christian He is not likely to be as gentle as He is usually pictured by the popular teachers. A sculptor does not use a manicure set to reduce the rude, unshapely marble to a thing of beauty. The saw, the hammer and the chisel are cruel tools, but without them the rough stone must remain forever formless and unbeautiful.

To do His supreme work of grace within you He will take from your heart everything you love most. Everything you trust in will go from you. Piles of ashes will lie where your most precious treasures used to be. TIC122-124

> *Lord, give me the grace to withstand "the saw, the hammer and the chisel." I submit myself today to Your working. Amen.*

HE
KNOWS

For we have not an high priest which cannot be touched with the feeling of our infirmities; but was in all points tempted like as we are, yet without sin. Let us therefore come boldly unto the throne of grace, that we may obtain mercy, and find grace to help in time of need.

—Hebrews 4:15-16

$\mathcal{D}$on't pity yourself. Don't be afraid to tell God your troubles. He knows all about your troubles. There is a little song that says, "Nobody knows the trouble I've seen," but there's Somebody who knows, all right. And our Fellow Sufferer still retains a fellow feeling for our pains and still remembers in the skies His tears, His agonies and cries, though He's now at the right hand of the Father Almighty, sitting crowned in glory, awaiting, of course, that great coronation day that yet is to come. But though He is there and though they cry all around Him, "Worthy is the Lamb" (Revelation 5:12), He hasn't forgotten us, and He hasn't forgotten the nails in His hands, the tears, the agonies and cries.

He knows everything about you. He knows! He knows when the doctor hates to tell you what's wrong with you and your friends come and try to be unnaturally encouraging. He knows!

With boldness, therefore, at the throne
Let us make all our sorrows known
And ask the aid of heavenly power
To help us in the evil hour. AOG094-095

Thank You, Lord, for this encouragement. Thank You that You know and understand. Amen.

GOOD IN THY SIGHT

And Samuel told him every whit, and hid nothing from him. And he said, It is the LORD: let him do what seemeth him good.

—1 Samuel 3:18

A determination to know what cannot be known always works harm to the Christian heart.

Ignorance in matters on our human level is never to be excused if there has been opportunity to correct it. But there are matters which are obviously "too high for us." These we should meet in trusting faith and say as Jesus said, "Even so, Father: for so it seemed good in thy sight" (Matthew 11:26). . . .

Human curiosity and pride often combine to drive us to try to understand acts of God which are plainly outside the field of human understanding. We dislike to admit that we do not know what is going on, so we torture our minds trying to fathom the mysterious ways of the Omniscient One. It's hard to conceive of a more fruitless task. . . .

A blind confidence which trusts without seeing is far dearer to God than any fancied knowledge that can explain everything. . . .

To the adoring heart, the best and most satisfying explanation for anything always will be, "It seemed good in thy sight."

NCA054-055

> *Lord, help me today, no matter what difficult circumstances I may face, to pray with Jesus, "for so it seemed good in Thy sight." Amen.*

THIS DOES NOT COME FROM GOD

Submit yourselves therefore to God. Resist the devil and he will flee from you.

—James 4:7

𝒥 have had times in my life and ministry when the burdens and the pressures seemed to be too much. Sometimes physical weariness adds to our problems and our temptation to give in to discouragement and doubt. At these times it seems that even in prayer it is impossible to rise above the load. More than once, by faith that seemed to have been imparted directly from heaven, the Lord has enabled me to claim all that I needed for body, soul and spirit. On my knees I have been given freedom and strength to pray, "Now, Lord, I have had enough of this—I refuse to take any more of this heaviness and oppression! This does not come from God—this comes from my enemy, the devil! Lord, in Jesus' name, I will not take it any longer—through Jesus Christ I am victor!" At these times, great burdens have just melted and rolled away—all at once!

Brethren, God never meant for us to be kicked around like a football. He wants us to be humble and let Him do the chastening when necessary. But when the devil starts tampering with you, dare to resist him! ITB015

Lord, help me to resist any attempt of Satan to defeat me today and to conquer in the victory You guarantee. Amen.

FAULTFINDERS

We are troubled on every side, yet not distressed; we are perplexed, but not in despair; persecuted, but not forsaken; cast down, but not destroyed.

—2 Corinthians 4:8-9

Nowhere else in the entire New Testament is the humanity of the great apostle [Paul] seen so clearly as when he staggers under the cruel attacks of the anti-Paul bloc in the Corinthian church. His sufferings are there the most poignant and nearest to the sufferings of Christ because they are inward and of the soul. For always the soul can suffer as the body cannot. . . .

But from Paul and his afflictions we may learn much truth, some of it depressing and some altogether elevating and wonderful. We may learn, for instance, that malice needs nothing to live on; it can feed on itself. A contentious spirit will find something to quarrel about. A faultfinder will find occasion to accuse a Christian even if his life is as chaste as an icicle and pure as snow. A man of ill will does not hesitate to attack, even if the object of his hatred be a prophet or the very Son of God Himself. If John comes fasting, he says he has a devil; if Christ comes eating and drinking, he says He is a winebibber and a glutton. Good men are made to appear evil by the simple trick of dredging up from his own heart the evil that is there and attributing it to them. WTA078-080

Deliver me from faultfinders and those of a contentious spirit. Silence them for Your glory. Amen.

CRITICISM AND ABUSE

But as we were allowed of God to be put in trust with the gospel, even so we speak; not as pleasing men, but God, which trieth our hearts.

—1 Thessalonians 2:4

"Let not thy peace depend on the tongues of men," said the wise old Christian mystic, Thomas à Kempis; "for whether they judge well or ill, thou art not on that account other than thyself."

One of the first things a Christian should get used to is abuse. . . .

To do nothing is to get abused for laziness, and to do anything is to get abused for not doing something else.

Was it not Voltaire who said that some people were like insects, they would never be noticed except that they sting? A traveler must make up his mind to go on regardless of the insects that make his trip miserable. . . .

One thing is certain, a Christian's standing before God does not depend upon his standing before men. A high reputation does not make a man dearer to God, nor does the tongue of the slanderer influence God's attitude toward His people in any way. He knows us each one, and we stand or fall in the light of His perfect knowledge. NCA094-095

Lord, I know this truth, but it's so hard to "let not thy peace depend on the tongues of men." The stinging insects are so annoying! Give me peace in Your approval today. Amen.

THE LABOR OF SELF-LOVE

For do I now persuade men, or God? or do I seek to please men? for if I yet pleased men, I should not be the servant of Christ.

—Galatians 1:10

The labor of self-love is a heavy one indeed. Think for yourself whether much of your sorrow has not arisen from someone speaking slightingly of you. As long as you set yourself up as a little god to which you must be loyal there will be those who will delight to offer affront to your idol. How then can you hope to have inward peace? The heart's fierce effort to protect itself from every slight, to shield its touchy honor from the bad opinion of friend and enemy, will never let the mind have rest. Continue this fight through the years and the burden will become intolerable. Yet the sons of earth are carrying this burden continually, challenging every word spoken against them, cringing under every criticism, smarting under each fancied slight, tossing sleepless if another is preferred before them.

Such a burden as this is not necessary to bear. Jesus calls us to His rest, and meekness is His method. The meek man cares not at all who is greater than he, for he has long ago decided that the esteem of the world is not worth the effort. POG105-106

Lord, give me this peace, this rest, this meek and humble spirit. Deliver me from concern for the esteem of this world. Give me victory over every trace of self-love. Amen.

IT WORKS!

Most gladly therefore will I rather glory in my infirmities, that the power of Christ may rest upon me. Therefore I take pleasure in infirmities, in reproaches, in necessities, in persecutions, in distresses for Christ's sake: for when I am weak, then am I strong.

—2 Corinthians 12:9-10

*T*en thousand enemies cannot stop a Christian, cannot even slow him down, if he meets them in an attitude of complete trust in God. They will become to him like the atmosphere that resists the airplane, but which because the plane's designer knew how to take advantage of that resistance, actually lifts the plane aloft and holds it there for a journey of 2,000 miles. What would have been an enemy to the plane becomes a helpful servant to aid it on its way. . . .

If this should seem like a bit of theorizing, remember that always the greatest Christians have come out of hard times and tough situations. Tribulations actually worked for their spiritual perfection in that they taught them to trust not in themselves but in the Lord who raised the dead. They learned that the enemy could not block their progress unless they surrendered to the urgings of the flesh and began to complain. And slowly, they learned to stop complaining and start praising. It is that simple—and it works! WTA032-033

Lord, I pray for Your grace to work within me that I might allow the trials to lift me aloft rather than press me down. Amen.

FEW LOVERS OF HIS CROSS

For ye have need of patience, that, after ye have done the will of God, ye might receive the promise.

—Hebrews 10:36

When God needs a person for His service—a good person, an effective person, a humble person—why does He most often turn to a person in deep trouble? Why does He seek out a person deep in the crucible of suffering, a person who is not the jovial, "happy-happy" kind? I can only say that this is the way of God with His human creation. . . .

Ezekiel did not come out of pleasant and favorable circumstances. The light had gone out in his heart. He probably thought that God takes a long time to work out His will.

Does not this same view surface in much of our Christian fellowship? We do not want to take the time to plow and to cultivate. We want the fruit and the harvest right away! We do not want to be engaged in any spiritual battle that takes us into the long night. We want the morning light right now! We do not want to go through the processes of planning and preparation and labor pains. We want the baby this instant!

We do not want the cross. We are more interested in the crown.

The condition is not peculiar to our century. Thomas à Kempis wrote long ago, "The Lord has many lovers of His crown but few lovers of His cross." MMG114-115

Lord, make me a lover of Your cross as well as a lover of Your crown. Amen.

EASTER WITHOUT GOOD FRIDAY

For unto you it is given in the behalf of Christ, not only to believe on him, but also to suffer for his sake.

—Philippians 1:29

*G*od will crucify without pity those whom He desires to raise without measure! . . .

God wants to crucify us from head to foot—making our own powers ridiculous and useless—in the desire to raise us without measure for His glory and for our eternal good. . . .

Willingness to suffer for Jesus' sake—this is what we have lost from the Christian church. We want our Easter to come without the necessity of a Good Friday. We forget that before the Redeemer could rise and sing among His brethren He must first bow His head and suffer among His brethren!

We forget so easily that in the spiritual life there must be the darkness of the night before there can be the radiance of the dawn. Before the life of resurrection can be known, there must be the death that ends the dominion of self. It is a serious but a blessed decision, this willingness to say, "I will follow Him no matter what the cost. I will take the cross no matter how it comes!" ITB096-099

Lord, I come before You on my knees to say, "I will follow [You] no matter what the cost. I will take the cross no matter how it comes!" Amen.

FORCED TO OUR KNEES

And lest I should be exalted above measure through the abundance of the revelations, there was given to me a thorn in the flesh, the messenger of Satan to buffet me, lest I should be exalted above measure.

—2 Corinthians 12:7

$\mathcal{T}$he experiences of men who walked with God in olden times agree to teach that the Lord cannot fully bless a man until He has first conquered him. The degree of blessing enjoyed by any man will correspond exactly with the completeness of God's victory over him. . . .

We might well pray for God to invade and conquer us, for until He does, we remain in peril from a thousand foes. We bear within us the seeds of our own disintegration. . . . Deliverance can come to us only by the defeat of our old life. Safety and peace come only after we have been forced to our knees. God rescues us by breaking us, by shattering our strength and wiping out our resistance. Then He invades our natures with that ancient and eternal life which is from the beginning. So He conquers us and by that benign conquest saves us for Himself. POM045-046, 050

Lord, indeed invade and conquer my heart today. Bring me to my knees in complete surrender; break me; shatter my strength and wipe out my resistance. Invade my nature today and conquer me for Your glory. Amen.

THE SHARP BLADE OF THE PLOW

Sow to yourselves in righteous-
ness, reap in mercy; break up
your fallow ground: for it is time
to seek the LORD, till he come and
rain righteousness upon you.

—Hosea 10:12

*T*he fallow field is smug, contented, protected from the shock of the plow and the agitation of the harrow.... But it is paying a terrible price for its tranquility: Never does it see the miracle of growth; never does it feel the motions of mounting life nor see the wonders of bursting seed nor the beauty of ripening grain. Fruit it can never know because it is afraid of the plow and the harrow.

In direct opposite to this, the cultivated field has yielded itself to the adventure of living. The protecting fence has opened to admit the plow, and the plow has come as plows always come, practical, cruel, business-like and in a hurry. Peace has been shattered by the shouting farmer and the rattle of machinery. The field has felt the travail of change; it has been upset, turned over, bruised and broken, but its rewards come hard upon its labors. The seed shoots up into the daylight its miracle of life, curious, exploring the new world above it. All over the field the hand of God is at work in the age-old and ever renewed service of creation. New things are born, to grow, mature and consummate the grand prophecy latent in the seed when it entered the ground. Nature's wonders follow the plow. PTP031-032

Lord, make me a cultivated field. Do the hard work of
the farmer in my life today. Amen.

THE NECESSITY OF WOUNDS

Before I was afflicted I went astray: but now have I kept thy word. . . . It is good for me that I have been afflicted; that I might learn thy statutes.

—Psalm 119:67, 71

*I*t is amazing to me! There are people within the ranks of Christianity who have been taught and who believe that Christ will shield His followers from wounds of every kind.

If the truth were known, the saints of God in every age were only effective after they had been wounded. They experienced the humbling wounds that brought contrition, compassion and a yearning for the knowledge of God. I could only wish that more among the followers of Christ knew what some of the early saints meant when they spoke of being wounded by the Holy Spirit. . . .

In every generation, the people who have found God have been those who have come to the end of themselves. Recognizing their hopelessness, they have been ready to throw themselves on the mercy and grace of a forgiving God. MMG059, 062

Lord, don't let me waste the humbling wounds. Do Your great work within me, and help me to respond properly and learn all You want me to learn through Your working. Amen.

THE BACK SIDE OF THE DESERT

Now Moses kept the flock of Jethro his father in law, the priest of Midian: and he led the flock to the backside of the desert, and came to the mountain of God, even to Horeb.

—Exodus 3:1

We should quickly review here the kinds of preparation Moses had gone through for his leadership role under God. Reared in Pharaoh's palace, he had been educated in all the wisdom of the Egyptians. He had the prerequisites for almost any kind of career. In our day a man with his qualifications would be sought for election as a bishop or the president of any of the great church denominations.

Then, too, Moses had a most unusual but highly effective postgraduate course. God took him out of the activity and the noise of Egypt and placed him in the silence of the open spaces. He kept the flock of Jethro, his father-in-law. Tending the sheep, he learned lessons of meditation and observation that he could only have learned in the silence.

Probably more important than anything else, Moses learned to know himself. That knowledge was a part of God's preparation of the man for his future tasks. We, today, know everything but ourselves. We never really come to know ourselves because we cannot get quiet enough. MMG070

Lord, I pray for the hurting pastor who is languishing in "the silence of the open spaces." Encourage him; instruct him; then show Him how You can use him mightily in Your way and in Your time. Amen.

HE PUTS ME FLAT DOWN

And it came to pass at the end of seven days, that the word of the LORD came unto me, saying, Son of man, I have made thee a watchman unto the house of Israel: therefore hear the word at my mouth, and give them warning from me.

—Ezekiel 3:16-17

I once heard a brother preach on the fact that the church should be without spot or wrinkle. To get the wrinkles out of a sack, he said, you fill it. To get a wrinkle out of a rug, you lay it down and walk on it. God sometimes fills us, the preacher continued, but sometimes He just puts us flat down so that everyone can walk on us!

King David long ago knew something of the latter method. He wrote, "The plowers plowed upon my back: they made long their furrows" (Psalm 129:3). I think David was talking about his enemies. And they must have been wearing hobnail boots!

Ezekiel had just come to this kind of a low-ebbed, humbling experience when God opened the heavens. In effect, God put His hand on him and said, "Now I can use you. I have some words and some plans that I want you to pass onto your country men." MMG117-118

Lord, whether You fill me or "put me flat down," I want to be fit to be Your servant. Use Your best methods on me, Father, as I submit myself for Your use and Your glory. Amen.

GOD SEND US TEARS

(For many walk, of whom I have told you often, and now tell you even weeping, that they are the enemies of the cross of Christ: whose end is destruction, whose God is their belly, and whose glory is in their shame, who mind earthly things.)

—Philippians 3:18-19

*T*he Bible was written in tears and to tears it will yield its best treasures. God has nothing to say to the frivolous man. . . .

The psalmists often wrote in tears, the prophets could hardly conceal their heavyheartedness, and the apostle Paul in his otherwise joyous epistle to the Philippians broke into tears when he thought of the many who were enemies of the cross of Christ and whose end was destruction. Those Christian leaders who shook the world were one and all men of sorrows whose witness to mankind welled out of heavy hearts. There is no power in tears per se, but tears and power ever lie close together in the Church of the Firstborn. . . .

The whole Christian family stands desperately in need of a restoration of penitence, humility and tears. May God send them soon. GTM002-003,006

This being so, Lord, I pray this morning that You would break me and send the tears. Amen.

WE MAY EXPECT TROUBLES

These things I have spoken unto you, that in me ye might have peace. In the world ye shall have tribulation: but be of good cheer; I have overcome the world.

—John 16:33

*W*e are all idealists. We picture to ourselves a life on earth completely free from every hindrance, a kind of spiritual Utopia where we can always control events, where we can move about as favorites of heaven, adjusting circumstances to suit ourselves. This we feel would be quite compatible with the life of faith and in keeping with the privileged place we hold as children of God.

In thinking thus we simply misplace ourselves; we mistake earth for heaven and expect conditions here below which can never be realized till we reach the better world above. While we live we may expect troubles, and plenty of them. We are never promised a life without problems as long as we remain among fallen men. . . .

What then are we to do about our problems? We must learn to live with them until such time as God delivers us from them. If we cannot remove them, then we must pray for grace to endure them without murmuring. Problems patiently endured will work for our spiritual perfecting. They harm us only when we resist them or endure them unwillingly. OGM121-122

Lord, I'm so homesick for heaven. But until You allow me to come home, I do indeed "pray for grace to endure [problems] without murmuring." Amen.

NOT YET "DUE TIME"

But he knoweth the way that I take: when he hath tried me, I shall come forth as gold.

—Job 23:10

$\mathcal{G}$od has said He will exalt you in due time, but remember, He is referring to His time and not yours!

Some of you are actually in a fiery furnace right now. You are in a special kind of spiritual testing. The pastor may not know it and others may not know it, but you have been praying and asking the Lord: "Why don't You get me out of this?"

In God's plan it is not yet "due time." When you have come through the fire, God will get you out and there will not be any smell of smoke on your garment and you will not have been harmed.

The only harm that can come will be from your insistence that God must get you out sooner than He plans.

The Lord has promised to exalt you in due time and He has always kept His promises to His people.

As children of God, we can always afford to wait. A saint of God does not have to be concerned about time when he is in the will of God. ICH116-117

> *Lord, I pray this morning for anyone who is "actually in a fiery furnace right now." Give great grace to endure until the "due time" when You bring release and exaltation. Amen.*

THE MINISTRY OF THE NIGHT

For his anger endureth but a moment; in his favour is life: weeping may endure for a night, but joy cometh in the morning.

—Psalm 30:5

*B*ut there is a limit to man's ability to live without joy. Even Christ could endure the cross only because of the joy set before Him. The strongest steel breaks if kept too long under unrelieved tension. God knows exactly how much pressure each one of us can take. He knows how long we can endure the night, so He gives the soul relief, first by welcome glimpses of the morning star and then by the fuller light that harbingers the morning.

Slowly you will discover God's love in your suffering. Your heart will begin to approve the whole thing. You will learn from yourself what all the schools in the world could not teach you—the healing action of faith without supporting pleasure. You will feel and understand the ministry of the night; its power to purify, to detach, to humble, to destroy the fear of death and, what is more important to you at the moment, the fear of life. And you will learn that sometimes pain can do what even joy cannot, such as exposing the vanity of earth's trifles and filling your heart with longing for the peace of heaven. TIC123-124

Thank You, Father, for the ministry of the night, for the lessons of pain. But thank You, too, that we're not alone in the night. Thank You for the morning star and the glimpse of the light of morning. Amen.

ORDERED BY THE LORD

The steps of a good man are or-
dered by the LORD: and he
delighteth in his way. Though he
fall, he shall not be utterly cast
down: for the LORD upholdeth
him with his hand.

—Psalm 37:23-24

*T*o the child of God, there is no such thing as accident. He travels an appointed way. The path he treads was chosen for him when as yet he was not, when as yet he had existence only in the mind of God.

Accidents may indeed appear to befall him and misfortune stalk his way; but these evils will be so in appearance only and will seem evil only because we cannot read the secret script of God's hidden providence and so cannot discover the ends at which He aims. . . .

The man of true faith may live in the absolute assurance that his steps are ordered by the Lord. For him, misfortune is out-side the bounds of possibility. He cannot be torn from this earth one hour ahead of the time which God has appointed, and he cannot be detained on earth one moment after God is done with him here. He is not a waif of the wide world, a foundling of time and space, but a saint of the Lord and the darling of His partic-ular care. WTA003-004

I worship and praise You for this: "the absolute assur-
ance that his steps are ordered by the Lord." And for the
fact that "misfortune is outside the bounds of possibility."
What a privilege to be "a darling of His particular
care." Wow! Amen.

HEARTACHE OR HAPPINESS

My brethren, count it all joy when ye fall into divers temptations; knowing this, that the trying of your faith worketh patience. But let patience have her perfect work, that ye may be perfect and entire, wanting nothing.

—James 1:2-4

*F*rom the trials and triumphs of Paul, we gather, too, that happiness is really not indispensable to a Christian. There are many ills worse than heartaches. It is scarcely too much to say that prolonged happiness may actually weaken us, especially if we *insist* upon being happy as the Jews insisted upon flesh in the wilderness. In so doing, we may try to avoid those spiritual responsibilities which would in the nature of them bring a certain measure of heaviness and affliction to the soul.

The best thing is neither to seek nor seek to avoid troubles but to follow Christ and take the bitter with the sweet as it may come. Whether we are happy or unhappy at any given time is not important. That we be in the will of God is all that matters. We may safely leave with Him the incident of heartache or happiness. He will know how much we need of either or both. WTA080

Lord, may I indeed be "in the will of God" today. I'll "leave with [You] the incident of heartache or happiness." I can trust You to decide wisely. Amen.

HAPPINESS IS NOT THE GOAL

See then that ye walk circum-spectly, not as fools, but as wise, redeeming the time, because the days are evil.

—Ephesians 5:15-16

*T*hat we are born to be happy is scarcely questioned by anyone. No one bothers to prove that fallen men have any moral right to happiness, or that they are in the long run any better off happy. The only question before the house is how to get the most happiness out of life. Almost all popular books and plays assume that personal happiness is the legitimate end of the dramatic human struggle.

Now I submit that the whole hectic scramble after happiness is an evil as certainly as is the scramble after money or fame or success. . . .

This . . . will be discovered easily by the simple act of reading the New Testament through once with meditation. There the emphasis is not upon happiness but upon holiness. God is more concerned with the state of people's hearts than with the state of their feelings. Undoubtedly the will of God brings final happiness to those who obey, but the most important matter is not how happy we are but how holy. The soldier does not seek to be happy in the field; he seeks rather to get the fighting over with, to win the war and get back home to his loved ones. OGM048-049

Oh, Lord, redirect my focus. Help me today to be a "good soldier of Jesus Christ." Amen.

WE FORGET

And these all, having obtained a good report through faith, received not the promise: God having provided some better thing for us, that they without us should not be made perfect.

—Hebrews 11:39-40

*T*hen there is the matter of constant consolation and peace—the promise of always feeling relaxed and at rest and enjoying ourselves inwardly.

This, I say, has been held up as being quite the proper goal to be sought in the evil hour in which we live. We forget that our Lord was a Man of sorrow and acquainted with grief. We forget the arrows of grief and pain which went through the heart of Jesus' mother, Mary. We forget that all of the apostles except John died a martyr's death. We forget that there were 13 million Christians slain during the first two generations of the Christian era. We forget that they languished in prison, that they were starved, were thrown over cliffs, were fed to the lions, were drowned, that they were sewn in sacks and thrown into the ocean. . . .

But there is something better than being comfortable, and the followers of Christ ought to find it out—the poor, soft, overstuffed Christians of our time ought to find it out! . . .

We Protestants have forgotten altogether that there is such a thing as discipline and suffering. WPJ017-019

> *Forgive me for complaining, Lord, about the few trials I've experienced. Amen.*

COOPERATE WITH THE INEVITABLE

Not that I speak in respect of want: for I have learned, in whatsoever state I am, therewith to be content.

—Philippians 4:11

This idea was once expressed better by a simple-hearted man who was asked how he managed to live in such a state of constant tranquility even though surrounded by circumstances anything but pleasant. His answer was as profound as it was simple: "I have learned," he said, "to cooperate with the inevitable." . . .

Though we cannot control the universe, we can determine our attitude toward it. We can accept God's will wherever it is expressed and take toward it an attitude of worshipful resignation. If my will is to do God's will, then there will be no controversy with anything that comes in the course of my daily walk. Inclement weather, unpleasant neighbors, physical handicaps, adverse political conditions—all these will be accepted as God's will for the time and surrendered to provisionally, subject to such alterations as God may see fit to make, either by His own sovereign providence or in answer to believing prayer. BAM064-065

How can I complain in the light of the wonderful gift of Your Son, born to give life—and victory? Work Your will in my life today as I celebrate the incarnation and all that it entails. Amen.

ANOTHER DAY OF PREPARATION

Beloved, now are we the sons of God, and it doth not yet appear what we shall be: but we know that, when he shall appear, we shall be like him; for we shall see him as he is. And every man that hath this hope in him purifieth himself, even as he is pure.

—1 John 3:2-3

*K*now that our living Lord is unspeakably pure. He is sinless, spotless, immaculate, stainless. In His person is an absolute fullness of purity that our words can never express. This fact alone changes our entire human and moral situation and outlook. We can always be sure of the most important of all positives: God is God and God is right. He is in control. Because He is God He will never change!

I repeat: God is right—always. That statement is the basis of all we are thinking about God.

When the eternal God Himself invites us to prepare ourselves to be with Him throughout the future ages, we can only bow in delight and gratitude, murmuring, "Oh, Lord, may Your will be done in this poor, unworthy life!"

I can only hope that you are wise enough, desirous enough and spiritual enough to face up to the truth that every day is another day of spiritual preparation, another day of testing and discipline with our heavenly destination in mind. JAF092-093

"Oh, Lord, may Your will be done in this poor, unworthy life!" Amen.

LONG ETERNITY TO ENJOY OURSELVES

Love not the world, neither the things that are in the world. If any man love the world, the love of the Father is not in him. . . . And the world passeth away, and the lust thereof: but he that doeth the will of God abideth for ever.

—1 John 2:15, 17

*A*ny appeal to the public in the name of Christ that rises no higher than an invitation to tranquillity must be recognized as mere humanism with a few words of Jesus thrown in to make it appear Christian. . . .

Christ calls men to carry a cross; we call them to have fun in His name. He calls them to forsake the world; we assure them that if they but accept Jesus the world is their oyster. He calls them to suffer; we call them to enjoy all the bourgeois comforts modern civilization affords. He calls them to self-abnegation and death; we call them to spread themselves like green bay trees or perchance even to become stars in a pitiful fifth-rate religious zodiac. He calls them to holiness; we call them to a cheap and tawdry happiness that would have been rejected with scorn by the least of the Stoic philosophers. . . .

We can afford to suffer now; we'll have a long eternity to enjoy ourselves. And our enjoyment will be valid and pure, for it will come in the right way at the right time. BAM141-142

Lord, may I be faithful to call people to that which is important to You, at whatever cost. Amen.

NOTHING TO FEAR

Thou wilt keep him in perfect peace, whose mind is stayed on thee: because he trusteth in thee.

—Isaiah 26:3

*T*he only fear I have is to fear to get out of the will of God. Outside of the will of God, there's nothing I want, and in the will of God there's nothing I fear, for God has sworn to keep me in His will. If I'm out of His will, that is another matter. But if I'm in His will, He's sworn to keep me.

And He's able to do it, He's wise enough to know how to do it and He's kind enough to want to do it. So really there's nothing to fear.

I get kidded by my family and friends about this, but I don't really think I'm afraid of anything. Someone may ask, "What about cancer? Do you ever fear that you'll die of cancer?" Maybe so, but it will have to hurry up, or I'll die of old age first. But I'm not too badly worried because a man who dies of cancer in the will of God, is not injured; he's just dead. You can't harm a man in the will of God. SAT080-081

Lord, "outside of the will of God, there's nothing I want, and in the will of God there's nothing I fear." Amen.

UNDERNEATH ARE THE EVERLASTING ARMS

> *The eternal God is thy refuge, and underneath are the everlasting arms: and he shall thrust out the enemy from before thee; and shall say, Destroy them.*
>
> —Deuteronomy 33:27

Surely Bible-reading Christians should be the last persons on earth to give way to hysteria. They are redeemed from their past offenses, kept in their present circumstances by the power of an all-powerful God, and their future is safe in His hands. God has promised to support them in the flood, protect them in the fire, feed them in famine, shield them against their enemies, hide them in His safe chambers until the indignation is past and receive them at last into eternal tabernacles.

If we are called upon to suffer, we may be perfectly sure that we shall be rewarded for every pain and blessed for every tear. Underneath will be the Everlasting Arms and within will be the deep assurance that all is well with our souls. Nothing can separate us from the love of God—not death, nor life, nor height, nor depth, nor any other creature.

This is a big old world, and it is full of the habitations of darkness, but nowhere in its vast expanse is there one thing of which a real Christian need be afraid. Surely a fear-ridden Christian has never examined his or her defenses. TWP007-008

Lord, I'll go today in the power of these awesome promises. I'll rest in these strong assurances. I'll face this "big old world" and its "habitations of darkness" in complete peace as I trust You completely today. Amen.

MOSES' PRAYER

So teach us to number our days, that we may apply our hearts unto wisdom.

—Psalm 90:12

A few days after these words appear in print the old year of our Lord will have gone to join the long procession of years and centuries that move on into the shadows of a past that can come no more.

In the year just gone the world has been writing history, not with ink only but with blood and tears; not in the quiet of the study but in violence, terror and death in city streets and along the borders of nations; and other and milder but more significant history has been written by incredible feats of power in sending man-made objects out to circle the moon and the sun. . . .

To each one fortunate enough to live out [this year], God will have given 365 days broken into 8,760 hours. Of these hours, 2,920 will have been spent in sleep, and about the same number at work. An equal number has been given us to spend in reverent preparation for the moment when days and years shall cease and time shall be no more. What prayer could be more spiritually appropriate than that of Moses, the man of God: "Teach us to number our days, that we may apply our hearts unto wisdom" (Psalm 90:12). WOS145-147

"So teach us to number our days, that we may apply our hearts unto wisdom." Amen.

PREPARED FOR WHATEVER

> *LORD, thou hast been our dwelling place in all generations. Before the mountains were brought forth, or ever thou hadst formed the earth and the world, even from everlasting to everlasting, thou art God.*
>
> —Psalm 90:1-2

*Y*et I do not advise that we end the year on a somber note. The march, not the dirge, has ever been the music of Christianity. If we are good students in the school of life, there is much that the years have to teach us. But the Christian is more than a student, more than a philosopher. He is a believer, and the object of his faith makes the difference, the mighty difference.

Of all persons the Christian should be best prepared for whatever the New Year brings. He has dealt with life at its source. In Christ he has disposed of a thousand enemies that other men must face alone and unprepared. He can face his tomorrow cheerful and unafraid because yesterday he turned his feet into the ways of peace and today he lives in God. The man who has made God his dwelling place will always have a safe habitation. wos148

Thank You, Father, for all You've taught me this past year. Thank You for the stretching experiences. Thank You for Tozer's wise counsel. Thank You for the privilege of serving You. Thank You for Your love and grace. Amen.

Reference Codes

REFERENCE CODES FOR BOOKS
AND BOOKLETS BY A.W. TOZER

Scripture Index

OLD TESTAMENT

JOB

PSALMS

ECCLESIASTES

ISAIAH

JEREMIAH

EZEKIEL

DANIEL

HOSEA

HABAKKUK

ZECHARIAH

NEW TESTAMENT

MATTHEW

PHILIPPIANS

COLOSSIANS

FIRST THESSALONIANS

Titles by A.W. Tozer available through your local Christian bookstore or on the Web at www.echurchdepot.com: